TRANSPORTATION AND THE PROSPECTS FOR IMPROVED EFFICIENCY

NATIONAL ACADEMY OF ENGINEERING

A Symposium sponsored by the
National Science Foundation
Department of Housing and Urban Development
Department of Transportation
and the
National Academy of Engineering
at its
Eighth Autumn Meeting
October 12 and 13, 1972

TRANSPORTATION AND THE PROSPECTS FOR IMPROVED EFFICIENCY

NATIONAL ACADEMY OF ENGINEERING
WASHINGTON, D.C.
1973

Available from

Printing and Publishing Office
National Academy of Sciences
2101 Constitution Avenue, N.W.
Washington, D.C.   20418

LIBRARY OF CONGRESS CATALOGING IN PUBLICATION DATA

Main entry under title:

Transportation and the prospects for improved efficiency.

A symposium sponsored by the National Science Foundation, and others, at the 8th autumn meeting of the National Academy of Engineering, Oct. 12–13, 1973.
1. Urban transportation–Congresses. I. National Academy of Engineering.
II. United States. National Science Foundation.
TA1205.T7   388.4   73-9501
ISBN 0-309-02120-0

Printed in the United States of America

NATIONAL ACADEMY OF ENGINEERING

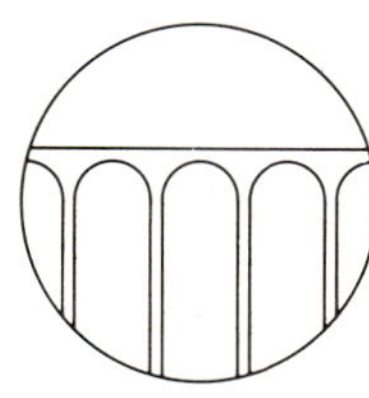

The National Academy of Engineering was established in December 1964. The Academy is independent and autonomous in its organization and election of members, and shares in the responsibility given the National Academy of Sciences under its congressional act of incorporation to advise the federal government, upon request, in all areas of science and engineering.

The National Academy of Engineering, aware of its responsibilities to the government, the engineering community, and the nation as a whole, is pledged:

1. To provide means of assessing the constantly changing needs of the nation and the technical resources that can and should be applied to them; to sponsor programs aimed at meeting these needs; and to encourage such engineering research as may be advisable in the national interest.

2. To explore means for promoting cooperation in engineering in the United States and abroad, with a view to securing concentration on problems significant to society and encouraging research and development aimed at meeting them.

3. To advise the Congress and the executive branch of the government, whenever called upon by any department or agency thereof, on matters of national importance pertinent to engineering.

4. To cooperate with the National Academy of Sciences on matters involving both science and engineering.

5. To serve the nation in other respects in connection with significant problems in engineering and technology.

6. To recognize in an appropriate manner outstanding contributions to the nation by leading engineers.

FOREWORD

Two major objectives of the Academy of Engineering are, first, to provide a means of assessing the constantly changing needs of the nation—and certainly the transportation needs are among these—and the technical resources that can and should be applied to them; and, second, to help solve significant national problems through the application of engineering and technology.

It was to further these objectives that the NAE Committee on Transportation undertook its study and prepared the report on Urban Transportation Research and Development and that the Academy has undertaken this symposium.

This symposium has been designed to concentrate on improving the understanding of urban transportation systems, of the related interfaces, and of the institutional barriers to progress in this area. The aim is to aid in overcoming some of the many impediments to improving the nation's transportation system, and we hope to bring forth, by hearing lessons already learned by experts in the field, ways to apply the accumulated knowledge of these lessons to improve future transportation decisions in both the public and private sector.

There must be a balance among the transportation modes that will help solve the transportation problems, but what the right balance is, where the interfaces occur, and how one gets public acceptance of the individual solutions are the real problems.

The symposium sessions will include discussions of modal interfaces involving people and freight movement. There are sessions on the interrelation of urban transportation and urban development and how private enterprise as well as government agencies work to overcome institutional barriers to transportation progress.

The hope is to stimulate urban transportation innovation and to foster a better quality of urban life, rather than just better transportation.

An exceptional group of speakers and panelists will be discussing the major issues related to achievement of the objectives I have outlined. We are certainly pleased that these outstanding individuals from the federal, state, and municipal level, from industry, and from the universities will present their views here.

I want to mention as well several organizational activities within the Academies; the Highway Research Board, the Maritime Transportation Research Board, the NAE Telecommunications Committee, and the NAE Aeronautics and Space Engineering Board, the Advisory Committee to the Department of Housing and Urban Development, and the NAE Committee on Transportation. All are contributors to the discussions through presentations or participation of panelists. We greatly appreciate their participation.

I want to express my appreciation to other members of our Program Committee: Erik Jonsson, former Mayor of Dallas, and Dr. Logan, President of Rose-Hulman Institute of Technology. Among us we have brought the government, industry, and university viewpoints into the planning for this meeting.

It is too much to expect that a meeting dealing with so complex a subject will come forth with dramatic new answers. The symposium and these proceedings are, however, valuable contributions to the continuing exchange of ideas and perspectives that are necessary foundations for solutions to improved urban transportation innovation and efficiency.

SEYMOUR W. HERWALD, *Chairman*
Program Committee

CONTENTS

LUNCHEON ADDRESS

SESSION II: URBAN DEVELOPMENT, DESIGN, AND
RENEWAL AND THE RELATION TO URBAN
TRANSPORTATION
  Panelists: *Harold B. Finger, Bernard Gifford,* and
  William L. Mertz

Contents   *ix*

Clarence H. Linder
President
National Academy
of Engineering

WELCOME

It is very gratifying for me to be present here today and to express the appreciation of the Academy to you for joining us on this occasion of the Eighth Autumn Meeting of the Academy of Engineering and the Symposium on Transportation.

The Academy is concerned with the definition of issues and the search for solutions to the important societal problems involving technology that face our country now and in the foreseeable future. At our autumn meetings we attempt to focus on problems of this nature by providing a forum for those of all interested disciplines in their search for understanding.

To some degree, this symposium is a follow-on to our meeting of a year ago, at which time we explored ways in which productivity in the service sector might be improved. In part, it is also derived from work accomplished by committees and boards of the National Academy of Engineering and the National Academy of Sciences.

We welcome this opportunity to have federal, state, and municipal officers and officials tell us how they view the current transportation problems. I think you will all agree that the outstanding speakers and panelists, and their choice of subjects, give every indication that we shall have an interesting and productive meeting.

I thank all of them for their willingness to share their time and knowledge with us.

INTRODUCTION

James M. Beggs

KEYNOTE ADDRESS: THE NEED TO DEVELOP INNOVATIVE SOLUTIONS TO TRANSPORTATION PROBLEMS

When I joined the Department of Transportation (DOT), after several years with the National Aeronautics and Space Administration, I remarked that going to the moon really seemed easier than trying to solve the problem of getting across town. No one has let me forget that remark, and—frankly—that's as it should be. Certainly, we can't let the problem get out of sight or out of focus—not if we ever hope to solve it. I assure you the challenge of congestion in our cities and the need for improved urban mobility are uppermost in our minds at DOT and hold a high place on the administration's list of domestic priorities.

I believe we have made some meaningful progress toward the decongestion of our cities. But we are a long way from the ultimate objective of our "urban Apollo" program, which is the attainment of a truly balanced transportation system with free-flowing corridors of travel and commerce in and through our cities.

The National Academy of Engineering report, *Urban Transportation Research and Development,* submitted to me last May, represents a searching examination of what's wrong with transportation in our cities today—along with some very cogent recommendations for changing the situation. I'm confident that this symposium will augment and amplify that report.

All it takes is one trip into Washington during the morning rush hour, or one trip across Manhattan any time of the day, to recognize that urban mobility is a subject in need of all the expertise and innovation that can be brought to bear. For with the greatest highway system in the world, and with 75 percent of Americans owning and operating their own "personal transit systems," we have more of the means of mobility

5

than any people on earth. Yet the traffic jams that are now commonplace—the 60 mph expressways that turn into parking lots twice a day—
make it all too obvious that the very popularity of the automobile now
seriously threatens its utility.

- According to the last census, 72 percent of our population now
live in urban areas that constitute about 3 percent of our total land.
- The major cities of America—those classified as Standard Metropolitan Statistical Areas (SMSA's)—contain two thirds of the 92 million automobiles registered in the United States. On the average, there
is one car for every 2.10 city dwellers, and that's not counting trucks
and motorcycles.
- One linear mile in every square mile of land is given over for
transportation purposes.
- America's transportation infrastructure—our roads and rails,
waterways and pipelines—is the most extensive in the world. Over the
network (we cannot honestly call it a system!) we perform 2,200 billion ton-miles of freight and 1.8 trillion passenger-miles of service—close
to half of that within the confines of cities.
- Of the 235 private transit companies that went bankrupt during
the 1960s, 146 went out of existence altogether. In the 10-year period,
rapid-rail ridership fell 13 percent; bus and trolley patronage declined
24 percent. Today 82 percent of all commuting workers use the automobile—54 percent of all car trips are less than 5 miles.

And there are other, equally far-reaching trends. We are convinced that
in the next decade we are going to be confronted with a petroleum
energy crisis of major proportions. Our transportation system uses
almost 60 percent of the petroleum energy consumed in this country;
our domestic supplies have finite limits, and our consumption continues
to increase.

At the same time, the now-familiar environmental crisis is upon us
and will be with us for a long time to come, until we solve the problems
of cleaning up our air and water and reducing the noise and other pollut-
ing factors in our environment. To solve the air pollution problem, the
automobile, a major contributor to urban air pollution, is being cleaned
up: Its engine cycle is being redesigned to reduce the pollutant output
to a very low level. In so doing, we are setting about reducing the efficiency of that engine by 25 percent, in order to meet the 1976 standards.
In the face of the aforementioned petroleum crisis, we not only are increasing consumption, but are reducing the efficiency of its use.

I might add that if you sat down with a group of engineers to design the most ill-conceived system for the kind of stop and start, idling-speed service that characterizes city traffic, you could not do better. It is a very poor system.

Last, and perhaps just as important, in the past decade we have constructed a number of new highways and freeways in our major cities. Today there is no room for more freeways and even if we were able to construct them, we would face rising alarm over what some of these highways might do to the cities. There just simply is no more land for this purpose in most of our cities; urban mobility demands, however, were never greater. And that indeed is the challenge that confronts us in our major cities. We face the necessity, therefore, to redesign, reconfigure, and reengineer the system, and perhaps even change the motivational factors and the social ground rules that shape the way our people live and work in our cities.

These are the things that concern us and often alarm us, because the problem in some places is immediate. This is not to say, however, that anything is intrinsically wrong with the system, or even the automobile; nor is it to say that there is anything wrong in the way that we have designed our cities, although some would claim that.

I simply think that we have gone too far in the expansion of the auto transportation system. The private automobile is, by its very nature, a grossly inefficient element in that system.

The urban transportation problem is a complex one. Transportation planning can no longer be conducted unilaterally or decisions made in isolation. Questions of urban land use, growth patterns, commerce and housing, jurisdictional prerogatives, the very social and cultural concerns of the community, are all related to the transportation issue and must weigh in every transportation deliberation.

But while the problems are complex, they are also compelling. Faced with curb-to-curb cars, inner-city decay, a shrinking tax base, and growing administrative costs, mayors and city councils today are hard pressed for answers. The challenges are immediate and urgent; the most attractive solutions long range, capital intensive, hard to breed, and slow to mature.

Our city fathers also find their options severely limited. They must rely on tried-and true technologies. The must build to some extent on the transportation infrastructure already in place. And they must go with systems that work—that will serve the people of the community and genuinely meet their needs. All of this, of course, within the framework of stiff time and budget constraints.

There is still another aspect to the problem, and that is the necessity to change people's transportation habits—in some cases, to alter their lifestyle. Given the density of the average city, it is virtually impossible to rework the means and modes of transportation without disrupting communities or inconveniencing their inhabitants. Projects that threaten to do that will understandably meet some resistance, but programs that would propose the wholesale transfer of commuters from cars to transit systems, for instance, must be prepared to offer strong inducements if vigorous public resistance is to be avoided or overcome.

So, recognizing these challenges and confronted by them, what are we doing to help America's mayors and city councils solve their urban transportation problems?

For one thing, we are exploring a variety of low- or non-capital-intensive alternatives: actions designed to increase the efficiency of existing systems at giveaway or bargain-basement prices.

An obvious example of such an alternative is affording priorities to high-occupancy vehicles (buses and car pools) and through other incentives that encourage the use of such vehicles.

There are other possibilities for short-term and low-cost urban benefits: increased regulation over the use of automobiles downtown, peak-period pricing for parking, greater use of staggered work hours, the restriction of some streets or certain hours for deliveries only, and so on.

There are certain nontransportation proposals that could have favorable effects on the urban transportation situation: the 4-day work week, for example, or the possibility that the work day might be spread over 24 hours, the work week "recycled" to include 7 days, or even the wider use of telecommunication capabilities to reduce the need for personal mobility.

Secondly, there are technical actions that can be taken to achieve better urban mobility. These entail considerable research, development, and demonstration work, involving new technologies or applying new twists to old ideas.

Probing technology has always been a fertile, but very bumpy field. The obstacles are mostly those relating to cost, together with the difficulties of superimposing new or replacement technologies over an existing system.

Still, there are enough examples of technological initiative already on the urban scene for us to be encouraged by the prospects for greater progress in this area.

The Bay Area Rapid Transit (BART) system in San Francisco, for example, is the first new rapid-rail system to be built in the United States in 60 years. It has all the "goodies"—the technical and cosmetic refinements needed to make a public transit system economic to operate, pleasant to ride, and attractive to the public.

But, good as it is, BART represents state-of-the-art technology, and it represents the kind of an investment—both in time and in money—not every city can afford. The root purpose of our DOT research, development, and demonstration program is to expand the options available to America's cities—to find technical shortcuts, if possible—and to evoke transit alternatives that are functional and economically feasible.

Later this month we will be inaugurating another public transit innovation—our personal rapid transit system (PRT) system in Morgantown, West Virginia. This concept comes closest, perhaps, to providing the personal convenience normally afforded by the car. Our announcement last week that Dallas–Fort Worth will build a PRT to connect the two cities with their new airport, and the announcement this week that we are funding a people-mover system for Denver are good indications that a number of "car-sick" U.S. cities will elect to invest in personal rapid transit. And the competition, in my judgment, will prove to be a real spur to people-mover technologies.

Another bright prospect on the technological horizon is the Tracked Air Cushion Vehicle. I won't dwell on the TACV's attributes—its magic-carpet-smooth ride, high speed, nonpolluting propulsion system—these are well known throughout the engineering fraternity. What *is* important today is that we are moving a big step closer to operational reality. Just this week the first state-of-the-art cars went on our high-speed test track in Pueblo, Colorado, for their initial test runs.

Federal funding for transportation research and development has increased each year of President Nixon's administration. From $114.2 million (1.7 percent of the DOT budget) in FY 1969, R&D program levels have risen to $387 million (4.5 percent of the budget) for FY 1973. We continue to believe that prudent investments in technical and engineering research pay some of the most rewarding dividends in terms of increased productivity and consumer benefits.

We also have high regard for the potentials of university research. Our university program this year is funded at the highest level in DOT's history. In keeping with President's Nixon's commitment to a 12 percent increase overall in funds for research and development work at universities and colleges, the agencies that are a part of DOT have budgeted $14 million for such projects. In addition, we have added a new program of university research, funded at $4 million, within the Office of the Secretary, in order to bring the expertise of America's outstanding colleges and universities to bear on the interdisciplinary, intermodal, and multimodal challenges facing us—especially in the areas of urban transportation. I consider this money well spent and an essential investment, if we expect to get a lead on the technical challenges at hand.

A third way to better urban mobility involves motivational forces:

We must persuade people that public transit is superior for urban travel—
a personal convenience and a community asset.

There has been a good deal of publicity given to the express bus service that has been operating for the past 2½ years over the Shirley Highway (in Northern Virginia) exclusive bus lanes. But that experiment is no gimmick. It offers ample evidence that bus transit *can* attract riders when it is made fast, frequent, and convenient. And the idea is being copied in other communities. When the Shirley express project began in 1969; 38 buses were sufficient to carry the fewer than 4,000 daily passengers. Today, 151 buses carry nearly 20,000 commuters over the express route every day, more than the number who commute by car.

Quality of service is probably a stronger influence than price in winning converts to public transit, but where price incentives have proved feasible, patronage generally has gone up. In Atlanta, for example, where the citizenry approved a 1 percent sales tax increase to underwrite improved public transportation, fares were cut from 40 cents to 15 cents and ridership has increased 20 percent.

The Southern California Rapid Transit District offers a monthly pass for 12 dollars, which entitles people to unlimited one-zone rides for an entire month.

As your committee so aptly observed in your *Urban Transportation Research and Development* report, state and local jurisdictions must take a larger and more cooperative role in renewing public transportation and in relating it to overal social goals. And, as you further suggest, the federal government does have a responsibility to lead and assist in that occupation.

We have held to the conviction that our capital grant programs serve larger purposes than the salvaging of faltering transit systems or the replenishing of hardware. It has been our view that just keeping transit wheels turning is not enough. We must move in new directions, turn to new ideas, and devote more resources and resourcefulness to improving the *function* of public transportation and its utility to the community.

Prior to 1969 mass transit was strictly a low-profile program in Washington. The Urban Mass Transportation Administration had a spartan staff, a shoestring budget, and no continuity of funding. From a budget of less than $135 million in FY 1969, public transportation has grown to the billion-dollar level in FY 1973, and Secretary Volpe recently recommended to the Congress that an additional $3 billion from the general fund be obligated and earmarked for public transportation programs through FY 1977.

So the trend under President Nixon's leadership is clear. Federal transportation investments are being intensified. To date, federal assistance has saved or stabilized public transit systems in 60 cities. To afford city leaders greater flexibility in meeting their urban transportation needs, we have lobbied long and hard in the Congress to make a portion of the Highway Trust Fund accessible to communities for *any* urban transportation need—road or rail, highway or busway. While we are disappointed that legislation to that effect was not enacted this session, we are equally confident that the principle is a valid one, and we will continue to seek ways to help city planners obtain the options, the technologies, and the resources they need to do the urban transportation job.

We believe that it is essential to give the city planners, the mayor, the councils, the opportunity to solve their problems as they see them, not as we see them here in Washington.

The challenge is a massive one. I know of no major city in America that pretends the job can be done by the automobile alone.

Our preeminent task is to demonstrate that public transportation systems *can* compete with the private automobile in quality and speed of service, in comfort and convience, and in cost. We must work toward that goal by whatever investment, technical, and motivational means we can muster, bearing in mind that the ultimate objective of our efforts is a better community for all who live, work, or travel there.

I am sure this symposium will serve those ideals.

Seymour W. Herwald

SYMPOSIUM APPROACH TO DEFINITION OF PROBLEMS AND TO IMPROVEMENTS OF URBAN DESIGN AND URBAN TRANSPORTATION

URBAN TRANSPORTATION RESEARCH AND DEVELOPMENT

Many of the problems and approaches to solutions that are associated with the three key elements of the urban transportation problem were explored in 1971 in a National Academy of Engineering workshop on transportation related to improved urban productivity. They were also studied during the past spring and summer by several NAE committees. I have had the pleasure to serve as Chairman of the Committee on Transportation, and I am pleased to have this opportunity to review the results of our study of urban transportation. This committee was created in 1970 by the NAE in response to a request from the Department of Transportation (DOT) for the NAE to provide engineering service in the field of transportation.

Our first task, a study of urban transportation and related urban development was completed earlier this year. A report on our findings was issued in April and is available from the NAE offices. We do not view this as a research report but rather as a presentation of the general consensus of the committee. The consensus is based on exploration of the broad issues with officials of DOT, the Department of Housing and Urban Development (HUD), other governmental agencies, and with many experts in these fields.

Two prime conclusions emerged early in the study and were reinforced throughout our evaluations:

- Urban transportation, including the interaction between transportation and urban development, is one of the most urgent problems facing our society,

* Urban transportation should be given the highest action priority by the Department of Transportation.

DEFINITION OF THE PROBLEM

General

The committee soon came to some general conclusions that help define the broad nature and scope of our urban transportation problems. There are growing indications that the urban transportation problem will worsen. This is readily understood simply from the continued growth of our population, particularly with the trend to population growth in the suburbs, and the evolving pattern of life styles and work locations. All seem to require greater mobility with regard to people, goods, and services. The general nature of these problems is not new, but they are becoming more severe and more urgent. The committee believes that a much greater effort will have to be expended to reverse these present adverse trends of increasing costs, declining transit services, and damaging side effects.

The concern for increasing our national, regional, and local efforts comes from the conviction that many of the underlying causes of transportation difficulties are beyond the problem of the systems themselves. They are intimately tied into the broader political, social, and economic considerations of urban decay and the processes of urban growth.

Cost

The cost of urban transportation in the United States is high and is rising. DOT estimates that approximately 20 percent of our gross national product goes to our total transportation activities. Approximately half of this total bill is associated with urban transportation. The realization of additional safety equipment, antipollution devices, and improvements to transport services will soon increase these direct costs by another 5 percent of our gross national product.

It is also obvious that many indirect and more subtle "costs" will have to, or ought to, be included in our transportation planning. For example, there are real "aesthetic" contributions that new, innovative systems should make to the urban and suburban scene. We cannot allow the system to degrade the visual concept of future cities.

In a similar vein, the positive enhancement of the "quality of life"

TABLE 1   Definition of Problem

1. General	
2. Cost	
Total transportation	20% GNP
Urban transportation	10% GNP
Safety equipment, antipollution devices, and improved service will increase costs	5% GNP
Cost impact on	Esthetics
	Quality of life
	Travel time
	Job access

of the urban environment must be considered. The real value of reduction in commuting time in terms of increased productivity for the community must be accepted as part of the cost equation.

Further, it is becoming more obvious every day that the increasing cost trends have a very serious impact on low-income urban families. (See Table 1.)

Declining Service

The predominant pattern of the evolving urban and suburban regions of our nation is almost totally based on the use of autos and trucks. For millions of people without cars, the *economic, social,* and *cultural* advantages of the urban region are out of reach because of the assumption that they can drive. Public transit for this setting is usually *inefficient, inadequate,* and exhibits *declining* service.

Most of the poor and the retired who have no automobile find that the time involved and the cost and inconvenience are serious obstacles to bettering, or even maintaining, their economic status and quality of life.

Damaging Side Effects

Perhaps the most serious and urgent aspects of the urban transportation problem are the subtle and not-so-subtle damaging side effects from our dependence on the automobile. These manifest themselves in many ways: from air pollution and noise to the intolerable human and material costs of accidents and the increased crime in the decaying cities.

The typical growth patterns for the suburbs all seem to lead to inefficient use of *energy, land,* and *resources* and to further fragmentation of the urban population.

The committee certainly agrees that there is an urgent need for a national growth policy that will enhance the quality of urban life.

Jurisdictional Considerations

Significant improvements in institutional and social arrangements are needed at all levels of government. As has been noted for some time, while there are technical and funding problems, a major difficulty in improving transportation lies in the institutional structures that function in our urban areas. The failure, the inadequacy, or the obsolescence of diverse institutional elements inject almost insurmountable difficulties to transportation and urban planning. Based on many discussions with individuals in this field, the committee feels that this problem is still very critical and intensive effort is needed to overcome it.

Research Effort

The complex problems I have just described are, in the view of the committee, amenable to an expanded and broadened research program. Transportation technology R & D needs to be significantly supplemented by work in all relevant disciplines, not just engineering and economics.

A creative effort to achieve new urban systems requires the information on which to base a design. Yet, not enough is known of the social, political, and economic consequences, either short or long term, of changes in transportation modes, systems, and services. Transportation, instead of being used to accommodate congestion should be used to serve urban growth and renewal.

The report points out that the lack of critical system design information and lack of performance cost–benefit relationships can only be overcome by an expanded, multidisciplinary R & D program. Such a program should be carried out by DOT in relation to the fundamental growth and functional criteria for our urban environments. R & D expenditures by DOT are low in relation to other federal agencies. The committee recommendation for an increased program and funding is generally consistent with that recommended by others outside the government.

Further, there is an extensive and varied experience in many foreign countries in rebuilding existing communities and building completely new ones. The DOT R & D program, as envisioned by the committee, can benefit materially from this ongoing worldwide experience.

RECOMMENDED ACTIONS

In summary, the committee feels that our view of urban transportation problems has been too narrow. Changes in urban transportation should assist in providing efficient economic activity, improved housing and public services, and access to recreational and educational opportunities and enhancing a healthful and pleasant urban environment. In view of these needs, the committee suggests the following course of action.

Action No. 1

Federal urban transportation programs should *focus* increasingly on providing better quality of urban life, *not* just better transportation. This requires additional activity so that the scope and scale of sponsored programs will demonstrate the influences of transportation systems and patterns of urban growth and development. The programs must consider the need for development of knowledge and follow a sound experimental approach.

Action No. 2

The increasing focus on the quality of life clearly calls for a better understanding of relationships between urban transportation systems and the *functions* of metropolitan areas. This, in turn, requires an enhanced program of analysis and real-world experimentation.

The committee report suggests several high-impact programs for using existing DOT demonstration authority to an even greater effect. In essence, these would call for a severalfold increase in the number and size of demonstrations of transportation system innovations aimed at gaining understanding of the interactions and relationships. In most cases these would also entail dedicated cooperation of the state and local communities. The complexity of the modern social urban structure precludes simple extrapolations from isolated experiences.

Action No. 3

The proper design of urban transportation experiments and the implementation of more effective investment programs also call for an increase in supporting social science thinking and analysis.

Of course, some research has been done in these areas, but much more work is required, particularly in the longer-range predictive situations. For example, work is needed to improve our understanding of the material, as well as social costs of the various system alternatives as they pertain to all segments of the urban society and to the range of movements of people, goods, and services. This work should be conducted within the social science frame of reference applying the concepts, insights, and findings of social science.

Action No. 4

Adequate support of increased DOT research, development, and demonstration activity requires further strengthened professional capability both inside and outside the department. In the committee's view, DOT should continue to form and develop concentrations of highly competent professional activity, where the overall emphasis should be on achieving critical size and quality of the groups rather than on the formation of a large number of small groups. These groups should include a broad spectrum of backgrounds to stimulate solutions of real-world problems within the context of the expanded research programs.

Action No. 5

With increased and improved resources and higher level of activity, the Secretary of DOT will be able to make specific assignments of responsibility within the department for implementing a more effective program of research, development, and demonstration in urban transportation.

The report emphasizes the sense of urgency with which these recommendations for action were made to the Secretary. In order to make a contribution to the improvement in the quality of urban life, the department's programs need increased funding and broad and continuing evaluation and review. A specific officer of the department should have the responsibility for developing detailed plans to implement the foregoing recommendations.

Action No. 6

With improved knowledge and increased resources, DOT could take the lead in encouraging state and local jurisdictions to accomplish program design, and it should consider doing so. The program could involve the overall physical and institutional transformation of a single metropolitan area—or several areas—as a demonstration of how changes in transportation can help fulfill broader social and urban objectives.

For example, it was suggested that DOT could join with HUD, the Department of Health, Education, and Welfare, and the Environmental Protection Agency in planning and joint funding of design competitions for up to 10 urban areas in each of three size classes. The purpose of such a competition, of course, would be to select the best proposals for full implementation.

There is a real need to establish guidelines for definition of the vital features and functions for urban areas. The committee report offers an example of what a typical program should be for the research, development, and demonstration of an urban design.

CONCLUSION

Much of the material I have presented is admittedly derivative in nature. There have been many studies in the past, and we fully realize that there are many programs under way already.

Yet the problems are staggering, and the conventional transportation investments in the cities have not met with notable success.

A central idea that this report may contribute toward the solution of the transportation problem is simply this: Given the new focus of transportation as it relates to urban goals, the mission of DOT should be looked upon as involving transportation not simply as a way to move people and goods but rather as a means of helping to create a better urban society.

Panelists:
Frank S. Besson, Jr.
William L. Everitt
and
Stanley P. E. Price

SESSION I:
GENERAL TRANSPORTATION PROBLEMS AND THE MODAL INTERFACE PROBLEMS RELATED TO URBAN TRANSPORTATION

René H. Miller

V/STOL AIRCRAFT: ITS FUTURE ROLE IN URBAN TRANSPORTATION AS A PICKUP AND DISTRIBUTION SYSTEM

INTRODUCTION

During the past two decades the per capita demand for transportation has doubled, while common-carrier transit travel has decreased by 50 percent. These changing travel patterns have generated acute problems of congestion over the shorter distances characteristic of intraurban and suburban trips where the highest concentration of travel occurs. This concentration is shown graphically in Figure 1, which also demonstrates the dominance of the automobile over the entire travel market, accounting for close to 90 percent of all passenger miles. This dominance is particularly evident for stage lengths of less than 50 miles, where it is estimated that 80–90 percent of all passenger trips are taken.

Accommodating this growing transportation demand by increasing automobile traffic density is becoming increasingly difficult, particularly in urban and suburban areas. In many such areas it is been estimated that 50 percent of the available land has to be dedicated to the automobile. Congestion increases yearly and now seems to exist throughout the day and not just at commuting peaks. But despite these and other factors that might be expected to inhibit the growth of motor vehicle traffic, the migration from common-carrier transit to the indivual automobile continues. It is by no means clear that newer concepts for urban mass transportation now being considered will be sufficiently attractive to reverse this trend voluntarily.

The great attractiveness of the automobile for the short-haul traveler stems from certain outstanding conveniences such as its door-to-door transportation capability, impossible to match with a common carrier,

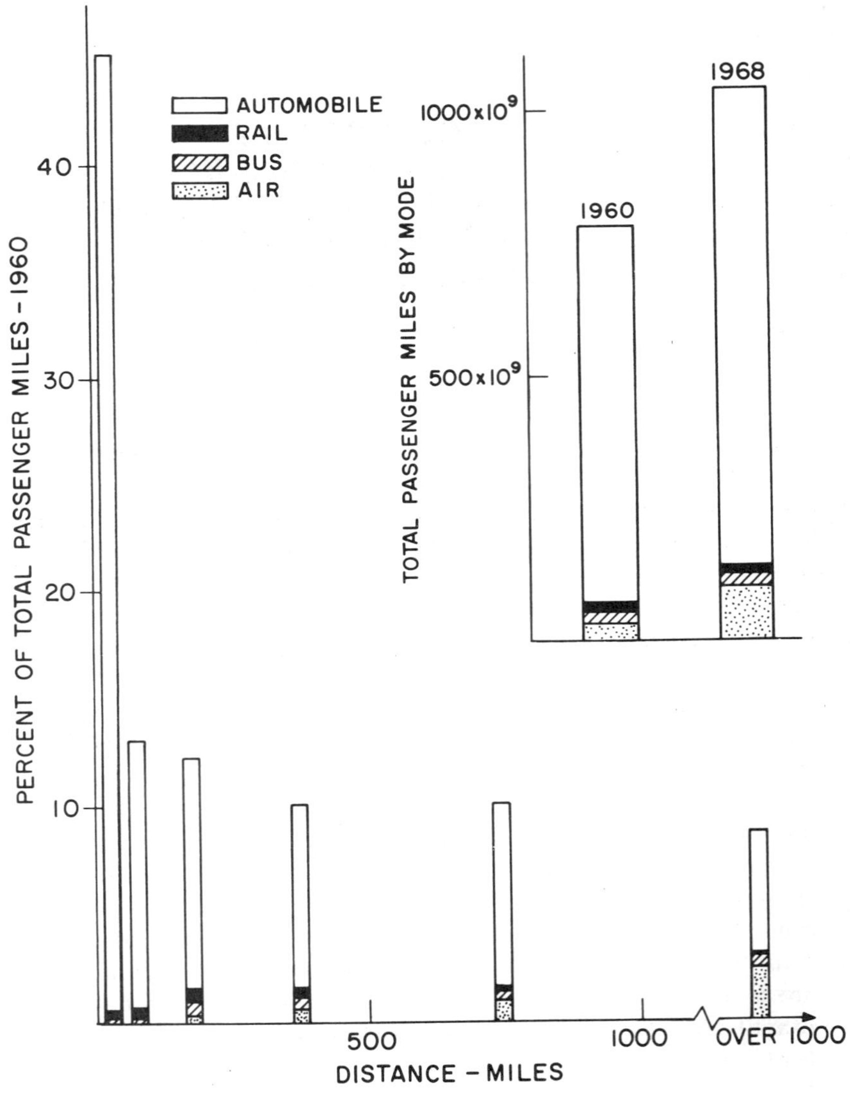

FIGURE 1   Estimated distribution of U.S. passenger miles for 1960 and comparison by mode of total intercity travel for 1960 and 1968.

except in the unusual circumstance of origin and destination both being close to a way station or terminal. In addition, the automobile provides a high degree of privacy and the freedom of choice associated with direct control of scheduling and routing.

In contrast to these overwhelming advantages our present common carriers in short-haul urban operations can offer very little in competition. They are, if anything, slower because of wait time and the need to make frequent stops. They are certainly less private, usually less comfortable, and frequently more expensive than the private automobile. Above all they require some means of collection and distribution of passengers to and from the stations or stops, a problem that has yet to be satisfactorily solved for any concept of urban mass transportation. The resistance of a traveler to a change in mode of transportation is known to be very high, and if he must walk or drive any distance to the station, he will elect to stay in his car and drive directly to his destination unless prevented from doing so by stringent parking bans and excessive highway congestion.

In searching for solutions to the mass urban transportation problem, it seemed logical to some of us to consider what air could offer as an alternative mode of short-haul travel. Certainly air transportation has had an outstanding success in recent years in satisfying the long-haul, common-carrier passenger demand (Figure 2), essentially without subsidy and at an average cost that, despite inflation, has remained substantially constant through the years. This success may be attributed in part to the high level of technology used in developing new air transportation concepts. It has been possible, in turn, to pay the tremendous cost of research, development, engineering, and testing required to support this technology because of the very much higher productivity of the newer advanced air vehicles as measured in passenger miles generated per hour. For example, aircraft costs are on the order of 70 dollars per pound of weight empty as compared to 2 dollars for surface transportation equipment, yet because of their high productivity, depreciation costs of modern jet equipment are amortized rapidly and thus represent less than 10 percent of total ticket price. These prices are competitive between air and ground. It seemed to us of interest to examine whether these advantages could be applied to the ultra-short-haul urban and suburban transportation market in a manner similar to their successful application to the medium- and long-haul markets.

We have been studying this question for several years and find that the answer could be in the affirmative, providing a solution to the ground interface problem of collection and distribution can be found, a problem for which we as yet see no completely satisfactory solution.

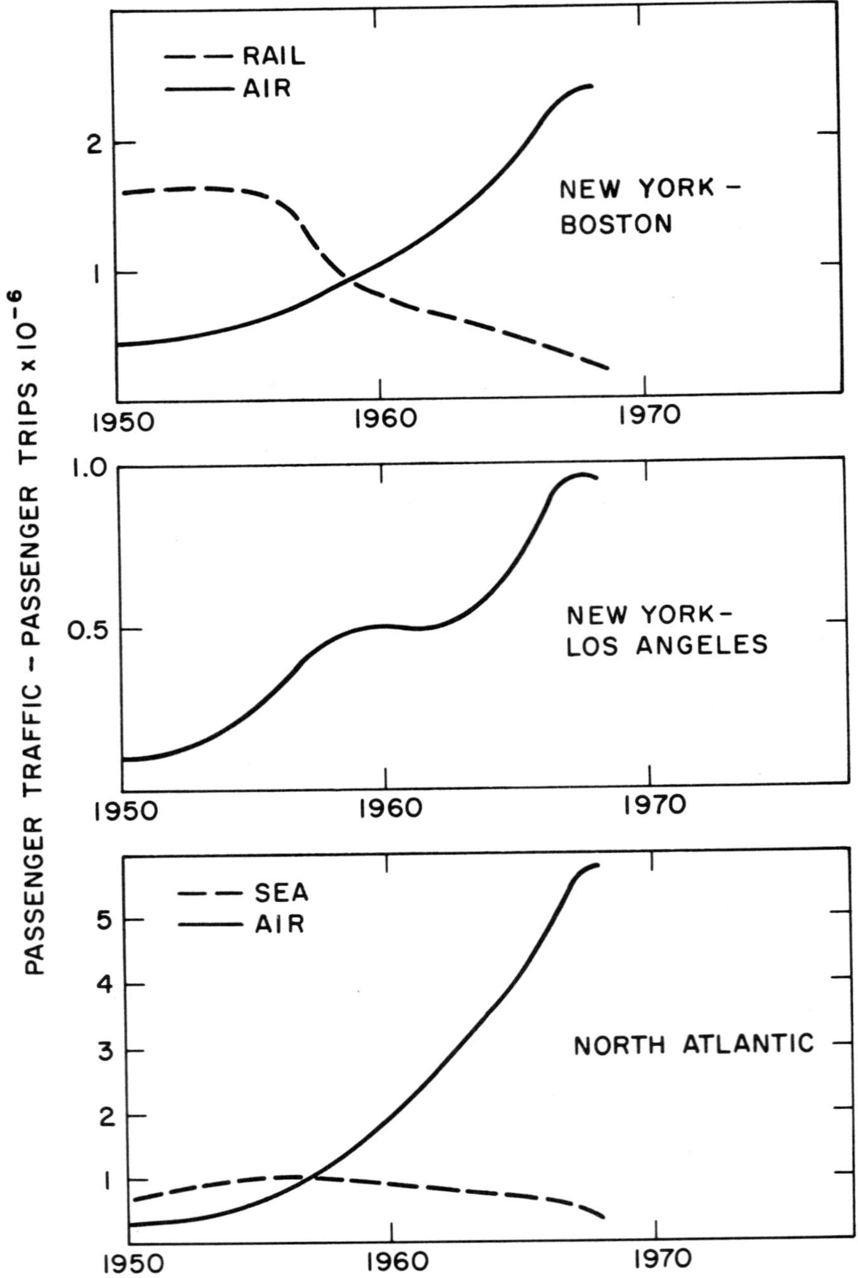

FIGURE 2   Growth of air travel for three typical travel markets.

It is certainly possible to develop aircraft and design a total air transportation system that will permit operation over distances of the order of 30 miles with block times of 5 minutes and ticket prices of the order of 3 dollars (10 cents a passenger mile), if the traffic density is sufficiently high. Over the same distances automobiles or buses, based on statistical studies of motor vehicle speeds in urban and suburban areas, would require block times of the order of 1 hour except in periods of light congestion, such as between 8 p.m. and 6 a.m. The apparent costs of the automobile for the same trip would be considerably less than air, on the order of 3 cents a mile or 60 cents for the trip. However, the true cost would be much higher, on the order of 20 cents a mile for typical urban insurance rates or a total of 6 dollars for the trip. These true costs include additional items not paid for at the time of travel, such as depreciation, the loss of return or interest on the capital invested in the automobile, its housing, maintenance, insurance, and taxes. Bus or transit costs could also be higher, depending on the amount of subsidy and stage length. Typical transit costs in the Boston area are of the order of 10 cents a passenger mile, an additional 10 cents being paid for by subsidy, although these costs drop rapidly to the order of 5 cents a passenger mile over the longer suburban distances as compared to intraurban travel.

One could conclude that air transportation is competitive with other modes of travel in cost, while at the same time providing a tremendous advantage in reduced trip time, and may therefore siphon off a large segment of the short-haul travel market from the automobile. It is believed, however, that this potential will only be achieved if the major problem of collection and distribution of passengers to and from the air terminals is solved satisfactorily. Any public carrier transportation network, whether operating in the air or on the ground, must have a finite number of modes, and, except in heavily built-up areas, these will probably not be spaced less than 5 or 10 miles apart. Otherwise trip speeds and more importantly passenger loading per departure will become too low to make the system economically viable. The collection and distribution problem then consists of providing some common carrier system to bring passengers to the stations over average distances of the order of 2 to 5 miles. If, and only if, this problem can be solved, will any public transportation system, air or ground, be competitive with the automobile.

Many solutions to this problem are conceivable: for example, a jitney system with dynamic scheduling in which small passenger vehicles are dispatched on demand, with a routing designed to minimize travel time and maximize load factor by means of a real-time computer optimization process.[14] Several such systems are currently under investigation and in demonstration programs. Alternatively one could consider the "disposable" car, a low-cost, electric-powered, one- or two-place vehicle activated by a coded card that computes charges on a time and mileage basis. The car is simply picked up at one point and left at another, using a multiplicity of small depots. Many other such schemes can be conceived of; the area is ripe for invention of a systems nature. The economics of such collection and distribution systems are very difficult to analyze and predict, and it is not at all certain that they will ever become feasible if required to compete on a cost basis with the private automobile. But the urgency of the transportation problem may be sufficiently acute to ensure their eventual development.

One may well ask why, if it is indeed possible to achieve a competitive short-haul air transportation system, have not the existing systems in New York, Chicago, San Francisco, and Los Angeles shown a greater growth. Why are ticket prices so much higher than those that have been quoted here? Certainly part of the answer lies in the problem of collection and distribution to, for example, the Wall Street terminal. If a cab is required, this vehicle will most likely be used for the entire trip to the airport in preference to change in mode. However, it is believed that the main reason for the discrepancy between fact and theory lies in the nature of the market served, which has not been large enough to warrant the frequency of service nor the development of the larger, faster vehicles necessary for economic operations. Turning again to the Boston area, the total trips into Boston by all modes and for all purposes amount to some 350 million per year and the total number of trips in the area served by the airport amount to some 500 million per year. On the other hand, travelers using the Boston airport account for only 10 million trips per year. If this number is increased to 30 million, as some of the figures indicate would be reasonable, to allow for visitors and employees, this still represents a small transportation market compared to the half billion trips in the area served by the airport. Airport service alone will probably never generate a sufficiently large market to support a common-carrier mass transportation system by itself, particularly a point-to-point city-center-to-airport transportation mode, since less than 50 percent of the airport users originate in the city center. It is believed that the only way in which a high-frequency, no-reservation, low-cost transportation system can be developed to serve the airport is by developing a total short-haul urban and suburban system, with the airport simply another node with links to all of the surrounding areas including the central business district. This total transportation system will satisfy a far greater need than airport service, while also providing rapid access to the airport from all points in the area and not just from the city center. Only then will the costs become competitive with other modes and be sufficiently attractive to draw an appreciable number of passengers away from the automobiles that now carry 70 percent of the passengers to airports. Furthermore, the very high indirect operating costs of air transportation systems (Figure 3) can only be reduced by such a high frequency, no-reservation

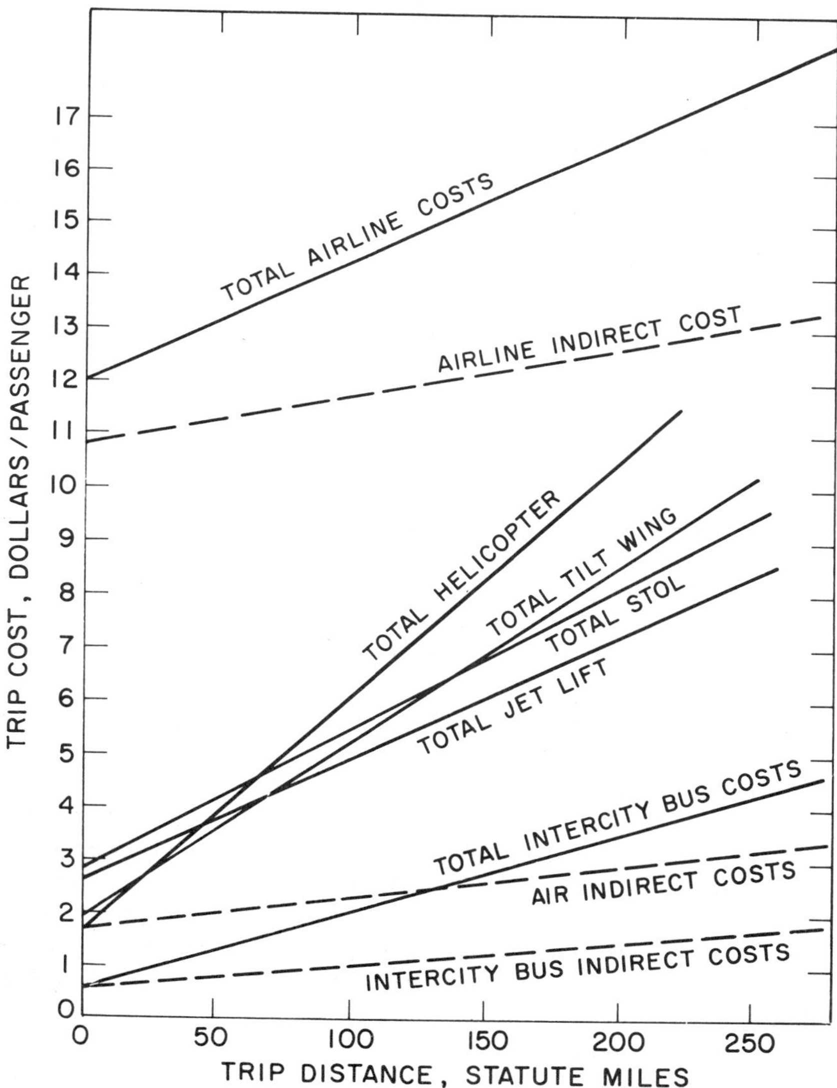

FIGURE 3 Comparison of direct and indirect travel costs—airline, intercity bus, and projected short-haul air.

air system. Currently, departure costs run to about 12 dollars per passenger emplaned, obviously a prohibitive cost over the shorter distances and one of the basic reasons why air transportation has never been competitive in the very short hauls. Analysis of these indirect operating costs[1] indicate a reasonable expectancy that they may be reduced to the point where the air transportation system will achieve the costs suggested earlier, but this will require a totally new concept of airline operation and a reasonably high market density.

METHOD OF ANALYSIS

The methodology by which the costs given above for the air transportation system were developed will be briefly described. The market examined is shown in Figure 4 and represents Boston and the surrounding suburban areas. First, a gravity-type model was selected to forecast the total travel demand of the type:

$$D_{ij} = K \, \frac{P_i P_j}{d_{ij}^{\gamma}} \, ,$$

where

D_{ij} is the daily one-way demand in person trips between areas i and j,
P_i is the population of area i,
P_j is the population of area j,
d_{ij} is the distance between i and j in miles,
γ is the distance elasticity of demand,
K is a proportionality constant.

The process of calibrating the demand model indicated that a value of 1 for the exponent γ rather than the usually assumed value close to 2 gave a better fit from the regression analysis.

In order to establish the distribution of this demand over the various competing travel modes, the concept of elasticity, which expresses the percent increase in demand as a function of a percent change in the cost or quality of a product, was used. In this case, the quality may include several factors such as convenience, comfort, cost, and speed, but the analysis was limited[2] to the more easily quantified items—total travel time (T) and cost (C).

The demand, D_n, for any travel mode, n, will be assumed to vary with T and C as

$$D_n = K C_n^{\alpha} T_n^{\beta}$$

where α and β are the elasticities with respect to cost and time, and K is constant.

The modal split prediction model will assume that T and C are the only two variables that the traveling public will use in choosing mode of travel and that the market share, M_n, of any mode, n, can be given by

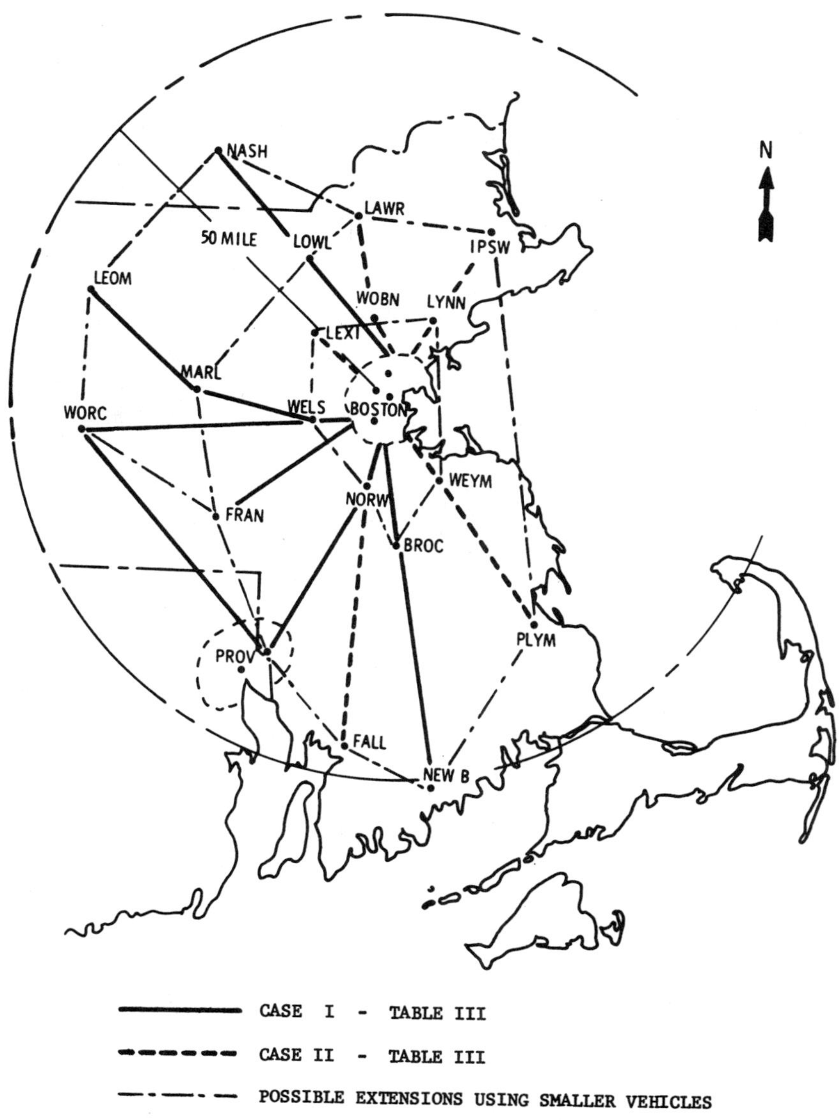

FIGURE 4 Boston suburban model showing air terminal locations and proposed air links.

$$M_n = \frac{D_n}{\Sigma_n D_n} = \frac{C_n T_n}{\Sigma_n CT} .$$

It was assumed that the total travel demand is fixed and hence is a secondary, or derived demand (i.e., represents required travel derived from some need other than the appeal of the travel itself). Introducing a new mode of transportation will then not increase the total amount of travel. This assumption appears to be justified for the shorter-haul travel by the New York–Boston data of Figure 2, where the total common carrier changed by only a small amount, attributable to population growth and variations in the economic situation. Evidently the nature of the North Atlantic travel market, also shown in Figure 2, is quite different and represents less of a derived demand (i.e., much of the travel is conducted for the sake of travel). Here the speed and comfort of the jets have generated a very large new demand. It is possible that the introduction of a new high-speed, comfortable, and convenient short-haul travel mode will similarly result in an increase in total travel in suburban areas due to demographic changes generated by this new capability, although such travel will almost certainly remain a derived and therefore a bound demand. Any such potential increase was conservatively ignored.

During the Northeast Corridor study of the Department of Transportation, travel information was obtained for city pairs in the area and from this statistical information the empirical values for α and β were determined to be $\alpha = -3.1$ and $\beta = -2.7$.

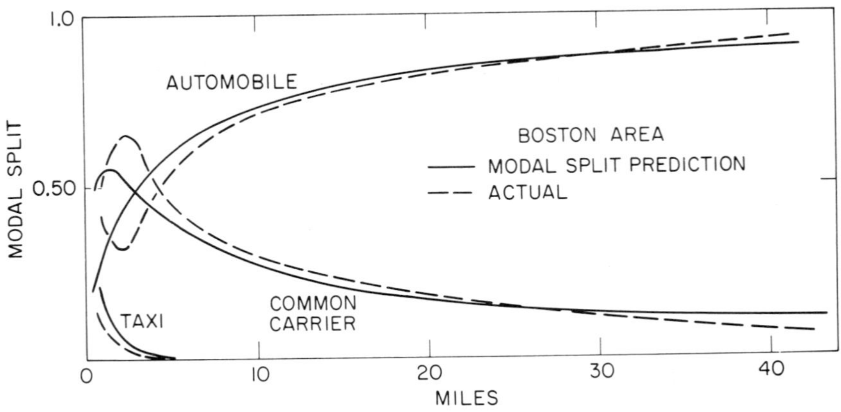

FIGURE 5   Predicted and actual modal split of traffic to and from Boston.

TABLE 1 Time and Cost Analysis for Various Modes of Travel

Code	Description	Cost($)	Time–Min
Air A	Helicopter	3.5 + 0.07D	22 + 0.28D
Air B	Tilt-rotor-wing	1.5 + 0.05D	22 + 0.16D
Auto A	Apparent costs	0.5 + 0.03D	10 + 2.4D
Auto B	True costs	1.0 + 0.20D	10 + 2.4D
Transit A	Existing subsidized	0.2 + 0.04D	20 + 4.8D
Transit B	Existing unsubsidized	0.35 + 0.07D	20 + 4.8D
Transit C	High speed subsidized	0.2 + 0.04D	20 + 1.5D
Transit D	High speed unsubsidized	0.35 + 0.07D	20 + 1.5D
Taxi	Conventional metered	0.60 + 0.70D	2 + 2.4D

Since these elasticities were computed from intercity travel data, it was necessary to check their applicability to the urban travel market in the Boston area. Figure 5 compares the actual modal split with that predicted using $\alpha = -2.7$ and $\beta = -3.1$. The agreement between the predicted and actual demand distribution is satisfactory, except for the shorter distances where the simple model used fails to account for the predilection for automobile travel over distances more suitable to walking. Since we are interested in travel segments greater than 5 miles, it was concluded that the empirically determined values were adequate.

Table 1 summarizes the values of T and C used in this study and discussed in more detail in Miller.[1] The last column gives the total time in transit including access time to reach the vehicle and, in the case of the common carrier, the wait time based on half the average headway. D is the travel distance in miles.

INTRAURBAN, SHORT-HAUL AIR TRANSPORTATION

Having established the nature of the existing short-haul ground transportation market and the demand elasticities that seemed appropriate, a hypothetical air transportation mode was added and an estimate made of the extent to which it could be expected to penetrate this market. It was assumed that the vehicles to be used would be capable of vertical takeoff and landing (VTOL) (and therefore able to land on any available area not much greater than the vehicle's maximum dimensions) and able to approach from any direction regardless of winds and steeply enough, even under Instrument Flight Rules (IFR) conditions, to be unconstrained by surrounding obstacles. Furthermore, their noise level would be of the order of ambient urban background noise levels (about 70 db), and they would be essentially nonpolluting. The justification for these assumptions, and the associated cost penalties, are discussed below.

As a result of several recent analyses of airline operating costs[3-10] reasonable projections as to the possible costs for a short-haul air system of the type to be considered here can be made. Extensive regression analyses were conducted[5] on airline indirect operating costs (IOC) separately for the domestic trunk and local service airlines. These costs are essentially passenger service, station costs, sales, and general administration. The direct operating costs (DOC) of several different types of aircraft operating at various altitudes and speeds were studied[4] by means of computerized design programs. A later report[8] expanded the study to include more advanced VTOL aircraft concepts such as the low disk loading tilt-wing-tilt-rotor. It was not the intent of either of these reports, nor is it the intent here, to select between the many competitive types of VTOL, V/STOL, and STOL aircraft that could be used for this transportation system. Each one has advantages and disadvantages, but one basic conlusion that can be drawn from the studies[4] is that there is little to choose in direct operating costs between configurations when viewed in the context of total costs, including indirects. This is clearly evident from Figure 3. For the purpose of this discussion the helicopter was selected as typical of existing VTOL transports and the tilt-wing rotor concept[8] as typical of a higher-speed VTOL aircraft that could be operational in the future and is well within the capabilities of present-day technology. Their total costs based on a 50 percent load factor were shown[1] to be $3.34 + 0.035D$ dollars per revenue passenger for the helicopter and $1.52 + 0.025D$ dollars per revenue passenger for the tilt-rotor-wing, where D is the trip distance in miles.

These costs are those that can be realistically expected during the present decade for advanced high-performance helicopters and for a tilt-rotor aircraft during the next decade operating in a region of high demand and under a management that takes advantage of modern techniques for decision making as to optimum scheduling for maximum utilization and load factor.[11-13] Taneja and Simpson[11] examine the concept of dynamic scheduling, in which aircraft are dispatched as demand dictates and subject to constraints such as a maximum waiting time for any passenger. It has been concluded that, whereas dynamic scheduling is attractive for a low-density market, scheduled flying generally results in higher revenues and better service for the passenger if the market justifies a high frequency of the order of 50 flights per operating day.

The block time consists of time to climb vertically, accelerate and climb to cruise altitude, cruise and descend from cruise altitude, decelerate and vertically land. No ground or air maneuvering time is included because of the anticipated method of terminal area operation discussed below. These block times are, for the helicopter, 1.0 + 0.23D minutes and, for the tilt wing, 1.0 + 0.14D minutes.

Since a few years of continuous operation will be required before the projected systems will reach their optimum schedules and fare structure, and in order to introduce a degree of conservatism into the air system analysis, the per mile costs were doubled in Miller.[1] The flight times were also increased by 20 percent to allow for a possible intermediate stop. The zero-length costs were left substantially unchanged since the indirect costs that dominate this parameter were felt to be reasonably well established by the referenced analyses based on experience with existing air transportation systems. The final values were therefore rounded off to $C = 3.5 + 0.07D$ and $T = 22 + 0.28D$, for the helicopter, and $C = 1.5 + 0.05D$ and $T = 22 + 0.16D$, for the advanced VTOL.

In both cases 20 minutes have been added to the total air times to allow for access to the terminal and wait time, as was also assumed for the ground transit system, and 1 minute added for access to the aircraft at the terminal. These points will be discussed further below.

THE DEMAND DISTRIBUTION

Figure 6 shows the results of several computer runs using the modal split relationship and keyed to Table 1.

From Figure 6A it is apparent that if a helicopter shuttle system (Case A for air) were introduced, operating over a radius of about 50 miles from the city center with indirect costs typical of airline operations, it would not substantially change the dominance of the automobile for shorter distances. Beyond 30 miles, however, it could be expected to assume a share of the market. A more advanced aircraft (Case B) such as a tilt-rotor, cruising at speeds of the order of 350 knots and operating at substantially lower indirect costs typical of a more mature system, could, however, be expected to take an appreciable share of the market away from the automobile beyond 30 miles, as shown in Figure 6B.

Figure 6C shows the effect of removing the subsidy from the ground system. Apparently this will simply increase automobile traffic without substantially affecting the air market, primarily because the transit share is, as might be expected, over shorter distances where air can offer little help. The undesirability of eliminating subsidy is apparent. It is particularly in the shorter distances that maximum congestion occurs, and an intolerable situation would probably develop if the transit traffic were transferred to the private automobile in these heavily built-up areas.

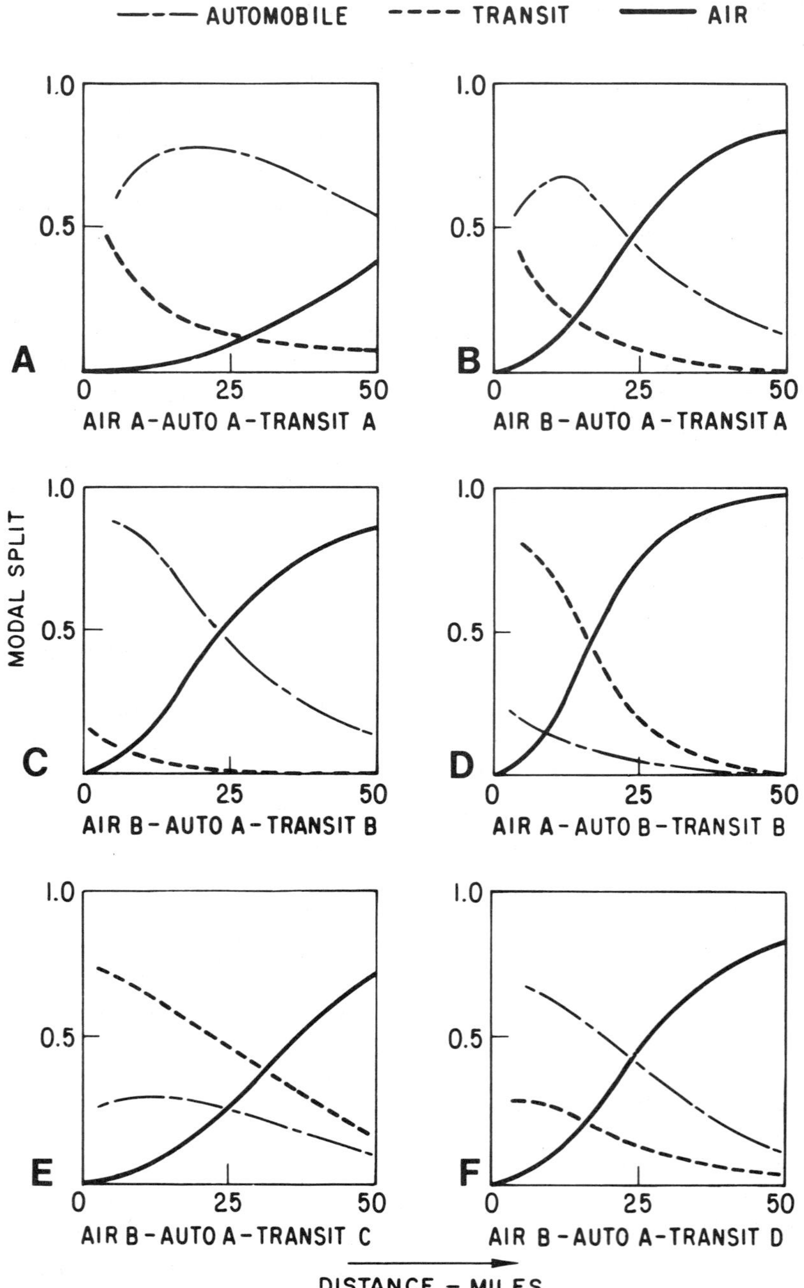

FIGURE 6   Effect of cost and time functions (Table 1) on modal shift.

However, if it is at all conceivable to allocate the true cost of ownership and operation each time an individual elects to travel by private automobile, then the picture changes radically. Figure 6D shows that even with the slower, more expensive air vehicle, such as the helicopter and an unsubsidized public transportation system, the automobile share would drop to a very small value. The market is then dominated by a logical combination of public ground transportation over shorter distance and common carrier over longer distances, probably an optimum system for minimum costs to society as a whole. However, it is improbable that this logic will prevail.

Although the modal split analysis biases the automobile for convenience in reducing the access time from 20 minutes to 10 minutes, the automobile has a much greater appeal that the simple demand model used does not fully simulate. The ability to control one's own destiny by route choice and change of destination if the whim occurs en route, plus the privacy and comfort of the modern automobile, will probably always drive the demand distribution toward that of Figure 6C rather than the true cost situation of Figure 6D.

Much interest has centered recently around concepts of high-speed ground transportation at costs comparable to present-day transit costs, but with block speeds considerably higher—of the order of 40 mph. Figure 6E shows that such a system, if subsidized, could be competitive with air transportation over the shorter distances and could be expected to share the market even at distances greater than 30 miles. Furthermore, it does serve the very useful purpose of reducing the automobile share of the market, based here on apparent costs, although Figure 6F would indicate that the subsidy is necessary in order to achieve this desirable reduction.

It is of interest to consider an ideal world in which each trip is charged according to its range rather than apparent costs regardless of mode. No funds are expended on a competing high-speed transit system, and advanced aircraft systems are developed. Figure 7 then shows clearly that, if such logic were to prevail, air would dominate at all distances beyond 10 miles, and the ground could be used for living and not for traveling. With quiet, pollution-free aircraft flying over distances of 20 miles at clock times of less than 5 minutes, and with no ground transportation to speak of (except for underground transit systems operating over short distances), our lives would certainly be pleasanter and better served than in the present cluttered cities and suburban areas dominated by a tangled automobile transportation system operating during periods of high congestion at speeds of the order of 10 mph.

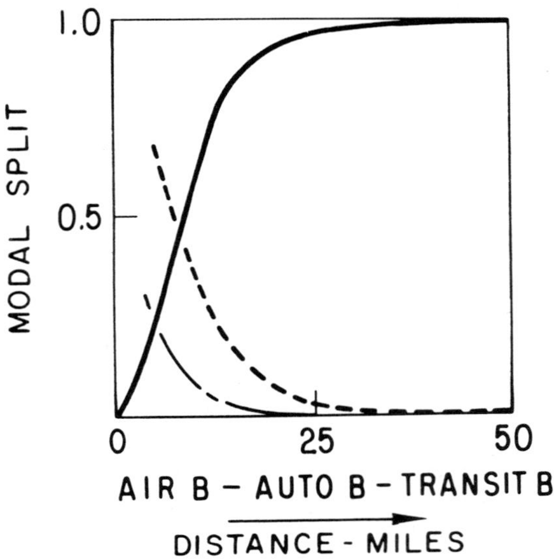

FIGURE 7   Modal split with advanced air system, existing
unsubsidized transit and true automobile costs.

THE COLLECTION AND DISTRIBUTION PROBLEM

In the modal split analyses a 20-minute access and wait time was assumed
for the common-carrier transportation systems, both air and ground, in
the interests of consistency and on the basis of the previous calibration
with existing systems. There is, however, a real question as to whether
such access times are achievable if a high-speed air or ground system is
introduced in a total suburban complex. In the transportation model
discussed below, catchment areas with a 10-mile radius around population centers, represented by the larger suburban towns and smaller cities
within a 50-mile radius from Boston center, seemed appropriate. At least
in this area, demand does not appear to justify a multitude of collection
points (stations or V-ports) in the outlying districts where such high-
speed systems would be attractive.

In these districts access to the terminals located at the suburban
population centers will initially have to be by private automobile.

Average car speeds in the suburban areas will be higher than in the
city, of the order of 40 mph. The average time required for access to
the terminal was then shown[1] to be 6 minutes and the corresponding
apparent cost to be 9 cents without parking.

Since the common carrier operates on a fixed schedule, the passenger need arrive only a few minutes, probably 5 at the maximum, before scheduled departure, particularly if dispatch reliability and frequency are both high, thus giving assurance that another vehicle will arrive in less than 20 minutes. For an operating day of 16 hours (7 a.m. to 11 p.m.), such a schedule requires a flight frequency of 50 flights per day.

The remaining 9 minutes of the 20 assumed for the common carrier allows for egress at destination, where transportation is available either by taxi, transit, or walking.

Clearly the choice of access and egress time is highly subjective and, like most opinions involving transportation, is colored by personal experience and circumstances. If the access time is increased by 10 minutes, analysis shows that the market share of the air system shown in Figure 6E will drop from 76 percent at 40 miles distance to 60 percent. A similar effect occurs by adding an access and egress cost that typically could vary from values of the order of 10 cents to over 3 dollars if a taxi is used at either end. For example, if a 1 dollar access and/or egress cost is added, the market share will drop another 10 points.

These reductions, applicable to both high-speed ground and air, point up the importance of considering the problem of microcollection and distribution before investing in an extensive advanced transportation system. Better methods of providing individual transportation are urgently required if we are to make effective use of present-day technology for improved transportation in urban and suburban areas.

Since the collection and distribution problem will be the same for any advanced transportation system, either air or ground, and no choice is apparent between these two systems from this consideration alone, it is interesting to examine what basis for choice does exist.

HIGH-SPEED GROUND VERSUS AIR SYSTEMS

For stage lengths below 50 miles, ground transit systems without the burden of capital amortization currently operate at lower costs than those postulated for air. If such costs could be projected to higher-speed tracked vehicles, then, as indicated by the modal split analyses discussed above, such systems could well become competitive with air systems and the private automobile. However, the ground transportation system requires a cleared right of way if block speeds of 40 mph are to be achieved. No cost analyses in depth are available for advanced ground systems because of the many unknowns involved, such as land values that vary greatly depending on population density. Universally applicable costs, comparable to those given above for air transportation, can therefore not be developed. Experience has shown, however, that the cost of acquiring and developing a right of way in a heavily built-up suburban area where such systems would be most applicable is high and requires a major initial capital investment. The true operating costs of new systems will therefore probably be much higher than those of existing public transit systems. On the other hand, no rights of way are required for air, the major capital investment being in the vehicles. It is thus possible to "grow" an air transportation system of small size, adding vehicles as the demand develops without a major initial capital investment, thereby incurring a much smaller risk. For example, the system described requires initially only 20 aircraft to serve the entire area. Also, since suburban V-ports need not be elaborate and the cost can be kept low, the choice of location could be determined experimentally and changed as the market demand changes seasonally or more slowly. No such flexibility exists in ground transportation systems; once the rails are laid down, the system is destined to serve the same points for the rest of its existence.

The air system costs were estimated[1] to be $112 million initially and $290 million for the complete system covering 360 miles or $800,000 per mile. This compares to costs of over $10 million per mile for new transit systems in the Boston area, even using existing rights of way.

Rail has a possible advantage in that it can make frequent stops along the line to pick up passengers. However, not many stops can be made if it is desired to maintain the 40 mph block speed. Experience with helicopter airlines has indicated that enroute stops can be made including approach, unloading, loading, and departure in less than 2 minutes and less than 1 minute of ground time. It is therefore unlikely that the major advantage in this regard will be with the ground vehicles. Furthermore, the ground system would require many radial lines extending from the hub to the suburban areas if their stations are to serve the 10-mile radius circular areas detailed above. Thus, we are not discussing the possibility of a single line but 5 to 10 such lines operating from the city center and clearly involving a major capital investment.

Although, in the light of present technology, a dispatch reliability under poor weather conditions appears to favor ground transportation, this is not necessarily so with the advanced concept in guidance and control discussed below. Indeed, in areas where snow is common, the advantage could well be with a VTOL air system that requires an area only slightly larger than its body dimensions for landing and not necessarily cleared of snow since no ground roll is required.

Of all these considerations it is felt that the most persuasive is the evolutionary growth possible with air transportation as opposed to the heavy initial capital investment required for a ground transportation system that the public may never choose to use as a mass common carrier.

A HYPOTHETICAL AIR TRANSPORTATION SYSTEM

In order to estimate the feasibility of operating an urban and suburban air-transportation common carrier, a hypothetical system was modeled for the greater Boston area shown in Figure 4. Nodes were chosen somewhat arbitrarily but essentially centered in areas of approximately 10 miles' radius.

Table 2 presents an analysis of the travel demand for the air transportation system, using the demand distribution corresponding to a transportation system in which existing public ground transportation is retained with subsidy (Transit A), an advanced mature air system operates without subsidy (Air B), and apparent automobile costs are used rather than the higher actual costs (Auto A). Two cases are shown, Case II corresponding to the case of Figure 6B and Case I with increased access costs of 1 dollar and an access/egress time of 30 minutes. The direct operating costs were based on 80-passenger vehicles, and, since the total costs assumed a 50 percent load factor, it is apparent that most of the Boston-bound trips would generate more than adequate demand for the postulated frequency of 50 flights a day. Some, as Providence–Boston, would justify a much higher frequency or alternatively multiple V-ports in the city centers.

On the other hand, the circular belt-type operations in the suburban areas clearly require a multiple stop service or service via Boston, except possibly for a few links between the larger towns. This, in turn, may be expected to increase station costs and travel times for some of the passengers, further reducing the demand.

Aircraft costs were based on a utilization of 2,300 hours per year, which agrees well with the prediction[10] for these stage lengths. This allows 50 flights per day over typical stage lengths with 100 percent standby equipment (float). Maintenance would be undertaken at night when the vehicles would be out of use. Approximately 20 vehicles would therefore be required for Case I and 60 for Case II.

The effect of a cyclic demand for the services will peak the loads at certain hours, but the assumed 50 percent load factor is probably a reasonable average over the entire day. Commuter travel, which causes the high peaking, represents of the order of 30 percent of the total trips in the Boston area, the remaining travel being distributed throughout the day. The peaking in demand, however, could well have a beneficial

TABLE 2   Analysis of Travel Demand for the Boston Suburban Area

Pair	Population (thousands)	Population (thousands)	Distance (mi)	Estimated 1960 Daily One-Way Demand	CASE I: $C = 2.5 + 0.05D$ $T = 30 + 0.16D$		CASE II: $C = 1.5 + 0.05D$ $T = 22 + 0.16D$	
					% Market	Load/Trip[a]	% Market	Load/Trip[a]
WORC–BOST	323	1,362	40	6,750	42	66	76	123
LOWL–BOST	161	1,362	23	5,749	14	20[b]	46	64
NASH–BOST	86	1,362	34	1,936	30	14[b]	68	32
PROV–BOST	816	1,362	42	15,700	44	167	78	294
LEOM–BOST	82	1,362	40	1,680	42	17[b]	76	31
MARL–BOST	121	1,362	27	3,600	20	18[b]	55	50
IPSW–BOST	107	1,362	26	3,349	18	15	52	42
NEWB–BOST	143	1,362	50	2,300	58	33[b]	83	46
BROC–BOST	146	1,362	20	5,982	9	13[b]	37	53
FRAN–BOST	169	1,362	26	3,350	43	36	77	64
LAWR–BOST	162	1,362	26	5,147	18	22	52	65
NORW–BOST	151	1,362	11	11,100	2	5	10	27[b]
FALL–BOST	100	1,362	46	1,796	58	25	80	35[b]
LYNN–BOST	243	1,362	11	17,500	2	8	12	51
WOBN–BOST	117	1,362	10	9,500	2	5	11	25
LEXI–BOST	140	1,362	13	9,000	4	9	17	37
WELS–BOST	108	1,362	10	8,744	2	4	11	23
WEYM–BOST	195	1,362	10	15,920	2	8	11	42[b]
PLYM–BOST	72	1,362	33	1,776	30	13	67	29[b]
LYNN–BROC	243	146	30	700	24	4	61	10
LEOM–WORC	82	323	20	800	11	2	37	7
LEXI–MARL	140	121	19	530	8	1	36	5
PROV–WORC	816	323	38	4,113	40	40	75	75
WORC–FRAN	323	109	26	816	18	4	52	10
PROV–FRAN	816	109	18	2,895	9	6	34	24
NEWB–PROV	143	816	30	2,320	24	13	61	34
MARL–WORC	121	323	13	1,700	4	2	18	7
LYNN–LEXI	243	146	15	1,350	4	1	21	7

[a]Based on 10 percent population increases and hence $(1.10)^2$ travel demand growth; frequency of 50 flights/day.
[b]Indicates one intermediate stop.

effect, since the aircraft in off hours would then be available for other revenue-producing uses such as express parcel delivery and mail. It is interesting to note that during the past 3 years a growing amount of mail has been carried by third-level air carriers, such as the air taxi, and in 1969 this represented 7 percent of the total air mail carried in the United States. At 40 cents a ton-mile, the revenue is equivalent to that obtainable from passenger carrying and could well represent a profitable and useful application of the short-haul air system in expediting mail delivery to suburban areas.

An examination of Table 2 indicates that the penalty of increased access cost and access time is particularly critical at the shorter distances. However, the more optimistic numbers (Case II) indicate a large volume of business over all the direct Boston links and some of the larger suburban complexes. Where the traffic is low, service could still be provided by multistop routing, possibly using smaller vehicles. A 20-passenger vehicle operating at 50 percent load factor, as assumed in the cost analysis, could certainly service profitably some of the more lightly loaded links and, at worst, would provide a useful feeder service into the more heavily loaded links. Optimization of a network of this type with multicommodity flows is an interesting exercise in transportation analysis for which the tools are only now being developed. Optimized scheduling for such a system will certainly develop a viable transportation network that may be expected to grow in a logical fashion given a high quality of service and dispatch reliability.

It may therefore be concluded that even in the relatively low population density area of Boston and vicinity an air transportation system could serve a useful function in relieving ground transportation and providing rapid communication between centers of population. However, the traveler is still left with the problem of reaching a terminal from his point of origin, be it home or office. Neither the market size nor the most optimistic demand predictions would indicate that a radical increase in the number of V-ports over those assumed in Table 2 could be expected in the near future. Access thus requires an increase in cost and a change in mode if a private automobile is used, as discussed above. Furthermore, the inconvenience of change in mode of transportation will quite probably increase the tendency to drive to the destination without stopping at the V-port.

These imponderables and the many factors involved in predicting the preferences and prejudices of the traveling public, as well as the potential unknown operating problems of a short-haul, high-speed air transportation system, would indicate the extreme desirability of initiating as soon as possible experimental programs and demonstration projects that will attempt to answer some of these vexing questions.[9]

NOISE

Probably no aspect of air transportation has received more concentrated attention during the recent past than that of noise. If the aircraft being considered for the short-haul, urban and suburban transportation system described above are ever to be acceptable in the built-up communities they are intended to serve, their noise level should not be much higher than ambient urban levels, or below 80 db.

In view of the high elasticity of demand with respect to cost projected for the short-haul suburban air transportation system, which amounts to approximately a 3 percent drop in travel for a 1 percent increase in cost, it is important to examine the cost penalties that would be associated with reducing the vehicle noise levels from those levels that correspond to optimum vehicle design for minimum direct operating cost. This was done[1] by designing new aircraft for lower noise levels and computing their direct operating costs.

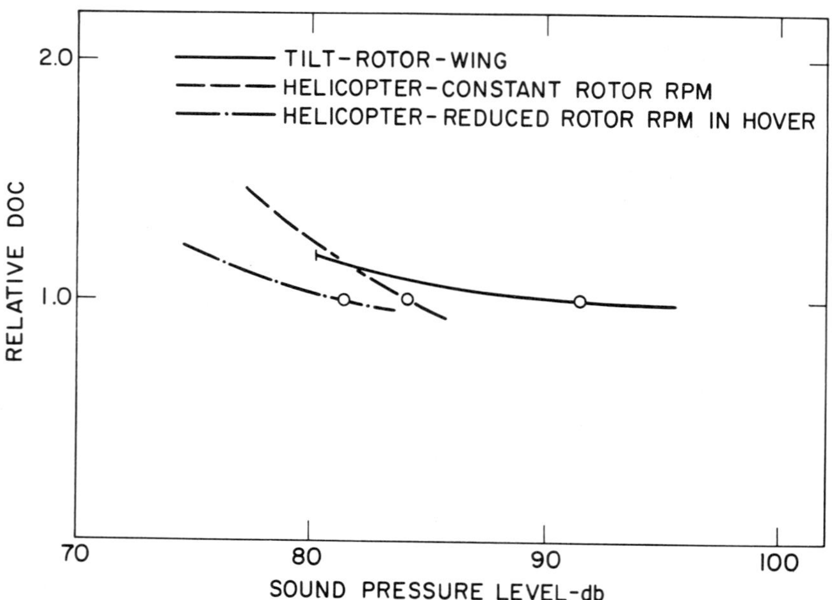

FIGURE 8 Variation of relative direct operating costs as a function of design noise level during hover flight.

Figure 8 shows the variation in direct operating cost normalized around the design points previously used. Evidently a penalty of approximately 20 percent in direct operating cost would be associated with the proposed noise reduction for the tilt-rotor. In context of the total, including indirect, costs, this is evidently a small increase. It may be concluded that aircraft designed for city-center operation with consideration given to noise constraints will not be appreciably more expensive to operate than aircraft designed for minimum direct operating cost. Recent success with quieting helicopters has resulted in spectacular reductions in noise, and there is every reason to believe that with sufficient design effort the noise levels of Figure 8 will be achieved for the helicopter and that levels of 70 db may be possible in approach and landing at 300 feet, with 60 db at 1,500 feet a not unreasonable goal in cruise flight.

POLLUTION

Air pollution resulting from the exhaust emissions of aircraft engines is probably the next most serious matter for concern in the public's mind when considering the operation of a multiplicity of aircraft in urban and suburban areas.

In cruise flight the gas turbine engine, unlike the reciprocating engine, operates at air-to-fuel ratios of the order of 60, approximately four times stoichiometric, whereas the reciprocating engine operates close to stoichiometric mixtures. Consequently, its combustion is far less complete than that of the turbine, and there is a much larger emission of carbon monoxide and particulates. The oxides of nitrogen are highly dependent on temperatures of combustion, and since the gas turbine engine must cool the combustion products rapidly before reaching the turbine in order to avoid excessive temperatures and structural failure of the high-loaded turbine blades, these pollutants are also appreciably lower than for the reciprocating engine.

Table 3 is a useful summary of the emission index for jets operating at various points of the landing and takeoff cycle and for the internal combustion engine. Evidently, other than at the lower power settings typical of idle and taxi, the emissions from the gas turbine engine are negligible. It is particularly important to note that the vehicles considered in this paper are vertical takeoff and landing vehicles that require no taxi prior to takeoff, if loading and unloading are performed on the landing pad, which is indicated[16] as the optimum way to operate a V-port in order to minimize access and egress time. Elimination of taxi time also reduces ground maneuvering time to zero,

TABLE 3 Pollutant Yields for Jets and Motor Vehicles

Engine Type	Operating Mode	Emission index (lb pollutant/1,000 lb fuel)					
		CO	HC	NO_x	Part.	Pb	SO_x
Turbojet	Idle and taxi	174	75	2.0	0.3	0	1.0
	Approach	8.7	16	2.7	1.0	0	1.0
	Landing, takeoff, and climbout	0.7	0.1	4.2	0.6	0	1.0
Automotive piston	Total average	300	55	27	4.5	0.4	2.3

thereby increasing block speeds. Since the aircraft can take off immediately when loaded, and since gas turbine engines require no idling time for warmup, low power operation of the engines will be minimal. Once a gas turbine engine is operating at or near full power, the lean mixtures indicated above will ensure the low emission index of Table 3. Consequently, at no point in its flight cycle will such an aircraft contribute any appreciable amount of pollution due to engine operation.

It is of interest to compare the contribution to pollution of the aircraft being considered here to the pollution caused by burning of hydrocarbon fuels in automobiles for the same travel distances. A typical car in urban areas operates at approximately 15 miles/gal or 4 lb/car mile, which, for the average load of 1.4 passengers, results in 0.285 lb of fuel per passenger mile. The tilt-rotor-wing vehicle consumes 520 lb of fuel for a stage length of 30 miles, and the helicopter consumes about the same amount. Since these are 80-passenger vehicles and the average load factor has been taken as 50 percent, this gives a fuel consumption of 0.45 lb per passenger mile. Referring to Table 3, it is evident that the emission per passenger mile of the automobile will be 280 times higher than the aircraft for CO, 350 times higher for hydrocarbons, and 4 times higher for the oxides of nitrogen. If for no other reason than pollution, the reduction of automobile transportation by the use of the common-carrier air transportation system considered here would be highly desirable as a means of reducing the pollution of the atmosphere in urban and suburban areas.

DISPATCH RELIABILITY AND SAFETY

For the suburban air transportation system we have been describing, it is essential that the aircraft maintain a high degree of dispatch reliability even under instrument flight conditions approaching zero visibility. A transportation system that is weather limited will never be viable because such a limitation implies the need for a backup system, clearly an impossible situation from consideration of economics alone. In addition to dispatch reliability the aircraft must maintain and exceed the enviable safety record of air transportation during the past years, which has resulted in fatalities per passenger mile of one tenth of the automobile's, its nearest competitor for the very-short-haul transportation market.

All aircraft considered in the study were designed for an engine out hover capability.[4,8] Although this involved a penalty in gross weight, it is believed mandatory that VTOL aircraft operating in an urban complex be capable of maintaining altitude and returning to the landing area in the event of an engine failure at any point in the landing and takeoff cycle. The ability to maintain altitude at some forward speed is not a sufficient safety criterion. With the provision of an engine out hover capability, the hazards involved in operations over built-up areas would be minimal.

In theory, the basic flight characteristics of VTOL aircraft should permit a high degree of reliability and safety in the landing mode, particularly during instrument flight conditions, because of their ability to achieve independent control of vertical and horizontal velocities. Touchdown could therefore be made at zero forward speed and with any control law desired in vertical flight; for example, constant height-velocity ratio. Because of its ability to fly very slowly or hover stationary in the air when in doubt, and in order to avoid other vehicles on the ground or in flight, air-traffic-control procedures should be far simpler than is the case for conventional aircraft.

Unfortunately in practice these inherent potentials of VTOL aircraft for safe, all-weather operation have frequently been masked by their poor handling qualities. However, artificial stabilization methods have now been developed[1] that will permit any desired control characteristics in the vehicle, providing sufficient control power is available. Although the need to rely on electronic stabilization systems under conditions where their failure could involve safety of flight may be questioned, the reliability of modern control equipment demonstrated in the space program, together with triplication of the critical channels, should insure that the total system reliability will be at least as high as that of mechanical control systems.

A VTOL aircraft, equipped with a control system[1] and providing both horizontal and vertical position stabilization, is a very simple vehicle to fly and land, even under instrument flight conditions without visual contact with the ground. With an inertial platform providing an essential reference for descent along steep paths, drift due to gusts is eliminated, and precise position may be held at any point along the flight path. Since the inertial system references the vehicle to the ground and not to the air mass through which it is moving, the loop is closed around the control target, that is, the landing spot or the microwave beam indicating the approach path. If the pilot commands zero velocity by neutralizing control, position is held regardless of gusts, and the danger of inadvertently drifting into obstacles in the vicinity of the approach path is eliminated. With such a control system it can be expected that all-weather operations will be possible even down to zero–zero conditions. The pilot could then feel his way in if necessary at any desired vertical and horizontal velocity.

In the design of any VTOL aircraft, primary consideration must also be given to adequate control power regardless of the wind direction. This is important not only to permit an approach from any direction as desired, but also to allow backing up as necessary to maintain position in hover. With this capability the aircraft may approach the landing pad without the need for an approach leg, or any air maneuvering, thereby considerably decreasing block time. Air and ground maneuvering times for conventional or STOL aircraft, which are required to line up with the runway and are sensitive to ambient winds, may involve as much as 5 minutes of air maneuvering time, thereby increasing the direct operating costs and considerably cutting down the acceptance rate of the terminal. The multiple-approach path possible with VTOL aircraft increases the acceptance rate of the terminal by an order of magnitude. The air-traffic-control problem is thus considerably alleviated, and, providing positive position information is available at all times either by inertial or microwave navigation systems, a large number of aircraft can be handled in a terminal area.

The smaller market postulated above (Case I, Table 2) could be served by some 10 vehicles in the air at any time, assuming a 20-minute schedule from eight suburban stations serving the core-city terminal. There would thus be a landing every 2 minutes if only one terminal were provided in Boston proper and all flights were nonstop. With multiple landing pads in the terminal, and by making use of the omnidirectional flight and tight position control capability of VTOL aircraft, the terminal area traffic could be handled without any congestion problems even for the larger market (Case II).

Because of the short flight times, it is quite possible that the aircraft positions can be scheduled at all times, not only in the terminal area, but in the total area being served, with the situation monitored from a central facility. An aircraft leaving a suburban terminal may thus plan

FIGURE 9   Artist's concept of tilt-rotor-wing transport landing in city center.

to arrive at destination knowing a block of space is available and the path is clear both en route and in the terminal area. Optimization of such an air-traffic-control system for maximum utilization and a high degree of safety presents no serious problem, and it therefore may be expected that the short-haul, suburban transportation system discussed above will operate with a high degree of dispatch reliability under all weather conditions.

Figure 9 is a pictorial representation of a possible air vehicle suitable for this new transportation concept. Figure 10 shows a typical urban center air terminal, and Figure 11 shows details of access and egress. The aircraft lands, unloads, and loads for takeoff at one spot, with passengers boarding through protected movable fingers. Figure 12 shows a typical, low-cost suburban terminal, easily relocated as market shifts may dictate.

CONCLUSION

In conclusion, systems analyses based on market projections and using existing vehicle technology indicate that an air transportation system can be developed to serve urban and suburban areas for less than $1

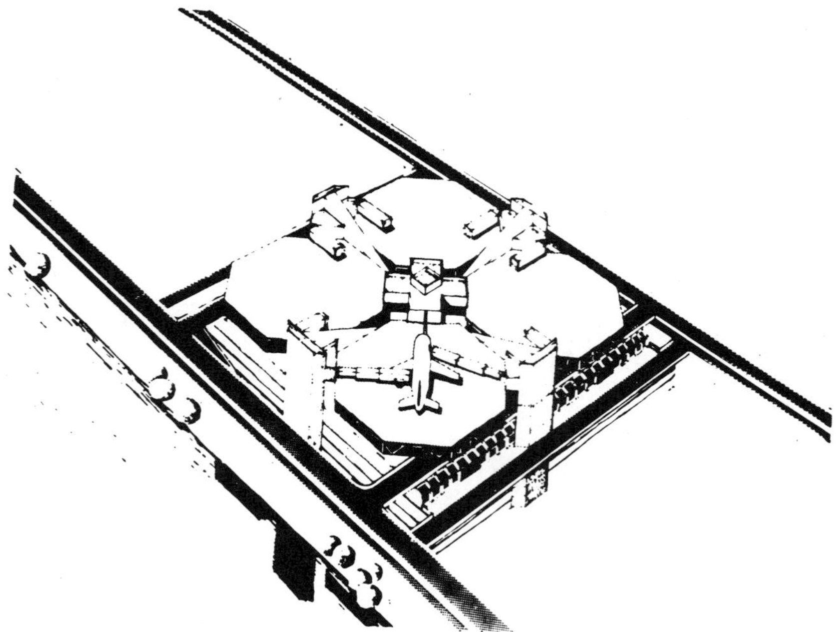

FIGURE 10   Possible layout for a hub V-port showing protected access to aircraft at landing pad.

million per mile, with ticket prices competitive with those of ground-based systems and operating at block speeds of the order of 10 times higher. Whether such an air system will ever be economically viable depends on a solution to the collection and distribution problem, but it must be recognized that this problem exists for any common-carrier system, whether air or ground. If it is concluded that a high-speed ground transportation system should be developed in a given suburban area, then the point of this paper is simply to suggest that a critical examination be made of the possibility of satisfying this need by a short-haul air transportation system. Such a system could well change our entire concept of urban complexes. The ability to travel 30 miles comfortably in 5 minutes at 10 cents a passenger mile would provide a new social tool permitting separation of living, manufacturing, travel, and business centers. Suburban living would be available to all, regardless of income, while still allowing urban living for those who may prefer a highly concentrated core city containing living, working, and recreational areas.

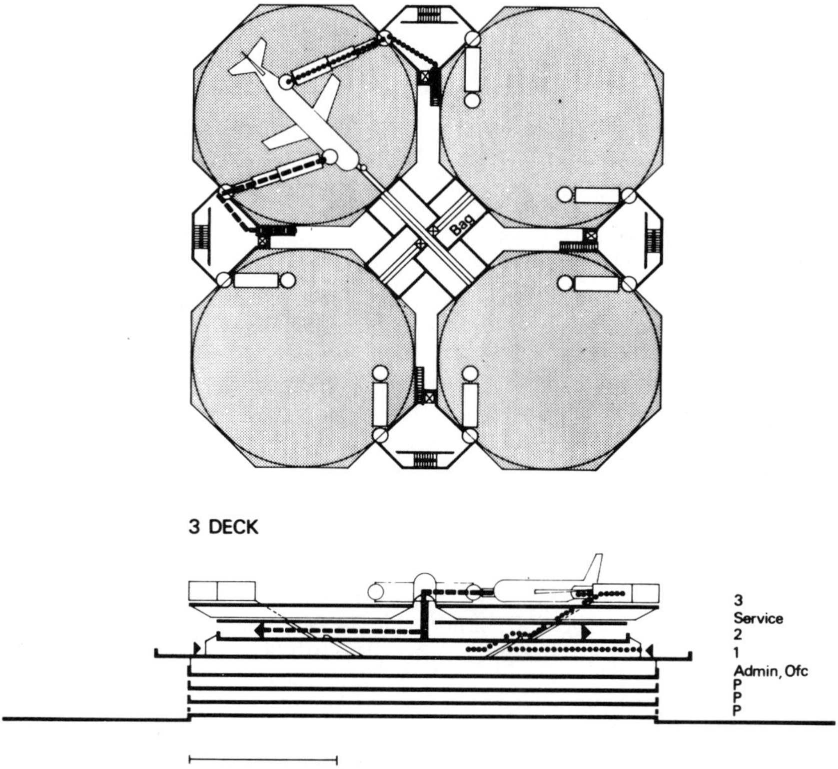

3 DECK

FIGURE 11   Details of V-port access.

FIGURE 12   Typical suburban V-port.

REFERENCES

1. Miller, R. H. 1971. Some air transportation concepts for the future, Aeronaut. J. R. Aeronaut Soc. 75(727):431–456.
2. Simpson, R. W., and M. J. Neuve Eglise. 1968. A method for determination of vehicle size and frequency of service for a short haul V/STOL air transport system. Report R-68-1. Flight Transportation Laboratory, Massachusetts Institute of Technology, Cambridge, Mass.
3. Flight Transportation Laboratory. 1970. Concept studies for future intracity air transportation systems. Report FTL R-70. Massachusetts Institute of Technology, Cambridge, Mass.
4. Flight Transportation Laboratory. 1965. A systems analysis of short haul air transportation. Technical Report 65-1. Massachusetts Institute of Technology, Cambridge, Mass.
5. Taneja, H. K., and R. W. Simpson. 1968. A multi-regression analysis of indirect operating costs. Report R-67-2. Flight Transportation Laboratory, Massachusetts Institute of Technology, Cambridge, Mass.
6. Miller, R. H. 1966. Air Transportation in the Eastern corridor. Report 660332, Society of Automotive Engineers.
7. Pearlman, C., and R. W. Simpson. 1966. Maintenance cost studies of present aircraft subsystems. Report FT-66-2. Flight Transportation Laboratory, Massachusetts Institute of Technology, Cambridge, Mass.
8. Gallant, R., M. Scully, and W. Lange. 1966. Analysis of V/STOL aircraft configurations for short haul air transportation systems. Report FT-66-1. Flight Transportation Laboratory, Massachusetts Institute of Technology, Cambridge, Mass.
9. Miller, R. H., and R. W. Simpson. 1968. V/STOL in the northeast corridor. Astronaut. Aeronaut. 6(9):28.
10. Stoessel, R. F., and J. E. Gallagher. 1967. A standard method for estimating V/STOL operating expense. Paper No. 67-828, AIAA.
11. Taneja, N. K., and R. W. Simpson. 1969. A simulation study of dynamic scheduling of a VTOL airport feeder system. Report FTL-R68-6. Flight Transportation Laboratory, Massachusetts Institute of Technology, Cambridge, Mass.
12. Levin, A. 1969. Some fleet routing and scheduling problems for air transportation systems. Report R-68-5. Flight Transportation Laboratory, Massachusetts Institute of Technology, Cambridge, Mass.
13. Simpson, R. W. 1969. Scheduling and routing models for airline systems. Report R-68-3. Flight Transportation Laboratory, Massachusetts Institute of Technology, Cambridge, Mass.
14. Wilson, N. H. M. 1967. CARS—Computer aided routing system. Report R67-12. Civil Engineering Systems Laboratory, Massachusetts Institute of Technology, Cambridge, Mass.
15. Sawyer, R. F. 1970. Reducing jet pollution before it becomes serious. Astronaut. Aeronaut. 8(4):62.
16. Allen, E., and R. W. Simpson. 1970. Ground facilities for a VTOL intercity air transportation system. Report FTL-R69-2. Flight Transportation Laboratory, Massachusetts Institute of Technology, Cambridge, Mass.

DISCUSSION

BESSON: I can see the flexibility of gathering the passengers, but it seems to me there will be a problem when passengers are dumped in the center of the city, a real problem of distribution unless the VTOL system is supplemented with some additional method of distribution inside the center of the city. I think this is a serious problem.

MILLER: I agree completely. That is the problem—collection and distribution. We are very concerned about it, and there is no happy answer to that.

EVERITT: There has been no discussion of the problem of safety here, and while I don't think the individual passenger is ever affected by the probability of getting killed—only his neighbors are going to get killed—there is a problem when you increase the amount of congestion in the air. This has resulted, I believe, in banning police helicopters over Manhattan and restricting the use of the heliports on the Pan American Building in New York and in Chicago on the Hilton Hotel roof. It seems to me that this is one of the things that must receive some attention, because of the very adverse reaction to crashes occuring in the city. I might add that a V/STOL system might greatly increase the cost of traffic control, and, as I understand it, air traffic control is subsidized by the government because airways are primarily a government function.

So this problem of safety disturbs me a little bit in that it seems not to have been discussed at all here.

MILLER: I am very sorry time did not permit sufficient reference to that problem, but safety is one of our major concerns. The vehicles that we considered for the computer analysis were all equipped with two or more engines so that with one engine out, the aircraft would still be able to maintain altitude.

Present helicopters don't have this capability, and we believe that vehicles put into this type of service must have it.

The question of dispatch reliability is extremely important; the vehicle must be able to take off and land regardless of the weather, and we do have such an all-weather system operating right now at Bedford Airport. The Boston Instrumentation Lab provides this capability through a program some of you may know about. The system uses an inertial platform in the helicopter that positions it in inertial space at all times. This provides all-weather capability and makes it very simple to fly such vehicles.

The market to be considered there is to be served by 60 aircraft, with 30 to be in the air at one time. The system has been costed out for an air-traffic-control system separate from that now existing, because we felt that we would have to operate at an altitude below that for established airways. The block utilization of the airspace would provide for a specified aircraft position at any instant in time with this inertial system, and, along with the aircraft and the terminals, we did add the cost of the aircraft control system.

I would like to speak for the airlines, who claim that the ticket tax does pay for their share of the ATC system.

EVERITT: With respect to this all-weather capability, I still question its capability in fog and some other situations.

The other point I would like to make is that I think the difference between the true cost and incremental cost is superficial as those who would patronize this type of transportation would have an automobile at home for other purposes. Therefore insurance and other associated costs would still be required, and so it represents an incremental cost.

MILLER: That is why we did not use the true costs, but instead used apparent costs in our analysis. I might say that many people have a second car for commuting, and for that case the total cost must be charged to the automobile transportation.

EVERITT: Most of us have a second car even if we don't commute.

PRICE: In your presentation you postulated that this form of transportation would be competitive with transit. I tried to visualize how that might fit. You also talked about the competitiveness of anything with the automobile. The problem of competing with the automobile, as you point out, arises from the fact that one can start from where he wishes and go to his destination in a car without changing modes or stopping.

However, think of the problem from the transit viewpoint in competing with the automobile, including the costs. We have high-capacity fixed route systems, such as the subway, in the city. To use it one must get to it, so one must think of supplementary forms of transportation. For example, a passenger could go by feeder-bus to the subway station, but the bus may not start right at the front door. Some thought is required about how to get to the feeder-bus. We might consider some kind of demand-responsive transportation.

Proceeding from the subway to the feeder-bus to the demand-responsive type of transportation, fewer and fewer people are carried per vehicle, and there is a driver who must be paid. In transit system operation more than 50 percent of the cost is associated with the driver; perhaps as much as 80 percent is labor if all labor is included. Therefore, to compete with the automobile, transit must provide some kind of economical multimodal system. I still don't understand how the V/STOL aircraft would fit into this multimodal picture economically.

MILLER: I agree completely with what you say. You have posed a major problem. We are conducting no further analysis because we see no solution to the difficulties that you have raised.

All we are saying is that we can provide a transportation system with catchment areas on about a 10-mile radius that can take people to the center of the city in a faster and more attractive way than can the auto. We still have no solution for the collection of people within that 10-mile radius and for transporting them to the terminal. When they arrive in the city center, there is no effective way to distribute them. I think we should develop some demand-sensitive system, some type of a portal-to terminal ground system.

We do require a ground link, the subways in the city, for example, to distribute people from the terminal to their destination within the city. Further, we need some type of low-density pick-up system in suburban areas that collects people for the trip to the terminals.

Only then will we keep people out of automobiles. Otherwise they will never go to the terminal, instead they will go right on into the cities by car.

We have only two messages here: (1) Let us try to solve this pick-up and distribution system problem by some common-carrier mode, recognizing the problem of getting people to the terminals; and (2) we believe it might be worthwhile to look at the air system and at the same time the high-speed ground system. They have similar problems, but the air systems are faster and are less capital-intensive.

There still remains the question of collection and distribution that must be solved.

FRIEDL: I see some limited application of V/STOL aircraft in interurban travel over short and perhaps medium distances, primarily to relieve the congestion that exists at the airports. However, we have the fundamental problem that a sizable percentage of the people simply don't want to fly. Has that aspect been taken sufficiently into account?

There are a number of reasons people may not want to fly. A primary one is the fear of flying and a second reason relates to physical discomfort and other personal reasons. A segment of the population has been effectively eliminated as air travelers because there are many areas in the United States, particularly in New England, that are just inaccessible by any means of transportation except the private car or a bus.

MILLER: One can only agree. Fifty percent of the people in the country have flown; youth fare has increased the acceptance of flying as a mode of transportation. However, there remains a resistance to flying on the part of many people.

KELLY: Professor Miller, I am a bit concerned about your time estimates. You indicate a fairly sizable shift of mode to V/STOL-type aircraft, if the end, or total, wait-time can be reduced from 30 to 22 minutes. Consider, for instance, a traveler from Cambridge, going either to Bedford Airport or to Boston Airport, then boarding a short-haul aircraft and proceeding to Worcester. Now compare that type trip with the time to move the distance from his home to Worcester by ground transit or auto. I think you will find the end-effect times are larger for the first case. I am sure that one of the major problems is the dead time at the end of the trip.

One other point, did you conduct your studies in terms of the transit time from home to destination, comparing that time with the total time required to get from home to airport to another airport to final destination?

MILLER: Yes, we looked at that in some detail; and all we are saying is that the access time to the terminal is extremely important and must be minimized. Once you have accessed any air terminal, then the preference will be for the air system because it is much faster. Any common-carrier system suffers from the delays in the collection and distribution system. I agree that if you want to go from Boston to Worcester, you would not drive to Bedford to pick up an airline; you would drive directly to Worcester. As your time doubles for the drive to Bedford, so the time saved on the trip overall is reduced, but there is a disinclination to change modes.

However, in the system we have postulated, I don't think that you would have to drive—the average passenger has to drive 2.5–3 miles—and I believe we stand a chance of convincing him not to drive for that segment of the trip, particularly if we can provide him with a competitive common-carrier mode.

I repeat, the major problem is the need for a simple common carrier accessing a terminal, whether that terminal be a BART terminal or a VTOL terminal of some type. Until we solve that problem, we will not have a viable common-carrier system that will penetrate the automobile market.

CRANE: Much of your discussion is based on consumer preference curves and the associated postulates that underlie your analysis. I would like to ask what assumptions you considered in plotting those curves?

MILLER: The critical factors are the time and cost functions. Those are explained in detail in the written version of my paper. The paper describes the various assumptions as to true and apparent costs, subsidized and unsubsidized, and gives very detailed projections on aircraft costs.

As far as the elasticities α and β referred to in the paper are concerned, they were determined from data obtained in the Northeast Corridor study on intercity demand, by mode. We checked that against the intracity information in Detroit and in Boston and were fairly convinced that the numbers are approximately right.

CRANE: Are the results here based upon some psychological studies, actual consumer preferences studies in real situations, or are they strictly cost related?

MILLER: They are based on the elasticity as determined from the choice of mode considered in the study.

QUESTION: I find the MIT research is extremely interesting, and I am for air transportation. However, I do feel that in the real world there is need for considerably more study.

Your study assumes almost instantaneous markets and that there would be this type of demand. It is assumed the public would be satisfied with the vehicle and with the system, but it does not take into consideration that risk capital is involved in developing the market. It does not take into consideration modal choice in terms of frequency of service. If you do not develop the demand at the same time that you provide frequency of service, demand will never exist.

Another theory that needs far more consideration in terms of vehicle adaptability is the number of units of aircraft that should be ordered at one time to enable a manufacturer to profitably engage in production.

I believe in terms of the type of aircraft that you described, a requirement would exist for firm orders for 200 to 500 units prior to production. I think much research is required in these areas prior to the time that we can consider this as a supplementary or alternative transportation system.

MILLER: I agree with what you have said. Costing for the vehicle is based upon a learning curve projection for 300 vehicles, and the market that I showed you utilizes only 60 of these vehicles. Obviously, we must consider similar markets all over the world to make it worthwhile for the manufacturer to undertake production of the vehicles.

That is a problem. One can't build these vehicles just for Boston. They must be built for Los Angeles, Vienna, Brussels, London, Paris, and other cities as well. We really require demonstration programs of this type of air system in order to find out where the mode should be located, what the true statistics of cost and speed are, and how the passengers will accept this type of transportation system. I think a projection of this approach should include demonstration programs for 1 or 2 years, followed by a building of a complete system. We do need real-life research.

Harry C. Brockel

DEEP-DRAFT PORTS: THEIR EFFECT ON MARITIME FREIGHT MOVEMENT AND RELATED INTERFACE PROBLEMS

Four hundred eighty years ago, Christopher Columbus reached the shores of the New World. Little is known about his flagship, the *Santa Maria,* but it is estimated to have been a ship in the range of 75–90 tons.

Almost on the same day, 480 years later, a Japanese shipyard will launch the greatest floating man-made mass in world history, a tanker of 477,000 deadweight tons (DWT). Three ships of this incredible size are already contracted for, and the first half-million ton ships are on the drafting tables. The Japanese Ministry of Transport has ordered a preliminary study for a proposed million-ton vessel.

Petroleum carriers of this incredible size, dry-bulk-cargo ships now approaching the 200,000-ton size, and the recent launching of a containership of 58,000 tons, are evidence of the shipping revolution that is one of the most radical phenomena in the entire economic history of the world.

The gigantic bulk carriers achieve economics in transport costs that a competitive world cannot resist. Transportation costs of raw materials can be reduced to one half, or perhaps to one fourth, of conventional cost levels, with these new leviathans capable of achieving tremendous annual delivery capacity by their combinations of great size and high speed. This class of ships is so profitable that venture capital is readily available, and they can be amortized after relatively few voyages.

The giant size of this new generation of ships gives them their inherent cost advantage, but it is also the factor that curtails their flexibility on world trade routes and their ports of call. Tankers require significantly deeper drafts as their deadweight tonnage increases. A loaded 100,000-ton tanker draws about 47 feet; the 300,000-tonner requires 73 feet under its keel, far more than any United States port can provide. The approaching 500,000-ton ship will need about 90 feet of draft, and if a million-ton ship ultimately appears (a very real possibility), its draft requirements are projected to be 100–110 feet.

No existing port in the world can provide draft in this range. Such ships cannot navigate the North Sea, nor negotiate the Malacca Straits between the Indian and Pacific oceans.

In mid-1971, there were in operation 167 tankers of 200,000 DWT or over. Believe it or not, 409 ships of this gigantic class were being built or were on order as of a year ago, and more have been programmed since. One estimate is that by 1980, there will be 800 ships afloat of more than 200,000-ton size.

A study by Litton Industries for the U.S. Maritime Administration projects about 3.4 billion tons of petroleum per year by 1983; a volume of over 13 billion tons by 2043 is projected. Dry cargo projections are a volume of 1.6 billion tons for 1983; nearly 22 billion tons by 2043. Litton projects world tanker-vessel tonnage to triple to 186 million tons by 1983; dry-cargo bottoms to go up by another half, to about 130 million tons. These far-flung projections obviously are based upon such assumptions as peaceful world trade, a population explosion, vast exploitation of natural resources, rising standards of consumption, and "developing nations" emerging into world trade.

The world's principal oil fields are mostly distant from great centers of population and industralization—the Arabian Peninsula, Libya, the Sahara, Lake Maracaibo, the Alaskan North Slope. The demand is, of course, in the industrialized areas of the world, and the geographic disparity between oil sources and oil markets has created the vast networks of ships and refineries to bring the two into balance.

As we have observed, these new giants of the sealanes have proven their economics beyond debate and are certainly indicators of world transport patterns of the future; but each new peak of vessel size presents new problems of draft and of port accommodation. In a few words, ship technology has run far ahead of port technology. The new generation of ships are too wide and too deep for the Panama Canal, the Suez, the St. Lawrence Seaway, the Kiel Canal, or any even slightly constricted passage such as the English Channel.

The new transport economics are also now asserting themselves in the Great Lakes. Two new ore carriers have just gone into service, of 48,000-ton and 52,000-ton size; they are limited to navigation on Lake Superior and Lake Michigan primarily. They cannot move through the Welland Canal, or through the seaway locks. Although the St.

Lawrence Seaway is only 13 years old, it already faces severe limits in that literally hundreds of new oceangoing vessels cannot enter it, and the new giant lake vessels cannot leave it.

America's ports face a serious dilemma. Fifty harbors in the world are—or will be—deep enough to handle tankers or other bulk carriers of 200,000 DWT. None of these are in the United States. The world tanker fleet already numbers 700 ships too large to enter any U.S. port.

Long Beach, California, and Seattle, Washington, can bring in the 100,000-ton ships in their 50-foot channels. Machias Bay, Maine, has deep water, but it is not an improved port—and Maine authorities have rejected, on environmental grounds, the plan to create one. Delaware has deep water 5 miles off shore, but it, too, has rejected plans for deep-water terminals there. The largest port, New York, apparently cannot go below 45 feet because of bedrock formations and underwater rail and highway tunnels. With a busy coast and 11 major ports, the best Texas can do is 40-foot channels at 5 of her 11 ports. Houston, third-ranking port of the nation, has 40 feet.

Very few places in the world have enough natural channel depth to serve the new generation of superships. Recognizing the critical role of oil in their economies, various governments and localities are spending huge sums to dredge deeper channels. Europort (Rotterdam), a huge refining center for wester Europe, will go to 70 feet to bring in the "medium" big ones. The port of Fos, near Marseilles, plans a 115-foot channel to serve the largest ships ever contemplated. The port of London is closing several of its historic dock basins and spending hundreds of millions to create a modern port complex at Tilbury, on the coast. Many other world ports are moving in various ways to meet the problem. It is reported that the Japanese government is, or hopes to be, dredging the Malacca Straits, connecting the Indian Ocean and the China Sea, to assure Japan the benefit of the largest ships afloat for her vital deliveries of ore, oil, coal, and grain.

With more than 100 ports of substantial scope on three seaboards, it is recognized that even profligate Uncle Sam cannot financially or economically consider deepening all of them, or even selected numbers, to supership channel requirements. The painful fact is that, as world shipyards turn out vessels in ever-increasing size and efficiency, the world's largest trading nation has not yet moved to solve the problem of the giant ship meeting the land. The U.S. Maritime Administration and the U.S. Army Corps of Engineers have ordered consultant studies dealing with projected shipping needs and alternate solutions for delivery systems.

A study by Arthur D. Little Co. for the Corps of Engineers has made some preliminary findings, suggesting at least eight alternatives for the United States in dealing with the supership:

1. Do nothing; continue status quo.
2. Plan to lighter the supercarriers from deep-water to inshore points.
3. Develop a deep-water transshipment terminal, not in U.S. waters.
4. Attempt design of a shallow-draft supercarrier.
5. Deepen and expand existing port industrial complexes.
6. Build new coastal U.S. transshipment terminal.
7. Build new offshore U.S. transshipment terminal.
8. Build new U.S. deep-water port industrial complex.

The maritime ports of eastern Canada and entrepreneurs in the Bahamas stand ready to serve the United States with new superports, with vessels of suitable draft acting as lighters to transship basic commodities into U.S. ports. Needless to say, this raises questions of the world's largest trading nation being in a position of total dependency on a foreign enterprise, vulnerable to future price squeezes as the dependency increases. Defense considerations are obviously thrust forward, as part of our long-range planning.

We can assume the impossibility of this nation to deepen and widen the channels, approaches, and anchorages at all major ports, as both physically impossible and financially prohibitive. Environmental considerations at large centers of population also work against the deep-draft tanker, new refining centers, ore smelters, and petrochemical complexes.

The ports of this nation obviously face painful choices in terms of the environment, enormous or prohibitive capital costs, and national defense considerations, particularly as to future fossil fuel and energy requirements.

The chief of the Corps of Engineers, some years ago, first hinted at a need to consider a wholly new concept—regional port complexes tailored to serve national, regional, or industrial needs as well as the deep-draft ship. A variant was the suggestion that instead of competitive duplication at scores of ports, there be considered on each seaboard a central petroleum complex, a bulk-cargo, raw material complex, and a centralized containership facility. The problems for U.S. and world ports can be summed up along the following lines.

Centralization—The larger ships become, the more they tend to concentrate at fewer major ports of call, to minimize costs, speed dispatch, and enhance earnings.

Finance—Billions of dollars are needed to finance deep-channel improvements and new port facilities, control environmental damage, and provide sophisticated equipment. The political climate favors social needs over capital improvement, as tax levies reach saturation.

Environment—The attitudes of environmentalists threaten not only harbor deepenings and port expansion, but shipping itself—the source of dreaded oil spills. There is hostility to industry, power plants, or any major intrusion into coastal zones, lake or ocean. In Maine and Delaware, as we have seen, these forces were decisive in their political effects.

Authority—Ports face new challenges in local, state, and federal moves toward coastal zone management. Ports may find their authority challenged or superseded by state, regional, or federal authority. Maryland recently took away the autonomous status of its port authority and made it a division of the Department of Transportation, under state control.

There is a growing body of opinion that our established ports can continue to do their job of serving the containership, the general cargo vessel, the moderate-sized bulk carrier, and the many special-purpose ships of medium size that are part of the changing world-shipping technology. Not only in our waters, but throughout the world, we must inevitably move toward a whole new delivery system for the giant bulk carrier, by means of offshore terminals in deep water. These can take several forms:

1. Long jetties, extending from shore the necessary number of miles out to deep water, where the giant ships can moor and transfer their cargo to pipeline or conveyors.

2. Single or multiple offshore mooring devices with connecting pipelines to the shore, usually submerged, primarily for the tanker.

3. Artificial islands that can range in concept from a single-purpose to a multipurpose port complex.

A proposed island in Delaware Bay for nonliquid bulk cargo, 300 acres in extent, at a cost of $160 million, was rejected for environmental reasons.

After intensive study, the U.S. Maritime Administration has proposed for the Atlantic Coast an offshore, deep-water supertanker terminal, about 9 miles east of the Delaware coast in 100 feet of water. Construction cost is estimated to be $1.3 billion, with 9 years for construction. A preliminary proposal is for federal assumption of one fifth of the cost for dredging and protective breakwaters. The remaining 80 percent would be assumed by the user industries, to pay for an artificial island, ship berths, oil transport, and pollution protection facilities. Preliminary indications are that the state of Delaware and Governor Peterson are reacting favorably to the deep-water offshore concept.

Indications are that two offshore terminal complexes may develop along the Gulf Coast, one in Louisiana waters and one to serve Texas. Eleven deep-water Texas ports now handle almost 200 million tons of cargo annually, much of it bulk liquids. Greatest draft capacity is now 40 feet—reasonable maximum draft capacity is 45 feet.

For the Pacific Coast, the picture is less clear. The ports of Long Beach and Seattle have limited deep-water capability. California is very environmentally sensitive and, it may be presumed, will take a hard look at any major port or petroleum proposals. At the same time, port competition on the Pacific Coast is spirited, and the economic benefits of the big ship will be sought by many, if not by all.

About 3 weeks ago the White House appointed a special task force to study offshore terminals: to determine whether man-made islands or other kinds of offshore "superports" should be built off the East or Gulf coasts to serve America's growing energy needs. The interdepartmental task force also came as a consequence of the recent decision to subsidize federally the construction of the first six American supertankers, a major feature of the national policy to build 30 new ships per year for the next 10 years to revitalize our languishing shipyards and our merchant marine.

The development of offshore terminals, as a new national policy, involves tremendous engineering design questions, i.e., how to build structures in water depths of 75 feet or more in coastal waters and depths of 100 feet at ocean sites. Geography, wind, and weather, bottom conditions, and ecology questions must be grappled with.

Political and jurisdictional questions arise immediately as to local, state, and national authority. If the regional port principle is adopted, a new bistate authority may be called for.

It can be assumed that many states will assert their port interest and port authority, but they must at the same time seek federal financing and must recognize industry's equity and obligations. To some degree, the petroleum industry has thrust its big carriers into a kind of governmental and port service vacuum.

Mr. Armour Armstrong, Chief, Office of Ports, U.S. Maritime Administration, succinctly described the management problem in these words:

What are the management alternatives? Should we rely on developmental and operational management by private enterprise; local port authority; regional port authority; state, bi-state or mult-state port authority; or should federal interests predominate in the management function if the facility is located in federal waters? Should there be a federal superport corporation similar to TVA or the St. Lawrence Seaway Corporation?

Mr. Armstrong further commented that the containership, apparently a great success story in its less than 10 years of history and carrying a large proportion of world general cargo, is a fine example of the interface between land and water. The 20- or 40-foot cargo container is weatherproof and usually pilfer-proof. Landed, it becomes a truck body, adapted to inland delivery, 1 mile or a thousand miles from the wharf. Placed on a rail flatcar, it becomes instant piggyback, ideal for inland rail movement and delivery to consignee.

The interface problem for bulk cargo is less well defined. Oil, coal, ore, fertilizers, grain, sulfur, and similar commodities have the advantage of automated loading, automated discharging, and mechanical handling for great distances, through conveyor or pipeline systems. However, the volumes already moving, and the volumes projected for the future, suggest the need for environmental controls and for large land areas for stock-piling, refining, or processing. The offshore-terminal concept suggests new locations, not proximate to established ports. The deep-draft ship forces this approach.

New regional ports, or new deep-draft offshore terminals raise important jurisdictional, economic, and financial questions in turn. If the ideal locations are remote and undeveloped, do we design new highway systems, new sanitary systems, and a planned industrial complex to serve each new development? Will the transport economies be nullified by tremendous costs for land acquisition, environmental controls, highways, and new utility systems? We have been talking for years in this country about decentralization of people, and ideally planned communities. Perhaps offshore-terminal development will provide the opportunity to test these ideas at several locations.

It seems clear, however, that more is involved here than a group of industries engineering low-cost transportation, while huge new responsibilities are thrust upon government. Perhaps as never before, there is an opportunity and a need for the best minds of industry and government—for the planner, the engineer, and the economist—to come together to analyze impressive new problems and to seek, hopefully, impressive new solutions.

Through the courtesy of the U.S. Maritime Administration the

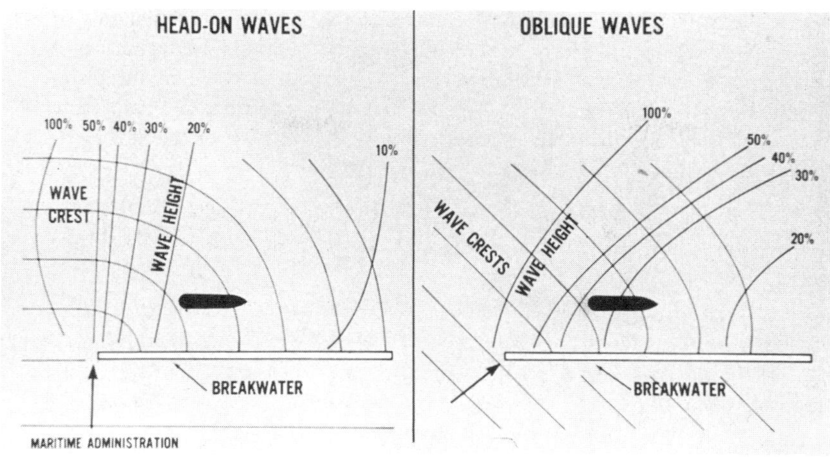

FIGURE 1 Breakwater effectiveness.

following graphics highlight the major areas of interest as well as some of the problem areas.

Figure 1 illustrates one concept of breakwater and wave effects at an offshore terminal.

Figure 2 is a graphic example of the type of wave effects expected in deep water 5 to 7 miles offshore and the kinds of sea conditions encountered when artificial islands or offshore mooring facilities are created.

FIGURE 2 Terminals–wave pattern diagram.

FIGURE 3   Port discharge and storage facilities.

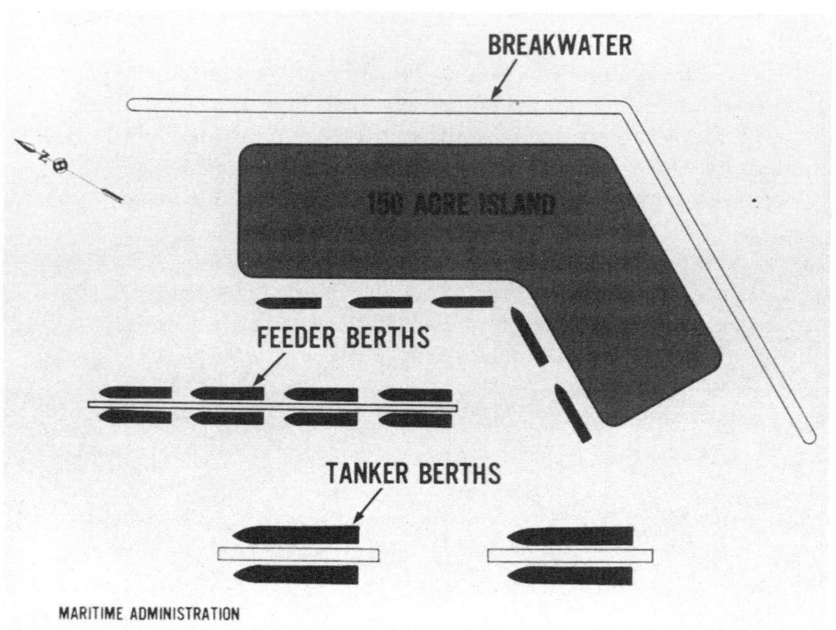

FIGURE 4   Representative offshore terminal–schematic.

FIGURE 5   Lightering operation for a supertanker.

Figure 3 is a theoretical concept of storage facilities combined with discharging facilities.

Figure 4 is an artificial creation in deep water of a breakwater properly designed to minimize wave effects. An artificial island is proposed with detached berths for ships of different sizes.

Figure 5 is an example of a 356,000-ton ship lightering to an 80,000-ton ship. The startling aspect here is that a few years ago 80,000-ton ships were considered huge. Now they act as lighters hauling petroleum from superships in Bantry Bay to Antwerp and Rotterdam.

Figure 6 shows the three principal alternatives for deepwater terminals: the fixed platform, the single-point mooring, and the floating stable platform, attached to the bottom by various anchorage devices. Obviously a great deal of design has to go into each one of these at each location.

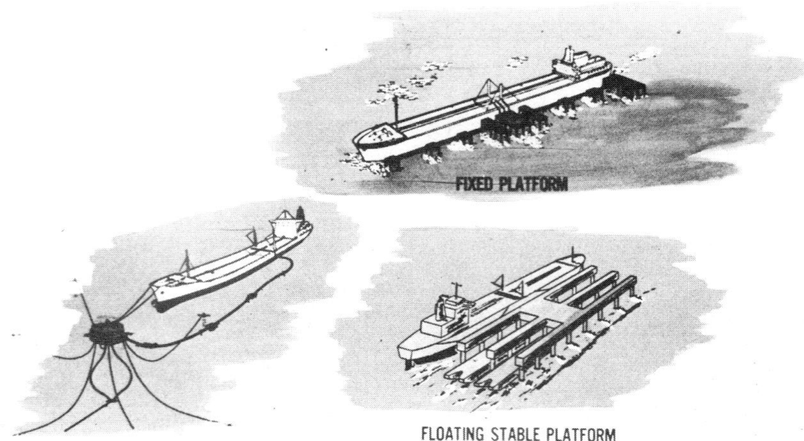

FIGURE 6   Deep-water terminal alternatives.

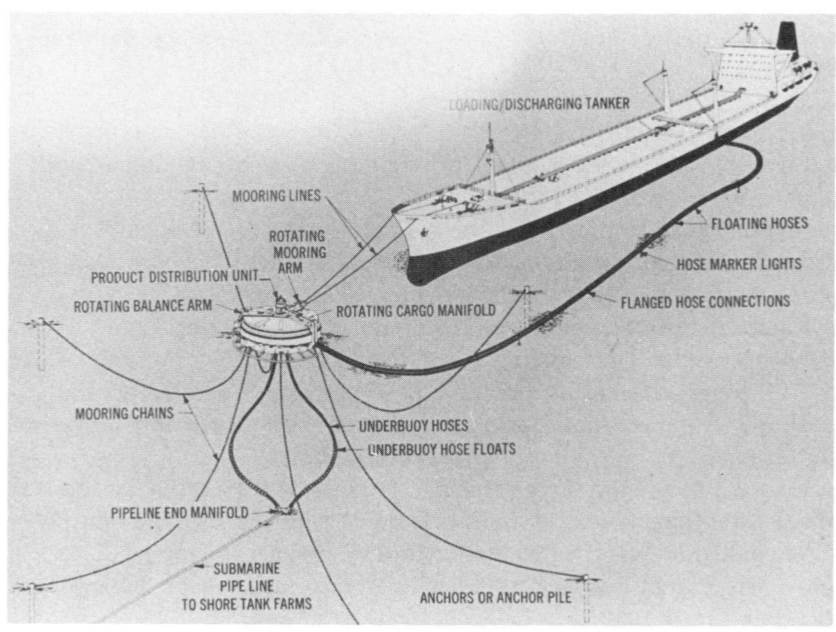

FIGURE 7   Single-point-mooring-buoy concept.

Figure 7 is an example of the single-point-mooring buoy, which has a number of advantages. It is limited in the sense it can handle one ship at a time, but that ship can float freely, responding to wind and wave and continue pumping through flexible lines, generally on the bottom of the ocean. There is much support for this approach and a number of these have been built. They are the lowest in cost, and perhaps the most flexible, considering the ship and what the ship must deal with.

Table 1 lists the ships over 200,000 tons. In mid-1971 there were 167 in operation and 409 on order. American shipyards are finally going to work and will attempt to build six 250,000-ton ships.

TABLE 1 Ships in Excess of 200,000
Deadweight Tons

Year	Number
1966	1 in operation
1971	167 in operation
1971	409 additional on order

Up to now the designs were pioneered in Japan and then adapted later in the shipyards of Sweden, Spain, Germany, and England. The superships are being built now at about half a dozen points in the world.

Table 2 shows what happens to the draft of ships. The famous American clipper ships drew about 14 feet of water and obviously could get into almost any place in the world. The *Globetik Tokyo*, launched October 12, is the last in the line, with a draft of about 92 feet, as compared to the 14 feet draft of the clipper. That is a 120-year progression of draft requirements in terms of ships and harbors.

TABLE 2 Increase in Ship Size

Year	Class	Loaded Draft	Tonnage
1850	clipper	14 feet	–
1942	T-2 tanker	30 feet	16,400
1946	dry bulk	34 feet, 4 inches	24,000
1950	dry bulk	41 feet, 5 inches	60,000
1960	dry bulk	45 feet	69,000
1965	dry bulk	50 feet, 6 inches	106,000
1968	supertanker	81 feet, 5 inches	326,585
1971	supertanker	89 feet	366,812
1974	supertanker	91 feet, 10 inches	477,000

FIGURE 8   Lightering operation in Bantry Bay, Ireland.

Figure 8 is another example of the giant ship and the lighter alongside. This is in Bantry Bay, Ireland, where the 356,000-ton ships come into deep water and lighter to the 80,000-ton ships that haul the oil to Antwerp, Rotterdam and other Western European refining centers.

Figure 9 is a quick progression in the years since World War II of what has happened to the deep-draft tanker. We have gone, in about 25 years, from the T-2 type (15,000 tons) to the *Globetik Tokyo* (477,000 tons). There has never been so important a development in such compressed time.

Figure 10 shows the same story in graphic form.

Figure 11 is another view of a giant ship at a platform.

Figure 12 is an artist's concept of the kind of things that can be done with a port.

The floating stable platform show in Figure 13 would be very flexible in adaptation; but the anchorage systems are critical in terms of what happens, because under maximum strains these might be in some jeopardy.

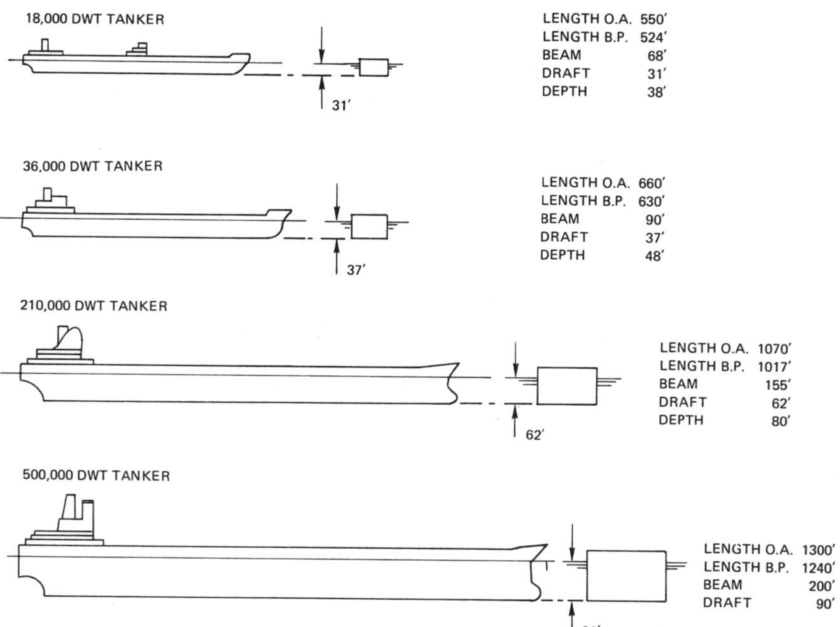

FIGURE 9   Comparison of ocean tankers.

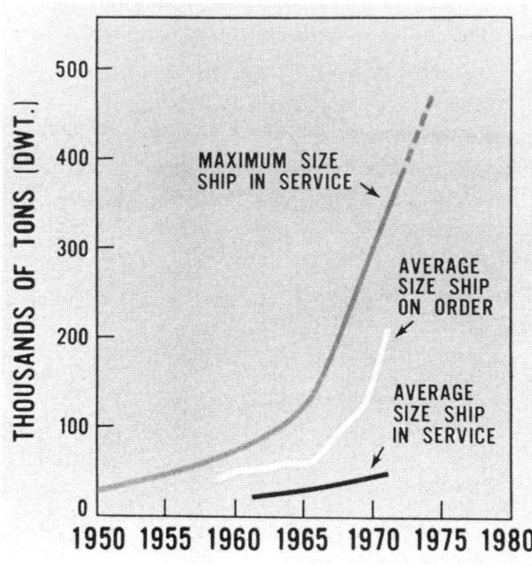

FIGURE 10   Growth in tanker size.

FIGURE 11 Supertanker at ocean platform.

FIGURE 12 Artist's concept of a port proposal.

FIGURE 13 Floating stable platform.

DISCUSSION

HERWALD: I would like to make three random comments relating to the reason for including a discussion of deep-water ports and maritime freight movement. The first one is very simple: Most of our cities have over 50 years of integrated movement. There is no way to change the investment in place in 1 year, that is, to accumulate the capital to do 50 years' worth of effort in a year. Pick any number you want as the amount an urban area can put in, but the number will probably be somewhere around 3 to 4 percent of invested capital per year.

Second, a high fraction of what helps to make the quality of life better in cities relates to the flow of people and goods and production of services, whether they are already there or must be brought in. Just a mention of the trucking traffic relative to passenger traffic in any urban area will make clear the interrelation.

If you are going to do any real long-range planning, say a 20- or 30-year cycle, the stragety must take account of immediate effects as well as the continuing good for 20 to 30 years ahead.

Third, there is an interrelationship between how much petroleum we are really going to use in our transportation system and how it is distributed as well as how the people and other freight move. I wanted to mention again the importance of considering all of the facets of urban transportation in consideration of the total problem.

EVERITT: One of Mr. Brockel's slides seemed to me to indicate the progressive lack of involvement of the American public in maritime operations. In the era of the clipper ship, a large portion of the people in New England were very actively involved in sailing the ships as well as operating the terminals. Today there is practically no involvement of American labor in the operation of our ships.

I wonder if this forecast increase in ship size would introduce economies that would permit American labor to be attracted back into the shipping industry. I also wonder if the degree of labor participation is related to laws passed that made it progressively more difficult for American seamen to be involved?

Is the current small degree of involvement of labor one of the reasons why it is difficult to get people excited about these things?

BROCKEL: We might begin by pointing out that the *Santa Maria* had a crew of 35. The *Globetik Tokyo* will carry 30 men.

In the containership trade, there are situations where one fast containership replaces eight conventional ships. One of the things that is happening—we didn't have time to talk about it—is that people have a much smaller stake in this kind of enterprise.

We talked about American people and their involvement with the clipper ships. The fact today is that of those 700 big ships you saw on the chart, none are of American registry, and many of them even have "gypsy" crews, that is, Chinese, Indian, or Spanish contract crews. The ship may be registered in Germany, operated by a London charter firm, crewed by Chinese, Indian, Spanish, or Italian sailors. They come as a unit, something of a revival of the Roman tradition of labor.

I would have to agree that the American involvement is less but our national government is trying hard to reverse this with a program of 300 new ships under the American flag. These are coming out of the yards at the rate of 10 a year and are to be American built, American manned, and American controlled. There is a national policy to attempt to revive the maritime tradition that helped build this country.

PRICE: I thought it was interesting that Mr. Brockel concerned himself very strongly with a factor that one wouldn't think would be of primary concern in a shipping topic. That was the effect on the environment, and I think that is typical of what the government is faced with these days. We have to concern ourselves with things other than those that seem to be the primary purpose of the undertaking.

In the Urban Mass Transportation Administration (UMTA), Mr. Villarreal, the administrator, and Dr. Hemmes, head of the R&D program, have insisted that we develop an explicit framework of measurements of the impacts of transit. We have identified four groups that are affected by transit and the impacts of changes. These are the rider, the transit operator, the manufacturers in the industry, and the public itself. When these other factors are taken into consideration, one often comes to different conclusions than would have been the case if one considered only the primary topic.

As an example, we looked at water demonstrations, an ancillary topic for us, where people and cities proposed that we consider instituting "over-the-water" transit service.

Through a program design study we had an independent and unbiased contractor look at this mode, and he found first that the Europeans have a great deal of experience in such systems, but that the quality of service provided isn't what the American public might accept.

The United States apparently has the most advanced technology through what we have done with our military craft such as the air-cushion vehicles, but that may be somewhat oversophisticated for a commercial market. Of course, there is the problem of peak-hour traffic. We might use such a craft during the peak hours, but what can we do with it after the peak hours? Will it be economically viable?

There is also the question of noise, perhaps not usually a primary impact, and the problem of debris in the water. Air-cushion vehicles looked promising with respect to avoidance of debris, but from our study of one type powered by two aircraft turboprop engines, we find it would be somewhat like having two propeller aircraft running here in the auditorium. The question is: Would we want that vehicle running up and down the rivers?

BROCKEL: Interestingly enough, the St. Lawrence Seaway Authorities of the United States and Canada recently made a noise study of transportation in certain urban areas in Canada along the St. Lawrence Seaway, and they found that it was possible to move astonishing quantities of goods per decibel of sound. The conventional ship has an incredible advantage over the train and truck.

Of course, it is perfectly obvious: A 30,000-ton ore ship doesn't make much noise, except when it whistles for a tug. So if we are concerned about noise, the conventional ship is the answer.

BESSON: Mr. Brockel has convinced me we have a staggering problem. Regrettably, but not surprisingly, I have no easy solution.

HERWALD: The issue of balancing all factors involved in anything we do is the most difficult part of the job, because we don't have the uniform public that has been mentioned. The public has divergent views of its own, and it is going to be very difficult to get the constituency—that is the users and supporters—to understand what the tradeoffs are, because they are not yet well defined. If somebody in the audience has the magic solution to that problem we would like to know about it. Anything we talk about involves tradeoffs, is either more good and less bad, or more bad and less good, and we have difficulty in communicating these shades of difference. I think it behooves all of us to be concerned about how we communicate with the public about these tradeoffs so that they have a voice in making the decision—not on technical terms, necessarily, but based on the issues that affect them. This discussion illustrates that problem, particularly for the UMTA case.

It was mentioned earlier in the day that 72 percent of our people live in urban areas. That is a different situation than that prevailing when our current transportation systems were put into place, when the highways were built to provide access for the rural areas to the city.

QUESTION: We have been told that in the future there will be less reliance on petroleum and fossil fuels, especially in the transportation field. We are talking about electric cars and atomic energy for electricity for the cities. What do you see in the future for the supertanker now being designed particularly for petroleum transportation?

BROCKEL: The possibility of the electric automobile and greater reliance on atomic energy or sun cells and so forth still seems to me to be very speculative.

The studies being made by the industry and by responsible federal agencies suggest that our imports of petroleum in the future will be at least four times the present level, along with a full exploitation of all of our domestic resources.

We are talking seriously about oil extraction from shale; that I think is perhaps closer to technical realization and economic realization than some of the other alternatives.

So for the next 50 years, I suggest petroleum will continue to be the primary source of energy. Everything I see points in that direction. Therefore, we have a fantastic interest in the big ship, the offshore terminal, the refining complexes, and what we are to do with them.

LEHAN: I would like to ask the speaker to comment on some-defense-related issues tied in with the supertankers-superships. One of his slides showed that a large supertanker is the equivalent of a large number of T-2's. This makes it a very attractive target, essentially a vulnerable target. Yet its speed makes it very difficult to operate in a convoy, and its size and draft may make it somewhat inflexible with respect to where you can use it. Would you comment on these three defense-related issues?

BROCKEL: My first comment would be to agree. One other comment, though, is that the giant ship means fewer ships, and this seems to be reassuring to a small degree to the environmentalists. In other words, if we can safely move the big ship and avoid *Torrey Canyon* situations, we can move a lot of goods with very large single deliveries.

I would have to agree with you, if we consider conventional warfare, the world could be brought to its knees with a relatively small number of well-placed bombs or torpedoes, because there would be fewer, but bigger, ships. You are quite right.

QUESTION: I am glad the speaker mentioned the *Torrey Canyon*. That was a relatively small tanker by today's standards, and the near-catastrophe it caused in the Channel, particularly on the beaches of Cornwall and the French Coast, is well known.

What happens then if we have a similar incident with a 450,000-ton tanker? What do we do, mop up the entire North Sea, for example? That is another order of magnitude.

What is the purpose of going to such outsize behemoths? Wouldn't smaller fleets of tankers be more practical? Oil spills are inevitable, bound to happen, and I can conceive of a 450,000-ton tanker breaking up as readily as a 25,000 tonner, or in fact, even more so, because the problems in naval architecture and construction are of another order of magnitude.

BROCKEL: Let me say that these considerations are very large in the minds of the government, the industry, and the ship operators. Many special precautions are being taken to improve harbor navigational techniques and navigation during fog. Special sealanes are being considered for these big ships to minimize the possibility of collision.

The economics, though, are overwhelming. The cost of transport in the

50,000-ton ship will be six or seven times per ton what it will be in the 500,000-ton class. I think you see national governments and the industries involved looking for lower costs, because they, too, are coping with inflation and creeping escalation of costs.

These are all matters of great concern; it is good to hear this audience take note of them, because I agree the world would reel at the results of a 500,000-ton oil spill, already having witnessed the results from a 100,000-ton ship. These problems can be dealt with—but at staggering cost.

KAVANAGH: The Academy is very much interested also in marine and ocean engineering, and I want to mention that there are other areas of offshore activity in transportation as well as in power and other fields. The possibility of offshore deep-water ports is paralleled by the possibility of having offshore airports, and certainly in New York, and other port authorities, this matter has been studied rather intensively.

In the field of power generation, for example, the chairman's company, Westinghouse, and Tenneco, formed a new development for the manufacture of nuclear floating platform-mounted power plants, which will string along our coasts from north to south and possibly along the Pacific as well.

There are other possibilities that include the building of petrochemical plants, sewage treatment plants, and all types of industrial facilities of that nature, which may eventually affect or have a great influence upon the urban and city problems that we face today.

BROCKEL: There is one consideration here we might take away with us related to making new land on the Continental Shelf. The cost is simply staggering in comparison to the availability of hundreds of millions of acres ashore.

It seems to me that the uses we make of offshore sites will be those forced by total necessity, by inescapable considerations, rather than by the economics of the situation. When we talk about making 300 acres of land in 100 feet of water, we are talking certainly in terms of hundreds of millions of dollars, or put another way, a land cost of several million dollars per acre. Six or 7 miles away, land may be available at $1,000, $5,000, $10,000, even $20,000 or $50,000, whatever the figure may be in a particular location.

The economics of this problem are going to be extremely interesting, and it is very good, I think, to see a group like this taking a look at it.

COMMENT: I just want to observe that automobile transportation in the United States alone accounts for 37 percent of the petroleum industry's market. The next largest market for the petroleum industry is the 10 percent for home-heating fuels. We should keep in mind that we bring all this oil over here to be used primarily for our automobile transportation. I think one has to question the building or even pressing ahead with these large tankers to fuel our automobiles.

HERWALD: That is precisely why the whole subject is being considered here. Going one step further, we find that, depending on whose estimates we take, anywhere from 60 percent to 90 percent of the fuel is used in an urban area. That shows even more exactly where we are consuming our petroleum.

Roger H. Gilman

PLANNING FOR IMPROVED TRANSPORTATION OF PEOPLE AND GOODS IN URBAN AREAS

The Port Authority of New York and New Jersey recently observed two anniversaries of projects, that, I believe, typify the bistate agency's diversified planning activities to improve the transportation of people and cargo in an urban area.

On September 1, the Port Authority marked the tenth anniversary of the start in 1962 of its operation of the Port Authority Trans-Hudson transit system, known as PATH, which today carries 145,000 daily passengers between New Jersey and New York on the first all air-conditioned, rail rapid-transit fleet in the world.

In August, the Port Authority observed the tenth anniversary of the opening of the first containership berths at its Elizabeth, New Jersey, Marine Terminal. In 1962 the opening of this partly developed facility heralded a new and revolutionary era in seaborne cargo transportation. Today, the Elizabeth terminal and adjoining Port Newark are recognized as the Container Capital of the world.

The World Trade Center, now under construction in lower Manhattan, is still another Port Authority project designed to improve the transportation of cargo and people in the New York–New Jersey Port District. Although it will not be entirely completed for another 2 years, the Trade Center already has as tenants 250 firms, all of them involved in the marketing, promotion, financing, document preparation, and other procedural steps necessary to the shipping of foreign commerce by ocean and air. In addition, the Trade Center will function as the hub of a worldwide information network that will enable exporters and importers to widen their markets.

First, what is the Port Authority of New York and New Jersey and what part does it play in urban transportation planning? The Port Authority was formed in 1921 as a joint public agency of the states of New York and New Jersey. The Compact creating the Port Authority charges it with two basic responsibilities: the promotion of commerce and trade through the bistate Port District; and the planning, development, and operation of public transportation, terminal, and other facilities of commerce in northern New Jersey and New York. In the Compact, the Port District is defined as the region where the two states have vital joint interests, embracing an area within a radius of about 25 miles from the Statue of Liberty and including important commercial and industrial centers in both states.

The rapid changes that are taking place in urban areas in the United States greatly increase the need for current and detailed information concerning not only the transportation flows that exist in the area, but also for a knowledge of the basic economic and demographic forces that combine to produce and direct these flows. In order to carry out its planning mission, the Port Authority is heavily engaged in the conduct of many different kinds of surveys designed to satisfy the urgent need for information.

The last 10 years have seen the development of increasingly sophisticated and accurate sampling techniques by our staff as efforts are made to obtain information concerning the identities and characteristics of both the commuting and noncommuting travelers in the region; a knowledge of the forces that motivate these travelers to select the routes and the modes of transportation they utilize; an understanding of their likely reactions to changes in service characteristics and the costs of travel; and also more down-to-earth information on hourly, directional, daily, and seasonal changes in the characteristics and composition of the region's traffic.

Household surveys, sophisticated attitude and motivation studies, continuous and carefully controlled origin and destination surveys of highway and rail facilities, inflight surveys, both personal interview and questionnaire-type surveys of transit passengers even during heavily crowded conditions, have all been utilized extensively by the Port Authority, and techniques for assuring the validity of the information developed by these surveys are continuously improving. Increasing use is also being made of various types of mechanical or electronic accounting, recording, and classifying devices in order to obtain more complete data covering the specifics of traffic flow in the region.

We have also found surveys to be an essential method for developing information necessary for planning cargo facilities. Different techniques are required in planning and conducting surveys of cargo, and over the years the Port Authority has developed efficient methods of research into source data such as U.S. Census Bureau figures on the movement of foreign trade, individual company records on the shipment of materials in and out of the Port of New York by rail, and dispatcher information on cargo flow by truck.

Where particularly detailed operational information is required for the movement of cargo, we have carried out sample surveys at pick-up and delivery points on piers, at air terminals, and at various kinds of railroad facilities in order to develop an understanding of the important characteristics of the freight and also to gather data concerning the flow volumes and operational problems involved.

We are at present working very closely with the airlines in the development of a survey technique to collect for the first time important data on the movement of air cargo on both domestic and foreign routes into and out of the port of New York. The survey will also provide information concerning the different modes by which their cargo arrives at or leaves the airports and the various modal interface problems that are involved.

One final survey effort for which we have extremely high hopes is the nationwide survey of U.S. foreign trade aimed at identifying the inland points of origin and destination of foreign cargo handled through each of the individual ports in the United States. We worked very closely with the U.S. Department of Transportation and the U.S. Bureau of the Census on developing the specifications for this survey, which was actually conducted by the Bureau of the Census.

Such comprehensive planning has provided the foundation for the Port Authority's development and operation of five basic types of transportation facilities. In 1921 railroads were the most important carriers of cargo in the Port District. Consequently, the study and report that led to the creation of the Port Authority in 1921 and the bistate agency's early planning activities emphasized improvements in rail freight service, including consolidation of trackage and terminals. However, the railroads, which were strong and well off in the 1920s, rejected these proposals; changing conditions have, of course, altered this emphasis.

Historically, our program therefore started with the development of six interstate vehicular bridges and tunnels linking New York and New Jersey. As highway transportation in the Port District expanded, we planned and developed two bus terminals in Manhattan for interstate commuter buses and three motor truck terminals, all designed to reduce traffic and, in the case of the bus terminals, eliminate the movement of interstate buses from Manhattan streets.

Since it is a port agency, planning for improved ocean transportation is a primary Port Authority concern. This is manifest through our six marine terminals that serve as the interfaces beteween ocean and land transportation of cargo and passengers in the Port District. Since the terms of the 1921 Compact provide that the Port Authority can take over municipally owned waterfront and other public properties only with the agreement of the municipality involved, our major port development responsibility did not begin until 1948 when, at the request of the City of Newark, New Jersey, the Port Authority took on the job of rehabilitating and operating under a long-term lease, the city's docks on Newark Bay on a self-sustaining basis. At the time of this acquisition, Port Newark was literally a structural shambles that had become a financial and economic liability to the city. Furthermore, the city had no funds to spare for redevelopment.

Previous Port Authority studies into every phase of pier operations had shown that the handling of trailer trucks was the key to efficient movement of cargo at these interfaces. We were therefore convinced that waterfront facilities should be of sufficient strength and size for such trucks to deliver and pick up cargo expeditiously.

The planning for Port Newark therefore included wide streets, wide pier sheds, and abundant truck-parking areas. The provision of such facilities would have been difficult, if not impossible, if Port Newark had been located near a built-up, crowded city center. Its position on the fringes of the port, near modern interstate highways, was a definite asset. In fact, this development has been largely responsible for the trend to transfer cargo shipping from the congested shores of Manhattan, where it had been traditionally located, to the Brooklyn, Staten Island, and New Jersey waterfronts.

Acceptance of the concept that the handling of trailer-trucks was the key to efficient cargo operations at ocean interfaces led to a revolutionary development in moving seaborne cargo during the 1950s. At that time, one of our Port Newark tenants came to the conclusion that the flagging coastal shipping industry could be revived if full containers hauled by tractor trucks could be loaded and unloaded on ships especially constructed to receive them. The first containerhsips to go into operation were constructed by rebuilding tankers with movable cranes on their decks and cells in their holds for receiving containers. An area in Port Newark was allocated for these ships and their cargoes.

When our studies showed that special containership terminals, with shore-based movable cranes would lead to more efficient operation, the Port Authority's Board of Commissioners, acting with great foresight, purchased in 1955 a tract of about 900 acres of swampland adjacent to Port Newark in Elizabeth, New Jersey, for development of container shipping facilities. This great area was on the fringe of the port and contiguous to major highway arteries and to railroads serving the New York–New Jersey metropolitan area. Above all, there was ample room for construction of terminals with adequate trailer parking areas and for facilities for consolidating cargo into containers, for building wide access roads leading to the terminals, for providing rail connections with trunkline railroads, and for erecting office and storage buildings.

By 1975, the development of the Elizabeth containership terminal complex, comprising over 3 miles of berthing space and 1,100 acres of supporting facilities, will be virtually completed. At that time, the two adjoining Port Authority marine terminals in Elizabeth and Newark, with 11,000 workers employed there, will be able to accommodate 22 modern containerships simultaneously, as well as many more break-bulk and other ships.

A week ago I watched the arrival of the newest containership at the New Jersey–New York port, some 946 feet long, with a beam of 105 feet, draft of anywhere from 33 to 35 feet, and a speed of over 30 knots. This ship in 19 hours unloaded and then loaded a combined total of 35,000 tons of cargo at its berth in Elizabeth. According to estimates by seasoned shipping men, the same volume of cargo on break-bulk ships would have required 20 days.

At the request of the city of New York, the Port Authority is currently building a new passenger-ship terminal on the Hudson River waterfront of mid Manhattan. The objective is to provide passengers of cruise ships and trans-Atlantic liners with a comfortable and convenient interface between their ocean voyages and the land transportation that will convey them to and from their homes. When completed in 1974, this terminal will be a dramatic improvement over the cold-in-the-winter, hot-in-the-summer, barn-like disgraceful piers that passengers now have to endure while going through the embarkation or debarkation process. Furthermore, cars and taxis bringing the travelers and their visitors will be accommodated on the terminal's roadways and parking areas, completely off Manhattan streets.

The most efficient marine or industrial waterfront terminal would be virtually useless if the waterway leading to it is inadequate or unsafe to accommodate the ships berthing there. Under its mandate from the two states to protect the commerce of the New York–New Jersey port, the Port Authority determines the port's general channel deficiencies and presents these needs for action by the Army Corps of Engineers, other federal agencies, and by the Congress.

In recent years our studies have shown that in the near future large volumes of the petroleum used in this country will be transported by huge supertankers with drafts of more than 50 feet. The studies have also shown that it would be difficult, tremendously expensive, and perhaps impossible to provide channels in the nation's ports deep enough to accommodate these mammoth ships. Accordingly, the Port Authority, through its membership in the American Association of Port Authorities, has participated in preliminary national studies of this transportation problem. From these efforts, studies are being undertaken by both the Corps of Engineers and the Maritime Administration of the feasibility of establishing regional deep-water oil terminals, possibly off shore, for serving the needs of the United States.

The Port Authority assumed responsibility for development of the airport system for the New York–New Jersey metropolitan region in 1947, after enabling legislation was approved by the two states. At the time, the states expressed their agreement that each air terminal in the region serves the entire Port Dsitrict, and they declared as their policy the integration of these air terminals into a unified regional system. The City of New York and the City of Newark then entered into long-term lease arrangements with the Port Authority under which the bistate agency has gone forward with the development of John F. Kennedy, LaGuardia, and Newark airports.

In planning for this unified system, we recognized that the type of service dictates the physical characteristics of an airport. Aircraft used to serve different kinds of markets have differing requirements. Thus, LaGuardia Airport serves the short-haul market to Boston and Washington, for example, and medium-haul travel to the Midwest, South, and Southwest. Newark International Airport handles the short- and medium-haul markets as well as the domestic long-haul flights, and is expected to handle an increasing number of international flights in the future. Kennedy International serves the domestic long-haul market and international traffic, plus a mixture of short-haul traffic providing connecting service. Kennedy is also the world's largest air-cargo center, handling approximately three quarters of the air freight shipped into and out of the region.

More than a decade ago, the Port Authority planning studies showed the need for additional airport capacity to maintain a continued high level of service. We found that the only politically acceptable solution to this problem was to secure greater, in fact, maximum, utilization of existing facilities. Our efforts here have fallen generally into two categories: physical and administrative.

First, we planned for the complete redevelopment of all three airports.

The Port Authority's redevelopment of LaGuardia was completed in 1967 when it opened a new three-story passenger terminal, seven times the size of the former terminal building. As part of the program, the airport's two runways were also extended over water to a length of 7,000 feet on a unique pile-supported platform.

Major redevelopment of Newark Airport is now under way. The work includes construction of three new terminal buildings, the first of which will be open in less than a year. These three buildings, each with three satellites, will provide a total of 83 aircraft gate positions, in contrast to the 32 positions at the present single terminal. Existing runways are being extended, and a new 8,200-foot instrument runway is under construction. Other improvements will include new parking facilities, hangars, and cargo-handling facilities.

Kennedy Airport already is operating at a level that exceeds by 20 percent the 1960 estimate of its maximum capacity. This expanded capacity, needed to accommodate the new generation of larger aircraft, was made possible by a series of costly improvements, including the expansion of the central terminal area from 655 to 840 acres, which permitted the enlargement of unit terminals, and the doubling of the size of the International Arrival Building.

Second, we have demonstrated an interest in the rapid development of a viable short takeoff and landing (STOL) system to serve the principal cities of the Northeast Corridor between Boston and Washington.

Thus, a study of feasible STOL-port sites in northern New Jersey is currently being undertaken by the New Jersey Department of Transportation with the cooperation of the Federal Aviation Administration and the Port Authority.

The provision of improved access to the regional airports is being given intensive attention. Arterial highway links are being built by the two states in cooperation with the Port Authority. Plans are being finalized for rail access to Kennedy and Newark Airports under joint studies by the Port Authority, the Metropolitan Transportation Authority in New York, and the New Jersey Department of Transportation.

As far as remedial administrative action goes, it first became necessary when congestion at high-density airports in the summer of 1968 caused a chain reaction that nearly brought the nation's air transportation system to a halt. Diversions, cancellations, and missed connections were commonplace. In some cases, flight delays at Kennedy, LaGuardia, and Newark reached 2 and 3 hours, backing up traffic at almost every other major airport in the country. To ease this situation, the Port Authority increased its minimum landing fee during peak hours from 5 to 25 dollars as a move to divert private aircraft movements to "reliever" airports in the region. A few months later the Federal Aviation Administration restricted the number of hourly flights at five of the nation's high-density airports, including our three regional airports, also to reduce congestion during peak hours.

As a result of these administrative remedies, the delay picture at our airports has improved considerably. Since 1968 the average number of flights delayed more than 30 minutes at Kennedy Airport has been reduced by as much as 75 percent on a typical day.

Rehabilitation and operation of our interstate transit line, PATH, illustrates the problems as well as the possibilities of rail transportation. The bankrupt Hudson & Manhattan Railroad, a 14-mile rail-rapid-transit system that connects Newark, Harrison, Jersey City, and Hoboken with New York City via tunnels under the Hudson River, was in an unbelievable state of decay when it was transferred to Port Authority operation and renamed PATH in 1962. In the first few months we scrubbed, painted, and undertook urgent repairs to make the line clean and safe for riders. At the same time, a massive reconstruction program was started, including the design and purchase of new rolling stock, the rebuilding of the signal system, the replacement of the electric traction power system, and the renovation of stations, maintenance shops, and car yards.

By the end of this year, PATH's fleet will total 298 air-conditioned cars. The Port Authority is also replacing two of the system's major terminals that have been completely inadequate and unsatisfactory for PATH service. Last year the new World Trade Center terminal in lower Manhattan went into operation as a replacement of the 62-year-old Hudson Terminal. Last month the cornerstone was laid for the new Journal Square Transportation Center, which is being built around PATH's new station in Jersey City. When completed in 1974, it will provide a combined rail–bus–auto parking terminal.

Over the past decade, the Port Authority, through its rail transit operating subsidiary, has invested $250 million in acquisition, rehabilitation, modernization, and operating deficits on the PATH system. PATH now carries over 70 percent of passengers entering New York City by rail from New Jersey. Traffic, which dropped to an all-time low of 26 million passengers in 1965, has grown to almost 30 million in 1971. Despite the increased ridership, however, the PATH deficit has steadily grown and reached $18 million last year.

Planning of commuter-rail-transportation improvements has a priority in the Port Authority. In 1970, Governor Rockefeller of New York and Governor Cahill of New Jersey appointed an Inter-Agency Task Force composed of the top executives of the Port Authority, the Metropolitan

Transportation Authority, and the New Jersey Department of Transportation to examine and develop recommendations for meeting future interstate public transportation needs. Extensive studies are almost completed on the provision of track connections and expanded rail facilities in New Jersey and improvements to Penn Station, New York, which can then accommodate additional direct commuter service to Manhattan.

At the same time, preliminary studies are being made on a proposed new trans-Hudson rail tunnel. These are focusing on forecasts of potential traffic by 1985 as well as operational plans and integrated train schedules for the commuter railroads involved, and design concepts of the tunnel, car yards, and connections. Preliminary cost estimates also are being prepared.

In planning for improved transportation the Port Authority has always followed a policy of working closely with other governmental agencies as well as with a great many civic and trade groups. In fact, we could not function efficiently or effectively without federal, state, and municipal government cooperation.

Cordial and close planning relationships have been maintained with the departments of transportation of the federal government and of the two states. Through this cooperation over the years we have improved the access to the Port Authority's bridges and tunnels, its airports, seaports, and other terminals.

Cooperative planning has been undertaken to achieve greater use of existing highways. For example, joint planning involving the Tri-State Regional Planning Commission, the New Jersey Department of Transportation, the New Jersey Turnpike Authority, and the Port Authority, with the aid of a $500,000 grant from the U.S. Department of Transportation, led to the opening in 1970 of an exclusive bus lane to handle morning commuter buses through the highly congested New Jersey approach to the Lincoln Tunnel. Use of this lane saves from 10 to 25 minutes of travel time for 25,000 daily New Jersey bus commuters to Manhattan. Its success has persuaded many former auto commuters to leave their cars home and travel by bus. Since then, agencies in New York City, Boston, and San Francisco have initiated similar exclusive commuter bus lanes. Of course, the Shirley Highway exclusive bus lanes near Washington, D.C. even preceded our own in New Jersey.

As another example, a joint planning effort by the New York State Thruway Authority, the New York State Bridge Authority, and the Port Authority led to the one-way toll collection system inaugurated in 1970 on 12 Hudson River and New York–New Jersey interstate crossings. This new procedure of collecting tolls only from eastbound traffic has speeded the flow of traffic and eased congestion, particularly during the evening commuter peak hours.

The Port Authority works harmoniously on a wide variety of programs and activities undertaken by the Tri-State Regional Planning Commission, which has been designated at the official regional planning agency by the states of New York, New Jersey, and Connecticut. In this capacity, the Commission processes from state and local jurisdictions, including the Port Authority, applications for federal grants of funds for transportation and many other types of projects. Thus, Tri-State was the agency that processed and administered the $500,000 federal grant for establishing the exclusive bus lane.

Many civic and business organizations in our region work closely with the public agencies in planning for improved transportation in the New York–New Jersey metropolitan area. For example, the Regional Plan Association has stimulated action on several proposals to improve transportation in the region. The Association was a strong supporter of construction of the Port Authority Bus Terminal, which has removed interstate buses from streets of Manhattan.

In the area of non-capital-intensive effort, staggered work hours has proved to be a constructive project for improving people transportation during peak hours. This program is currently being sponsored jointly by the Downtown-Lower Manhattan Association and the Port Authority. Some 100,000 workers of 250 companies in lower Manhattan have abandoned the traditional 9–5 work hours for either earlier or later schedules. This has spread commuter travel in the area substantially and has significantly reduced the congestion on PATH and New York City subway lines. The program is now being extended to midtown Manhattan through the cooperation of a task force composed principally of representatives of many business associations in the midtown area.

To summarize, the Port Authority has been directly concerned with planning for improved transportation of people and cargo since it was established 51 years ago. By consistently adopting new management and planning techniques as they have evolved, and by working closely and harmoniously with other governmental and private planning groups, modern and efficient facilities have been provided for improved transportation of people and goods in the New York–New Jersey metropolitan region.

Arthur Goldsmith

THE RELATIONSHIP OF TELECOMMUNICATIONS TO URBAN TRANSPORTATION

The keynote address by Mr. Beggs covered the need to develop innovative solutions to transportation problems. As he indicated, a good many of these involve telecommunications in some form or other. Let me define my use of telecommunications, since it means many things to many people. We start with the International Telecommunications Union definition—"any transmission, emission or reception of signs, signals, writing, images and sounds or intelligence of any nature by wire, radio, or other electromagnetic systems"—and extend it to include sonics and ultrasonics. Thus we include all means used for communications, navigation, surveillance, and command and control as connected with transportation.

We normally think of urban transportation as those means required to get around the city, i.e., buses, rapid transit, automobiles, trucks, and some innovative means such as personal rapid transit. However, in the Department of Transportation (DOT), we plan for the entire trip, that is, from origin to destination. This involves local as well as long-haul means such as conventional aircraft, trains, and highway vehicles and the attendant interface problems.

Let us for a moment consider the importance of transportation in our modern industrial society. The transportation industry accounts for almost 20 percent of the gross national product, about equally divided between freight and passenger transport. A good portion of the congestion and pollution in the urban areas is caused by the internal combustion engine of the approximately 110 million registered motor vehicles (automobiles, buses, and trucks). A recent study by DOT's Federal Highway Administration (FHWA) showed that the distribution of automobiles is about the same as the population. About 75 percent of our population lives in urban areas. This means that three fourths of the motor vehicles move primarily on the 15 percent of the U.S. road miles in the metropolitan areas. That is approximately one vehicle for every 35 feet of road.

With the U.S. population expected to grow from its current 210 million to approximately 300 million by 1990, transportation requirements can only go up. In fact, they are expected to double in the next 20 years. The problem is meeting these requirements, and innovative R & D holds the answer.

Transportation has been identified as one of the five areas of technical opportunity where a breakthrough is most likely to make a great difference in the lives of the general public. To emphasize this, the 1973 federal budget allocates about $650 million for R & D in the field of transportation. A major portion of this is DOT's approximately $450 million for research, development, and demonstrations, amounting to approximately 5 percent of our total budget, with the percentage increasing over the past several years. The Highway Trust Fund, which is primarily for roadway construction, accounts for almost two thirds of the DOT budget. If the distorting effect of this fund, whose expenditures are fixed by law, is removed, the R & D percentage increases to 11, comparing very favorably with the R & D expenditures of other high technology industries.

However, simply increasing the capacity of present means is not the answer. Let us take the automobile as an example: Downtown Los Angeles has about one fourth of its total area devoted to streets, freeways, and parking. If much more is paved over, its reason for existence will cease. In the New York metropolitan area, if the capacity of every bridge, tunnel and freeway were doubled and as much road and parking space provided as there is presently in Los Angeles, only 22 percent of the present commuters could be accommodated in private vehicles. Thus, it is obvious that pouring concrete is not the answer. Better and more efficient transportation must be found, that, among other things, will not contribute to environmental pollution. A possible means involving heavy emphasis on telecommunications would provide the needed improvements in transportation system operations, in efficiency, in safety, in scheduling, and in the availability of other amenities. Another solution is to decrease the need for transportation by substituting telecommunications.

Transportation and telecommunications are not strangers. There have been crude types of signaling systems from the early days to assist in the orderly flow of transportation. The railroads, for example, started with trackside semaphores and have gradually evolved into sophisticated block-type controls utilizing electronic means to communicate directly with the driver. Certain modern systems of transportation would be completely inoperable without the current control systems. Try to imagine, if you will, helicopters landing in the midst of a large city without some type of air-traffic-control and landing aids.

To date, the major use of telecommunications has been for two-way radio and for navigation systems. At the present time, there are approximately four million radio transmitters in the mobile services licensed by the Federal Communications Commission (FCC). A large portion (43 percent) of the radio frequency spectrum from 10 kHz to 100 GHz is assigned to the mobile services, including aeronautical fixed radio location, mobile navigation, and satellite services. In addition to communications, transportation is increasingly making use of electronics for command and control purposes.

The Department of Transportation is a leader in sponsoring and implementing transportation research. Before detailing some specific projects, let me briefly cover the organization and areas of responsibility within DOT. The Office of the Secretary is responsible for the general direction of all programs, establishes policy, monitors progress and output, and provides guidance. The specific responsibility for research, development, and demonstration is vested in the Assistant Secretary for Systems Development and Technology to whom the Office of Telecommunications reports. Also within the Department are the operating administrations, each responsible for certain transportation areas and each having its own R & D group.

There are four operating administrations concerned with ground transportation. The Urban Mass Transportation Administration (UMTA), as its name implies, is primarily responsible for various forms of mass transportation, i.e., rapid transit and buses in the urban area. It is also concerned with other forms of urban public transportation such as personal rapid transit systems and demand responsive transportation systems. The Federal Highway Administration (FHWA) is concerned with roads and vehicular traffic. In spite of the "highway" connotation, its responsibilities include the urban streets and arteries. The Federal Railroad Administration is primarily concerned with long-distance and high-speed rail and unconventional transportation systems using guideways. However, they work very closely with UMTA on the technological problems of rapid-transit systems. The National Highway Traffic Safety Administration deals with the safe movement of motor traffic whether it be rural or urban.

Although their interest is slightly peripheral to urban transportation problems, the Federal Aviation Administration (FAA) and the Coast Guard nevertheless interface closely with the urban area. The FAA is responsible for air-traffic control that, in the case of the quiet short-haul air traffic systems, impinges directly on the urban area. They are also concerned with problems of airport access and the surface movement of passengers to and from the airport. The Coast Guard has responsibilities for safe operation in the harbor and has recently been given authority similar to that of the FAA for control of harbor traffic under the Ports and Waterways Safety Act of 1972.

A number of ways are utilized by DOT to implement our research and development activities. Several in-house research facilities are maintained such as the Transportation Systems Center in Cambridge, the National Aviation Facilities Experimental Center in Atlantic City, the Coast Guard Electronics Engineering Center in Wildwood, and FHWA's Fairbanks Highway Research Center in McLean, Virginia. In addition to in-house R&D efforts, a considerable portion of the R&D funds are also expended in direct contracts with industry, and through grants-in-aid to state and local governments, universities, and other not-for-profit organizations. Finally, there is the indirect method of encouraging industry to pursue certain lines of research endeavor.

To illustrate the uses of telecommunications and show the relationship of telecommunications to transportation, I will describe several urban projects. Many of these have been funded wholly or in part by DOT. Let us consider the first completely new metropolitan rail transportation system that has gone into operation in the United States in the past 60 years. I am referring to the San Francisco Bay Area Rapid Transit, commonly known as BART, which began revenue services just last month.

The BART system, with its top speed of 80 mph and average speed, including station stops, of 45 mph, 90-second headway between trains, en route telecommunications, and automated fare collection would not be possible without telecommunications. All BART system operations are under supervisory computer control. A central computer collects status information and controls all operations throughout the system in a coordinated manner. It is in communication with an individual train only when it is at a station. At that time, a miniature computer aboard the train is updated and the train speed and station dwell time programmed until it reaches the next station. In between, there are local control units relating to safety that the computer cannot override: protective train spacing, overspeed prevention, and the locking of switches to prevent misrouting. An attendant aboard the train takes over only in case of emergency. There is also a communications system through which the dispatcher can have two-way communications with the train attendant. He can also make announcements directly to the passengers on one or a group of trains. Passengers can talk to the train attendant via an intercom. In addition, the fare system is completely automated. A vending machine dispenses a magnetically striped ticket that stores its cash value. At the entry turnstile, the station is recorded on the ticket. On leaving, the passenger again has to pass through a turnstile. If there is sufficient cash value on the ticket, the amount is subtracted; if not, the passenger has to make up the difference. This is just a brief description of the many ways electronics is being used to improve the safety and efficiency of the latest urban mass transportation system.

Let us now consider a few command and control projects. The systems usually also involve communications, but this is an adjunct to the primary purpose.

Automatic vehicle monitoring (AVM) is one of the areas in which there is considerable interest. One of the largest systems is the pilot project with the Chicago Transit Authority, known as Monitor-CTA. This system consists of a number of low-powered transmitters, each having a unique call sign, located at about 2-mile intervals along bus routes. A bus passing one of these transmitters, called sign posts, receives and records its identification and also makes note of the time when it passed that location. Each bus is also equipped with two-way radios for communication with the central station. Under computer control, each vehicle is queried in turn and responds with its identification number, the location of the sign post most recently passed, and time at which it passed that location. Approximately 500 buses out of a fleet of 3,300 have been equipped for this pilot experiment. In addition to the location feature that enables the dispatcher to check schedule adherence, each bus is also equipped for two-way communication between the driver and dispatcher, and a silent alarm for informing the dispatcher of the bus location in case of emergency situations aboard the bus. This system is currently undergoing evaluation. The CTA-estimates that through improved scheduling, better service, and decrease of vehicles required for "turn around" that the system will pay for itself in approximately 3 years.

A second series of AVM experiments has been conducted in Philadelphia to investigate the technical feasibility of vehicle location on an areawide basis. (The CTA system is good only for vehicles on fixed routes.) Three technologies were tested: The first used a group of transmitters operating at approximately 10.5 GHz, each transmitter having a unique identification code. The vehicle was equipped to detect the closest transmitter and record its identification. On query from the central station, that information, together with the vehicle's identification, was transmitted. Such a system requires a large number of sign posts, the exact number depending upon the size of the area to be covered and the accuracy of the location required. The second system tested depends on a signal being transmitted to the vehicle and the vehicle transmitting this signal. The signal is then received at a number of locations and the difference in time of receipt of the signal is used to compute the vehicle location by trilateration. The third method uses existing navigation signals, in this case, Loran-C. The vehicle needs the necessary equipment to determine its location or transmits the raw Loran data, and the central computer does the required calculations. This, incidentally, is a cross-modal use of telecommunications, since Loran-C is basically a maritime system. The latter two systems encounter considerable difficulty in the built-up urban area due to multipath and other propagation problems. While the final reports are not in, preliminary indications are that accuracy of the order of 1,000 feet (95% CPE) can be expected from these systems. There is a good possibility that a fourth system, using dead reckoning (odometer and compass), together with a computer program to eliminate errors, may be tested in Philadelphia by its manufacturer.

A system for vehicular traffic control, known as the Urban Traffic Control System, is currently being installed in Washington, D.C. Approximately 120 intersections in the western portion of downtown Washington as well as several approach corridors have been instrumented. From one to five sensors have been buried in the pavement. These are connected to a central computer and the computer, in turn, connected to the traffic-signal controller at that intersection. This system has been designed with high flexibility so that a number of computer programs can be checked and strategies developed for real-time control of street traffic in a major urban area. An additional feature is the bus priority system. Approximately 35 intersections have a different type of sensor that can be actuated by a transmitter on board the bus. The bus driver has a switch to indicate whether he plans to stop or go through the particular intersection. If traffic permits, the bus may be given up to 10 seconds of additional green time, but the bus transmitter cannot change the traffic signal. The system is expected to be fully operational about November of this year.

As a result of the recent passage of the Ports and Waterways Safety Act of 1972, the Coast Guard has been given authority similar to the FAA for "terminal" areas. To implement this authority, the Coast Guard is working on several vessel traffic-control systems; these are designed to assure positive control of ship traffic in a harbor. The most sophisticated of these systems is in San Francisco harbor; here two radars keep track of all ships in the harbor; each target ship is identified on the control panels and the vessel movements are directed by means of VHF radio. For the deep-draft ports and their approaches, the Coast Guard has been looking into various navigational schemes to provide the desired navigation accuracy. The leading contender for the offshore areas known as the coastal confluence region is Loran-C.

The use of quiet short-haul air transportation systems in the urban areas raises a number of air-traffic-control problems. The FAA has several projects looking into present traffic control and landing schemes as well as improved methods for control of this type of aircraft.

DOT is working on a number of communications systems. The main ones of urban interest are several types of motorist information systems, both one- and two-way. Some are designed to provide information directly to the motorist. Others will summon aid to a motorist in distress, while the most sophisticated will provide two-way communications to all motorists.

Communicating to the motorist presents an ever-increasing problem. The profusion of signs at many intersections only serves to confuse rather than help. There is also the problem of advising the motorist of changed road or traffic conditions or the existence of emergencies. An incidental problem is the growing tendency of the motorist to shut himself off from audio contact with his surroundings by closing the car windows and having the radio or stereo on at high volume. The result is that, in many cases, he does not hear the approach of emergency vehicles. One series of experiments proposes the use of the existing receiver that is now found in about 95 percent of all vehicles. By means of short-range roadside transmitters, messages can be given by the driver through his radio. Several types of systems are under consideration: In one, a roadside sign will advise the motorist to tune to a particular frequency in order to obtain emergency information. To ease the tuning task, tests are being considered for both low and high ends of the broadcast band. The Los Angeles airport is currently planning such a test along the road approaching the airport and on the road that connects the terminal buildings; messages on traffic and parking situations will be provided to the motorist. A more sophisticated system under consideration would enable emergency messages to preempt the receiver so as to assure the message coming through. In such a system, an emergency vehicle would also be provided with a transmitter.

A motorist aid system recently evaluated by DOT is called IVAC (In-

Vehicular Assistance Communications). IVAC is a complete two-way communication system with a series of repeaters strung along the roadway. The repeaters serve two purposes: to relay the messages along the system to the dispatcher; and to pick up transmissions from any vehicle in its area. A motorist pushes a button on his set indicating the type of assistance he requires. The dispatcher, on receiving the message acknowledges it. If necessary, he can also "enable" the vehiclular equipment and establish two-way communication between himself and the motorist. In addition, the dispatcher can identify the repeater that picked up the message; thus, he has, in effect, what amounts to a vehicle-locating system. One advantage of the system is that only two frequencies would be required nationwide. Unfortunately, all vehicles would require special equipment.

The discussion of communications leads naturally into one of the other problem areas requiring consideration, that is, frequency spectrum utilization. The frequency spectrum is a limited and scarce source; DOT has been working in a number of areas to make greater use of existing frequency bands, to open new ones to meet the increasing demand for services, and to develop schemes that would require little or no frequency spectrum usage. These include the implementation of single-side band, communications splitting the VHF communication and navigation channels, development of equipment to use UHF in addition to VHF for all mobile services, and experimenting with the use of "near-field" communication systems. In the UHF area a number of companies are also working on so-called cellular systems, whereby repeated use of frequency channels will be made in a geographical area by keeping the power down and changing frequency on the vehicle as it moves from cell to cell.

Finally, I believe the substitution of telecommunications for transportation shows the greatest promise for meeting transportation requirements.

The commercial for the Yellow Pages, "Let your fingers do the walking" is familiar to most. This is telecommunications–transportation substitution in its simplest form, that is, using the telephone to obtain information rather than shopping in person. One study by the National Academy of Engineering claims that 18 percent of urban travel was for the purpose of exchange of information. Actually, the total physical movement of people and goods would not decrease, but the implementation of telecommunications–transportation substitution can keep the increase down to a reasonable rate. Considerable improvements can be made even in simple areas. For example, many times a person wishing to determine bus routes or scheduling in order to utilize public transportation gets either a busy signal or finds the information unavailable when he attempts to contact the bus company. The AC Transit Company in Oakland, California, credits greater usage of its buses to several telephone "information hotlines" installed in the downtown area.

A number of experiments and operating installations are in existence to test the substitutability of telecommunications for transportation. Both telephone conferencing and video conferencing could be equivalent to personal travel and remote terminals for access to data banks could be available to obtain information. Several commercial companies have already or are planning to install video-conferencing circuits. The British Post Office has a system called Confravision serving five locations in the United Kingdom. Anyone can rent the studios and set up a video conference between any two locations. Up to five people can participate at either end, and there is provision for viewing documents between the two locations. These examples are intercity, but each intercity trip also requires a certain amount of intraurban transportation.

Considerable experimentation on the basic problems involved in communications between people is now in progress. What types of meetings are amenable to replacement by telecommunications, and what forms of telecommunications are needed? The British government has been greatly concerned with decentralizing some of its activities, and such separation of offices naturally leads to increased travel for face-to-face meetings. In many cases, their studies have found that most remote conferencing between people who have worked together can be accomplished by audio means, and the additional cost of providing video will, in many cases, not be justified. However, as the length of the communication line increases between electronic audio and video conferencing and for physical travel, the comparative costs decrease. At present, local travel can be accomplished at lesser cost than elaborate video interconnection. However, with concepts such as the "wired city," replacement of even local travel by electronic means becomes feasible. The use of interactive terminals opens the way for providing medical, educational, and similar services remotely. The future in this area would appear to be limited only by imagination and, of course, by costs. Radio broadcasts, television, and the rapid burgeoning field of cable television have also had a profound effect on local travel to theaters and other entertainment media. In fact, they have caused a complete revolution in the entertainment industry.

Research, development, and demonstrations are only the first steps in the implementation of ideas. There are a number of steps that have to be taken before use is widespread. For a number of the DOT projects previously mentioned, there are two categories of end user: In the first category DOT itself is the end user. This would involve such projects as air- and vessel-traffic-control systems where it has the responsibility for system operation. Here it becomes a matter of funding in order to put such systems into operation. In this category a number of the other types of systems, such as improvements in urban transit would fall. In the second category the local transit company would be the end user, and for implementation of these systems, funds are available through capital grants programs, usually on a share basis. In either case, results of all DOT-funded studies are made available to the public.

Although a major factor, costs are not the only impediments to implementation. There are often institutional or regulatory constraints. In many cases, the public acceptability of a new system is part of the study. In the telecommunications area, regulatory aspects also arise. For example, there are at present no radio frequencies allocated for automatic vehicle monitoring, although a Notice of Inquiry (FCC Docket 18302) has been filed by DOT. Here the Department works through the FCC in attempting to obtain the necessary frequency allocations for these services. Thus, our work does not stop with just the research and development.

Telecommunications plays an important role in transportation in general and in urban transportation in particular. It can be expected to play an ever-increasing role in improving safety and efficiency and, in my opinion, replacing transportation. Some of the social implications still remain to be determined. As the old-timer said, "Yep, people get where they're going a darn sight faster these days, but they're just as stupid as before, when they arrive." Perhaps with the aid of telecommunications we can also make them smarter when they arrive.

PRICE: It sounds as if the Port of New York and New Jersey Authority is fairly healthy, financially; they took over the bankrupt Hudson and Manhattan Railroad and spent $250 million in 10 years to refurbish it. I wonder if any of the money for that comes from tolls?

GILMAN: That is the only way we could undertake it. The money comes from charges for all our facilities—airports, bridges, tunnels, and seaports, though not too much from the latter, and from our other terminals. Under this concept, we have a general fund to which all revenues go, so the deficit in effect is borne by the user-charges from the use of all of our facilities.

PRICE: That sounds as if it is really a transfer from the auto, that the auto user pays for it.

GILMAN: It certainly is part of it.

PRICE: The Golden Gate Bridge is apparently in a similiar condition. It is a good money maker, but transit in the Bay Area doesn't have enough money. Perhaps this is a concept that can be fostered.

GILMAN: The Metropolitan Transportation Authority (MTA), as you know, includes the Tri-Borough Bridge and Tunnel Authority, and, again, revenues from those bridges and tunnels that are located wholly within the city of New York contribute toward the operation of MTA. I think this is a concept that is developing.

BESSON: The one comment that I have on Mr. Gilman's presentation is that as I see the terminal problems and the air congestion problems in the Washington-to-Boston corridor, there seems to be a considerable opportunity for AMTRAK to operate in this area.

EVERITT: I have been impressed by Mr. Gilman's paper and also by other interactions that I have had with the Port Authority operations. It is one of the best examples in the country of really good planning by engineers in terms of an interdisciplinary approach to very many problems.

One of the most interesting things to me is the fact that apparently through more freedom from control by political groups and so forth, they have been able to develop a viable operation that is substantially financially self-supporting.

They are doing all the things that we are told can't be done because they cost too much. In our Telecommunications Committee, for instance, we conducted a meeting with city mayors, and they said: "Well, you have made a lot of fine suggestions, but we have absolutely no money, we can't do anything unless we get all the money from the federal government.

The Port Authority has been able to accomplish many projects and apparently has always had money in the bank. Therefore, it is able to start undertaking new projects and integrate its entire operation, complete with consideration for social consequences. I am particularly impressed by the financial operation, and I would like to hear further comment on this from Mr. Gilman.

In terms of telecommunications, Dr. Goldsmith mentioned our report (*Communications Technology for Urban Improvement*) in which we concluded that to a large extent improvements in transportation must be obtained by moving from the individual car to urban centralized transportation.

Further, I think that the greatest problem we have, in terms of the substitution of telecommunication for transportation, is in attracting people to use it. It is also difficult to get people to change from automobiles to other types of transportation. These changes are going to involve incentives. In this connection, I believe that we need a study on how to persuade people to do things rather than forcing them to comply.

In the substitution of telecommunications for transportation, some of the newer methods, particularly the use of wide-band systems appear to offer the greatest advantages as they provide more information. I might add that feedback is necessary. One of the things we have learned from feedback systems is that a delay in the feedback can have a major effect upon whether you break into oscillation or get stability out of feedback.

The picturephone and other similar types of equipment are going to be involved in the future. They provide a great deal more information than you realize, because the way you look carries perhaps a lot more information than what you say. This could develop into one application of the substitution of telecommunication for transportation.

PRICE: I want to mention that in our authorizing legislation for R&D in UMTA, it basically says that we have two charters. One is to improve mass transportation services, and the other is to reduce the need for transportation. Virtually our entire program to date—last year $63 million and this year $95 million—is devoted to improving mass transportation services. This implies that we take things the way they are now and try to improve them.

We have done virtually nothing so far, except to start a study looking at the other aspect, that of reducing the need. That is a completely open area. We received proposals recently that suggested a return to the cottage-industries concept as one way of reducing the need for travel. We have one contractor on the West Coast who does just that. He doesn't make his people travel to work, and he is one of our most effective analysts. He expects each of his professional people to produce one page of the final report every day, and he doesn't care whether they get to the office or not as long as the results appear.

HERWALD: I happened to be in on the picturephone experiment. The most important thing that had not occurred to me came about because I could see into the office that I was calling and know whether somebody was there or not. Just telephoning doesn't reveal that necessarily.

MURRAY: Why hasn't AMTRAK taken some steps to see that government employees ride on that system instead of using the airlines, where air travel may not be necessary?

FINGER: It is my understanding that the Joint Travel Regulations inhibit government employees from traveling by rail. I don't know the status of the negotiations between AMTRAK and the government concerning the holders of government–joint travel regulation travel requests aimed at easing those restrictions.

QUESTION: Excuse my being contrary, but just within the last week I went by rail from Los Angeles to El Paso. It is time-consuming, but on a weekend it was fine. I think that AMTRAK, with the government as a partner, could encourage some of its civilian and military personnel to use the system to the overall benefit of the government.

FINGER: I don't believe the government services can be in the position of favoring one mode of transportation over another. They certainly should not inhibit the use of satisfactory transportation, but because of a quirk in the way the Joint Travel Regulations were written, this inhibition did in fact exist. I do not know whether it has been removed yet or not.

QUESTION: I recall the comment, I think made by Dean Everitt, concerning feedback. If the feedback is late in coming under consideration, there is not much response to it. There was an earlier comment to the effect that if drivers or automobile travelers knew the actual costs of owning an automobile in urban areas, their responses might be quite different.

I wonder if any studies are being made in the use of telecommunications to communicate to people just what the actual costs are and thus to make costs more painful where they exist. For instance, when I get on a transit system, I must take 45 cents out of my pocket, and I am very much aware of that. When I pay my gasoline bill once a month, I tend to forget about it for the rest of the time.

Are telecommunications being used for anything like this?

EVERITT: In our studies on telecommunications, we have not dealt in any detail on instructing people. That is somewhat similar to a study of what it costs to borrow money. Laws were eventually passed in that area, and, as a result, people discovered that costs were much higher than they expected.

My earlier comment was that when you compare costs between the automobile and other types of communication, you must grant that most of the population is going to have an automobile anyway. They are only interested in incremental costs: How much to drive a mile in an automobile compared to not driving it. They are not greatly concerned about the overall cost.

I don't believe it is the job of a telecommunications committee to study whether people ought to know more about an infinite number of things. They can learn about such things through telecommunications or through newspapers and magazines as they choose.

MERTZ: In regard to that specific question, though, the Federal Highway Administration did recently study and release through all the news media information about the total cost of owning and operating an automobile.

FINGER: One part relates to owning and the other to operating. Most people are going to own an auto anyway. I will mention two points. It is not only an economic problem. It will be absolutely necessary, as we go further and further into the future and find that our energy-producing resources and resources in terms of land and of air space are increasingly saturated, to better inform the public.

EVERITT: My feeling is that the U.S. public responds only to crises. I see a crisis approaching in terms of use of other than mass transportation in the near future, and that is going to turn people, as the crisis develops, back to mass transportation.

GIFFORD: I might say, parochially, in the New York–New Jersey region we have been a supporter for the past decade of the whole Northeast Corridor project and the AMTRAK development. For the reasons that have been suggested, the air lanes can just accommodate so much traffic. The type of ground transportation service that was described this morning is highly desirable to handle whatever portion of the total volume will use rail as opposed to air.

HERWALD: I might just comment that the view held by the NAE Committee on Transportation was that, basically, we were going to need a balanced transportation system. There is a tough question as to where the right balance points are, and that is what we are really talking about here.

All the discussion is centered on the one interface of the automobile in the urban area, not what it does outside of that difficult point. Other than in urban areas we are hard pressed to devise something that it as convenient for the people.

The other point noted was that what it costs to own an automobile is only partly relevant. The public probably knows their personal costs fairly well but they just don't care and are willing to pay. Of course, there is a threshold of pain beyond which the public may flip in the other direction. As a fair number of people begin to think the cost is too high, then you begin to gather constituency faster than the costs go up. That tends to push the people in the other direction. The total costs, including environmental, may become better known and that will add to the trend. If you think it is desirable, the difficult problem is to anticipate where the interfaces are or what the balance ought to be 10 or 20 years from now. We perhaps would agree with most that has been said about what needs to be done, but we don't yet know the proper timing. Petroleum costs are going to go up, but just when and how much relative to other fuels, is the tough issue.

EVERITT: I would like to restate my question to Mr. Gilman. I would like to know how the Port Authority is able to do so many things with its own money that everybody else says it can't afford to do?

GILMAN: We have to measure the transportation demand—the public need—against the ability to go down to Wall Street and borrow the money, like some private company. From that standpoint, based entirely on revenue bonds without tax funds, we think we have over the years, through generally prudent management, been able to build up a credit rating that permits us to finance projects that could not be financed without that good rating.

There is always the matter of balance that has been suggested here. It was on that basis that we undertook the takeover of the Hudson–Manhattan Railroad and the development of PATH within the framework of our total financial capability. This approach does not permit you to go "whole-hog," of course, into the entire transit or commuter revenue system.

HERWALD: Would you agree that you have the relatively unique situation of having under your control a reasonably balanced transportation system? In effect, what you lose on one operation, you make up on the others?

GILMAN: I think this is true. As I said right at the outset, we are more than what is generally known as a "Port Authority," which, as Harry Brockel would say, is his port of Milwaukee. We have a broad range of transportation projects that have given balance, both in the handling of people and in the production of funds.

EVERITT: It seems to me that when Mr. Gilman says there is good management, it includes planning, and they seem to be able to do a longer-range planning than most areas are able to do that are politically controlled. Would you agree?

GILMAN: No, I could not agree with that view. I should mention that the Port Authority is a completely nonpolitical, permanent, career-type program, which does not vary with changes in administration, as many other functions of government properly should.

The Port Authority is a public business of running transportation projects, and there is not a Republican or a Democratic way of running a tunnel or bridge or airport or a marine tunnel. The important thing is that we do have the continuity, which has been probably as productive as anything in this field.

COMMENT: I would like to comment on the overall problem of optimizing the transportation and reducing the costs. One of the things that is very important and has not really been considered very thoroughly is the fact that the automobile is used by people because it provides better transportation to the average person for the average trip than any other means of transportation. If one is going to get people to use an alternative, there ought to be an alternative that offers as good transportation, or there will be a net loss to the community or the economy by substituting something poorer for the automobile.

The essential characteristic of the automobile is that it can go from any point to any other point, and most of the travel is in urban areas. But travel in urban areas is not from suburbs to downtown anymore. It used to be, but it is now distributed throughout the whole metropolitan area, and the public transportation that has been devised and has been available to people has been built to serve the central city, and it does not serve the present transportation needs.

Only about 7 to 10 percent of total trips are going to downtown now, and the rest are distributed throughout the area. If you are going to do anything about solving this problem, you have to provide widespread service with good access and high-frequency service anywhere in the metropolitan area. One cannot provide that kind of service and have paid drivers for the vehicles.

I think there really is no solution that does not involve the use of automatic vehicles that are operating on a network that pretty well covers the metropolitan area.

One of the major programs in the Department of Transportation is to provide these systems of circulation and distribution; the emphasis in that area is still very small, and it is apparent that unless major improvements in costs of these systems can be made, they will turn out to be so expensive in initial capital investment that they cannot be installed. Therefore, it seems that if there is going to be any real solution to this problem, it has to involve a much larger research and development effort in automatic circulation and distribution systems.

COSGRAVE: I was struck by the fact that every time we turn around it seems there is a host of reasons something can't be done. We heard this today, and we have heard of the problems from the mayors.

Several years ago, before the advent of the Department of Transportation, Bob Baker, in the Bureau of Public Roads, had the Commerce Department appoint a committee to study the general transportation picture, and at that time one of the ideas was to provide a truly all-weather transportation capability—primarily at that time for the automobile.

This was discussed and there were hundreds of people who said: "It will be altogether too costly; it isn't practical." In the Midwest, for example, Columbus, Ohio, with a population of around 750,000 to a million people, each winter salt is spread on the streets by the city and causes about $100 per vehicle per year loss. If one were to multiply this by half a million automobiles, you have something in the neighborhood of $50 million. If that expense could be saved, the $50 million could be available for new types of transportation; all-weather transportation being only one to consider.

I think we should approach this from a far more optimistic point of view, perhaps in terms of money, in terms of alternatives. I agree with the idea of research, but I just was wondering if the speakers would have any comments along optimistic lines, imaginative lines, for revenue, for overcoming old problems?

PRICE: I guess this and the last question, plus the introductory speech by Mr. Beggs and our chairman, made me wish that we had a session here to talk about the UMTA program, because we are optimistic. We have a very ambitious, large-scale program, which is devoted both to the near term and the longer term. This is not the place to go into the entire program, and I will save the details for another time.

HERWALD: First of all, the statistics on where the problem is don't come out of gross statistics. The important thing is to alleviate the peak traffic problem. That still occurs in the center or near-center of most cities, and the real problem there is not alleviated by the utility of the automobile for doing all the missions that were pretty well outlined here. Even the greatest automobile advocates don't say that it handles well the last 2 miles into this coagulated work center. It is in this congested area that UMTA is particularly concentrating and trying to devise efficient transfer of some kind where it provides as convenient or better service than that currently available.

Using the gross statistics in talking about the automobile puts it in a more pessimistic light. This bothers most people who are trying to solve transportation problems. I believe, though, that the people who work with UMTA are a lot more hopeful that we can make better use of fuel, land, and people's time. UMTA's programs are aimed at trying to alleviate those problems we have discussed today.

PRICE: That is true, and of course we recognize the difficulty of it and especially the institutional difficulties that were mentioned in the earlier speeches.

The European experience, by the way, is something we are studying, especially the case of Hamberg, Germany, where they have an integrated transit system, and of London, England. In London a very high percentage, around 70 to 90 percent of the people, commute and use transit. So there is hope.

LUNCHEON ADDRESS

Secor D. Browne   **NEW TECHNOLOGICAL POSSIBILITIES IN TRANSPORTATION**

There are all kinds of new technological possibilities in transportation, but so far there is no way to use most of them. The United States essentially relies on two modes of transportation—the car and the airplane. This is not to say that other possibilities are not fascinating, exciting, or forthcoming; tracked air-cushion vehicles, linear induction and other electrical propulsion systems, steam or gas turbine-propelled vehicles, and other less conventional systems all have much promise. However, at our current pace, implementation of these transport system innovations is a long way off.

Vertical takeoff and landing systems and short takeoff and landing systems, the air bus, the short-haul transport we need for interurban service systems, the SST, and clean quiet engines have all been on the horizon for a long time and will remain there, unless they are developed outside the United States. I regret and I emphasize that this hardware is not coming from us.

The problems of allocation of funding sources and responsibility have been prominent in the surface transportation systems that have been discussed. The Department of Transportation (DOT) has done, and is doing, a magnificent job "making bricks with very little straw." The DOT transportation studies and the demonstration projects are being funded at minimum levels, and there is very little prospect of funding levels that would allow any massive introduction of new systems and new facilities in the future.

Aside from the present investment in highways (subsidized by the Highway Trust Fund), future investments in other forms of high-speed or personal rapid transit surface transportation will require large investments in both fixed guideways and equipment. High-speed ground transportation systems have cost the French government approximately $900 million, the British and Japanese governments approximately $400 million each, and the Dutch government $75 million. The high cost of these systems dictates that here the United States Congress must subsidize their expense. But to my knowledge no one in Congress is prepared to appropriate these kinds of funds for these types of projects.

Our airlines are also facing such serious financial problems for the future that I wonder if they can survive. These problems really fall in two areas, costs and capital. Labor costs are a severe problem; at present 46 cents of each expense dollar spent by the air carriers is for wages. Few people realize that the rate of wage increase in the airline industry has been 50 percent higher than of the construction industry. In addition, most of the air carriers will face major labor negotiations in the coming year, and if the 29.5 percent wage increase settlement of the Northwest Airlines strike this year is any indication of things to come, then the air carriers will have even more serious financial problems. Effective labor legislation supplementing the present wage and price control legislation is needed. Increased landing fees, municipal head taxes, and other charges relating to airlines, ground facilities, and airline operations are also contributing to the air carriers' financial problems.

Noise pollution controls are highly desirable and also costly. If we want these controls we will have to pay for them either with increased fares or freight charges or with reduced airline revenues and services.

Finally, there are the effects of air piracy. The human, as well as the economic, costs can mean disaster for the air carrier, the passengers, and the flight crews. We must pay whatever price necessary to ensure the safety of our airports and airways, and the responsibility for the safety is rightly in the hands of the federal government. However, there still remains some burden that must be borne by the air carriers, and that will add to overall air transportation costs.

The availability of capital is another area of concern. Without subsidization, continued high operating costs will lead to the decline of air carrier profits, followed by a loss of confidence in the airlines as an investment medium, resulting in eventual bankruptcy and governmentalization.

Under present statutes, the Civil Aeronautics Board must maintain (i.e., subsidize) air carrier service where it is in the public interest, including a margin of profit for those providing the service. At this moment, however, we subsidize only local air services that are simply not profitable. Unless we find the answers to the questions of increased operating costs, availability of capital, and allocation of transportation system responsibility, our efficient air transportation system may collapse as our fixed guideway system has done, forcing a governmental allocation of transportation resources, which I think no one wants.

DISCUSSION

RUMMEL: In order to avoid the type of circumstances you currently project, i.e., the conflict between cost and capital, and considering the economic environment in which we operate, what would be a reasonable return to expect on investment?

BROWNE: The Board, in its domestic passenger fare investigation has determined a return on investment of 12 percent as being justified for an air carrier. This is substantially below that prevailing in many other industries. However, this was found to be in the public interest whether you looked at it as transportation cost, attraction of capital, fair return to the investor, and so on. In 1970, air carriers as a group lost about $200 million. In the 1972 calendar year, after taxes, a conservative estimate is that they will make $200 million. You have a swing of about $400 million even with taxes. That is very encouraging, but it is nothing like a 12 percent return on investment. I suspect it is currently within the area of between 4 and 5 percent; therefore, we have a long way to go.

GILMAN: Would you comment on the prospects of VTOL commercial service?

BROWNE: I read Professor Miller's abstract, but unfortunately was not able to hear his remarks. I gather we again remain encouraged and recognize those practical problems of getting a system demonstrated, as well as the problems of continued development. However, we have problems of distribution once the passenters arrive at the pad downtown by helicopter. The helicopter, like the airplane, is only part of the system. We just don't have the whole system, nor is anyone likely to give us the money to prove it in the immediate future.

QUESTION: With reference to the increase of wages in the airplane business, are there wage and price control measures to cope with this aspect?

BROWNE: I hope there are, particularly in light of the 29 percent increase that Northwest has negotiated. There are people that are supposed to cope with it. The problem of controls is also related to what to do if the people go on strike anyway. There is compulsory arbitration—which is great—but if the people walk out and the leaders are thrown in jail, we are still left without docks, airlines, or trains. The British, French, and others have taught that to us many times.

QUESTION: If in the airlines industry 46 cents of the expense dollar is for labor, in a rapid transit system, would it run as much as 100 cents on the dollar?

BROWNE: Yes, that is true. The equipment is obtained somewhat differently, and most of the operating expense is labor.

QUESTION: What is the situation with respect to mergers?

BROWNE: Mergers are a very interesting phenomenon and are usually associated with a poor economy, whether the mergers involve drug stores or airlines. The

Board does have a couple of mergers pending that are of long standing. To effect a merger decision that will stand up in the courts we must hear all parties concerned, and this takes about 9 months. In any case there has not been a new merger floated by the Board in many months. The loss of interest in mergers came about with the upturn in airline fortunes. Mergers—unless they are forced by the government—place one in the position of allocation of joint resources, and after looking at the British experience in this area, it does not appear to be a very good solution.

QUESTION: Would you discuss the relationship of railroads to the total transportation system, especially in the Northeast where the Metroliner seems to have taken some traffic from the airlines?

BROWNE: The increase of passengers on the Metroliner, compared to the general traffic growth of airlines, may not be too impressive. I have a very narrow view of fixed guideway systems, which is, simply, that for urban and suburban use they are satisfactory systems. For longer transportation needs, the way to do it is with the total air system. By that I mean airport access, traffic control, a suitable vehicle, and all the essential parts. I frankly don't see a high-speed guideway system in the Northeast Corridor for the future. I think that if the arithmetic is done correctly, it will indicate that Congress will never put that amount of money into a subsidy for that kind of construction costs. I think we are going to wind up with the private car and the airplane, and that is where I came in.

PRICE: I wouldn't want to disagree with Mr. Browne, since he was formerly the Assistant Secretary for Research and Technology, prior to Bob Cannon, but I think we in the Department of Transportation believe that in the heavily traveled corridors, the studies have shown that various types of guided trackway transportation are going to be the answer. That will be true because you will run out of the ability to control large numbers of comparatively small-capacity aircraft. In going from city center to city center, I find even today that I can get from my office downtown to downtown Philadelphia faster by the Metroliner than I can by going to the Washington airport, landing in South Philadelphia, and having to go to downtown Philadelphia.

In getting to New York, times are just about equal at the moment, if you don't happen to run into a traffic jam on the way from the airport. And just improving the roadbed for the conventional Metroliner would cut down on the train time considerably. Other advanced systems that we are working on—the tracked air-cushion vehicle and, somewhat still further in the future, experiments with magnetic levitation—may provide even faster ground travel in the corridor.

Panelists:
Harold B. Finger
Bernard Gifford
and
William L. Mertz

SESSION II: URBAN DEVELOPMENT, DESIGN, AND RENEWAL AND THE RELATION TO URBAN TRANSPORTATION

Morton Hoppenfeld   **TRANSPORTATION AS
A PART OF THE
COMMUNITY-BUILDING
PROCESS**

The principles that guide The Rouse Company and me have led us into
certain kinds of urban development activities that I believe are relevant
to the interests of any group concerned with transportation, and that I
certainly think are relevant to the nation's interests as related to the
quality of American cities. The real problem that we have to address is
why those interests are not being served. What are the hurdles?

The Rouse Company is engaged in the urban-development process.
Its reason for being is to create useful places where none existed before—
to build. Its set of three goals are interesting and important because they
condition our work, the way we go about it, and the results we achieve:

1. Improvement of the quality of life in the United States by helping
to build a better environment

2. Improvement and creation of opportunities for the personal growth
and development of the people working within the company

3. Creation in that process of a profit sufficient for the company to
grow and attract investment capital

It seems to me that that is what any civilization is about—or should
be about (give or take the concern about profit and investment capital).

The three goals are usually in tension, the pure pursuit of one tending
to deny the others. The most difficult task is to continue creatively to
keep them in balance.

I am sure that you are all familiar with the current phenomenon of
urban growth and the fact that all over the world people have left the
farm and small town to go to the city. Why do people move to cities?

113

They find their rural environment lacking in opportunities for earning a living, for learning and for maintaining a decent home and enjoying good health. In general, they seek opportunities to enhance their life.

They come to the cities where the opportunities are greater and where there is a greater choice. That is the history of the growth of cities and the dynamic behind their getting bigger: the reason New York City continues to get larger instead of smaller even though it seems to get more and more oppressive; and the reason Philadelphia, Baltimore, and Washington continue to grow. Of course, by city, I no longer mean the political jurisdiction that is called Philadelphia or New York City. I now mean the millions of people who live in a metropolitan area—the old city (the core) and the new city (the suburbs).

Cities are meant to serve fundamentally the quest of individuals and families to improve their personal lives. That is what urban development is for, and that is what this country is supposed to be about. The fact that we are an urban country now, and becoming even more so, means that our city-building processes must improve; otherwise the individual quest of every citizen is going to be frustrated. Whether our cities will prove sufficient to the needs of our people is the great test. If not, if they fail, then that will be where our civilization fails.

The subject of this meeting, your common interest—transportation— is just a part of that whole urban-development process. Transportation, properly viewed, is simply a means of bringing individuals in touch with the resources that they need for growth.

To return to the principles that guide our company, if our purpose is to build well, then we must plan. In order to create value on a continuing basis, we must evaluate and check to see whether what we have built is working, thereby improving the product (the community) and ultimately whether the community is growing as a capable development entity.

This process of planning, development, and evaluation is the life-giving process of urbanization. In most situations, those three activities are totally separated in principle and in fact. Most cities do not have real community-development capability, though they do, as a rule, have some limited planning capability that does not directly influence development decisions. That is in the hands of many small individual entrepreneurs, or of a municipality acting like an individual entrepreneur. In those cases, the municipality does a piece—it builds a building, a school; at its boldest, it builds a subway or a highway. The largest integrated thing that cities have undertaken in recent times has been the attempt at urban renewal (a couple of blocks at a time).

Traditionally, therefore, the ability to plan for the comprehensive activities of development is limited, and there is no feedback to speak of. The question of how the environment influences the quality of individual or family life remains largely unanswered.

I would assert that the connection between planning, development, and evaluation must result in a single entity, a community development body or corporation. This phenomenon needs to be reproduced in this country, in fact, in the world, a thousand times over. Only a few such organizations exist today, here and elsewhere in the world; unfortunately, they do not always concentrate on the purpose of development, the enhancement of human condition.

The obstacles to better communities, cities, and regions exist largely because American cities have lacked a way to deal with their problems. Public and private interests are locked into their separate jurisdictions, powerless to attack the problems that respect no such boundary. We do not have a community-development process enabling us to work together across all boundaries—public and private, town and city, black and white, rich and poor.

Only a new way of thinking and working can be useful in the monumental tasks of community renewal and development in the American city and its surrounding towns. The following are eight basic operating principles to illustrate that way of thinking. These have emerged out of the experiences of The Rouse Company in building the new city of Columbia and establishing the Hartford Process*:

1. *Bring the essential parties to the table.* The job of improving the quality of life cannot be accomplished by any one, or even several, of the leadership elements of the region. Local government cannot reach beyond jurisdictional lines and thus cannot take direct action on problems originating beyond its borders. Similarly, the private sector cannot deal with issues in the public realm—education, police, urban renewal, etc. All elements having power in a community or region, either positive or negative power, have to be engaged in the process of improving their environment.

2. *Set forth a believable image of a community, or a region, that works.* To motivate people to support the overall task, it is necessary to project a believable image of a place as people would like it to be;

---

*The Hartford Process refers to the planning and organizational methods used in approaching the redevelopment of the greater Hartford, Connecticut, area. See the report, "The Greater Hartford Process," The American City Corporation, American City Building, Columbia, Maryland.

this is a way of releasing new energies to work toward that objective. The image is built from a set of common goals shared by all affected persons, rich and poor, black and white, resident of city and suburb. Crystallizing these goals is a first step in developing the broad base of political support necessary to carry out the needed changes.

3. *Unite planning and development with a commitment to carry out the plans.* There must be a unified process of planning and action so that the people can in fact expect to see plans carried out. Historically, in this country, many of the best minds have tackled some of the most serious urban problems; the result has been one more study on the shelf.

The connection between planning and development capabilities is crucial. Economic and social feasibility must be continually reassessed, and plans must be altered if not feasible. A plan that does not, in fact, guide and generate development is not a good plan. The planning and development processes must continually interact; neither planning nor development is "finished" until the entire project is complete. Until then, planning and development considerations each take their turn affecting decisions in the other's jurisdiction.

4. *Recognize the inseparability of social, economic, and physical planning and development.* With every moon shot, we recognize the situation of "all systems go"—where inadequate fuel, the oxygen or navigation system, or communication system could jeopardize the whole endeavor. In life on earth, we don't act as if we understand how one system impinges on another; we act as if infant mortality has everything to de with prenatal care and hospitals and nothing to do with bringing the baby home to an apartment where there is no heat, where the mother's diet is poor, where health care is inadequate, and where the man of the family is chronically the last to be hired and first to be fired. It is necessary to deal with social, economic, and physical systems in all areas simultaneously, recognizing their mutual support.

5. *Use physical development as the opportunity for positive social change.* Physical development has always had an impact on the quality of life, sometimes positive, sometimes negative. But the occasion of major physical development should be deliberately used as the opportunity to analyze social and economic systems, to introduce new programs, or even restructure entire social systems.

This simply means the physical world is already strongly disciplined by the needs of financing and scheduling—the need to demonstrate feasibility in order to gain financing, the need to keep precise schedules because of interest paid on borrowed money, etc. Social planning, on the other hand, has generally shown a less than precise regard for costs and timetables. With physical and social development linked, questions about the social realm will be raised at the same time as are questions about physical change, and they must be answered in the same disciplined fashion.

This principle operates in both renewal and new development. It is possible to rethink the whole idea of what a school should be, if in fact a new school is to be built. If a certain number of new housing units are to be built, it becomes essential to decide, in social terms, where we want those units to be in relation to other housing, what kind we want them to be, and what else the community should make possible in the lives of its residents.

6. *Work on a large enough scale.* Twenty-five years of housing and redevelopment projects have demonstrated that isolated projects consume the scarce resources of time, money, and civic energy without significantly improving the quality of life in the region. In order to have impact, and in order to command the human and financial resources needed, programs must operate on a regionwide basis, must deal with large parts of the central city, and must plan for whole new communities outside the city.

Some of our most urgent concerns have regionwide components—a good system of health care, for instance, needs nearby facilities serving a small number of people on a daily basis and also needs the highly specialized hospitals and programs that can only exist for the large population of the whole region. The labor market is not contained within town boundaries, a transportation system must extend throughout the region, and so on. None of these problems can be solved on a strictly local basis.

The question of scale also dictates the need to build whole new communities and renew whole sections of the central city. Dealing with a large enough part of the central city insures that small projects won't be overrun by adjacent deterioration.

7. *Create and capture values.* Land values will increase as the community is assembled, planned, zoned, and developed. These increases in land values are then "captured" by the community developer and by the town governments and recycled to the social and economic development process. Similarly, investments to improve social and economic systems will enhance people's capability to be self-sufficient, taxpaying, and independent. This, in turn, will make the geographic area more attractive to private investment and further enhance the value of the land.

8. *Establish a continuing process.* Community engagement in planning must be established on a continuing basis. The object is not to accomplish a specific project, but to set in motion a new way of thinking

and working by which the community may constantly renew itself—may engage in a continuing self-examination. It is a way for a community to face up to decisions rather than let decisions go by default.

This assumes the essential working premise that the planning process must be open. No longer can planning be done in a back room and a finished product brought forth to the people who will have to live with it; any complex proposal for the future must have the active involvement of the people who will carry it out and the people who will be affected by it.

What is the importance of all this to transportation? Among other things, we are probably the most mobile people on earth—we love to and are able to go from place to place. The problem that is emerging concerns the purpose of the trip. Too many of us are moving away from one place in search of a better one, and the search seems to become less and less rewarding. We must reassess our sense of purpose and recognize that we are building communities to serve the needs and aspirations of people. Moving within and between communities and whole regions is part of serving the needs and aspirations of people. If the movement systems we build work to make possible and strengthen good communities and good regions, if they serve human purpose, to that extent they should be developed. Outside that context, they become dubious.

Sound community development has lagged greatly in this nation behind highway building. I would assert that a truly sound transportation system can be conceived and built only in the context of communities and regions that work for people.

In closing, let me refer to principle number 5: physical development as a lever or engine to move social system development. This country is in a constant love affair with building—it really loves to build things, including, until recently, roads and travel systems. The energy behind transportation-system building can affect sound community and regional development, and vice versa, if we think in synergistic terms.

In building a transportation system, enormous new values are created in areas given new access. Since this value is created by public investment, the increased value should be returned to the public and utilized to defray the cost of the system. A program of land acquisition should be undertaken for appropriate community development at the station stops and interchanges; acquisition of this land would be simultaneous with route acquisition. This land would be sold to qualified community developers, with development programs agreed to in advance by the developer and the town involved. Such a program would not only facilitate sound community and regional development patterns but would also help insure ridership for the success of the movement systems.

Our mutual task, then, is to put it all together, to create community development entities—public, private, and combinations of the two—that would be able to put to work a new way of thinking about cities and that would utilize the principles I describe to build the next America.

DISCUSSION

HERWALD: Our NAE Committee on Transportation, somewhat painfully, because in our discussions with a number of the social scientists we became convinced that the social stresses were severe in urban areas, took the position that transportation really is a key ingredient in the building of a better urban quality of life. Mr. Hoppenfeld presented the situation within a different framework than that of many social scientists and gave us a different perspective on the whole question and the solutions to problems we have described as institutional and social barriers. We, as a committee, felt that a balanced approach is important and that some kind of integrated effort is required in order to achieve desired objectives.

FINGER: First, it is important that I express my views on the activities of The Rouse Company, the American City Corporation, and the Urban Life Center, which are all associated in the activities that Mr. Hoppenfeld is involved with. In my view, there is no effort now under way that is as comprehensive as that Mr. Hoppenfeld described for the Greater Hartford Process.

To some extent, that effort contradicts some of the initial design and motivation of Columbia as a new town itself or at least approaches the concept of urbanization from a very different and much broader point of view. It also differs, I believe, from the Staten Island Project.

The important point is that the people with whom Mr. Hoppenfeld is associated were asked to come into the city of Hartford and try to help solve, in North Hartford, all of those problems that we normally think of as related to the concentration of poor and minorities in central cities.

North Hartford is a compact area, high density, primarily minority populated, primarily black, very low income, deteriorating, and declining, with very little job base.

Upon examining Hartford, their group quickly came to the conclusions that you can't treat the problems of North Hartford in North Hartford alone, nor really in Hartford alone. One must consider the problems on a broad regional basis.

The Hartford Process right now is a major large-scale experiment that is under way; it is strongly supported by the Greater Hartford community—government, industry, and the community groups themselves—and, therefore, has to be given every support in order to determine what can be created through that approach.

The point is, we are not certain we can put it all together and make it work. Yet, we think the effort should be made because of the problems of the decaying core. The question is: Can we restore that core and revitalize it or should we accept the fact that some parts of this broad region may in fact decay and decline? Should we look at it overall to try to assure that everyone has an opportunity to live decently in a good environment with job opportunity and educational opportunities anywhere he chooses to settle in this broad region?

Looking at new cities alone, for example, Columbia, and relating that to the transportation issue, I have to ask: How does a new city become an old city? As it begins to develop, will it incur the same kinds of problems that we now face in old cities?

For example, in Columbia, how has transportation been incorporated in that design to provide for problem-free and easy access to all of the opportunities that should be available to all of the people? How do you assure that what is new today, and is sharp and interesting and motivates the people who reside there, will remain that way and not end up with decaying cores?

HOPPENFELD: In answer to the specific question about the role that transportation played in the design and subsequent development of Columbia, I can say that transportation was a fundamental ingredient.

There was a preceding step, however. We tried to analyze the basic institutional ingredients of a supported community and then to develop the facility requirements and to determine the relationship between those facilities and the institutions. We tried to diagram a community that would work better than others have, and I think we did that.

We planned centers or clusters of activity to provide for the fundamental facility and institutional requirements of community life. What resulted was a whole set or overlapping sets of centers, as opposed to a network or grid form of distribution.

The premise was not that centers are good in and of themselves. Rather, it was that in the centering and bringing together of certain activities, such as schools, libraries, shopping centers, basic recreation facilities, certain kinds of office activities, and religious facilities, there was an extraordinary benefit to be gained, that is, ready access.

Based upon that premise, we then said that if only one center were available to the people, it would have limited value. Consequently, we decided that we would develop a system of public transportation routes connecting all the several main centers. The city was designed with a spine of higher-density housing permitting half of the people to live within a 600- to 900-foot walk of station stops. At certain of those station stops would be the seven or eight major centers, as well as a number of smaller centers. Along the route were also the centers of employment.

That is the way the city was designed and is now being developed. The problem, of course, is in the creation of that public transportation. We have not been able to do that in the manner we had anticipated.

We had many ideas for that public transportation system, but they didn't materialize. For example, we have separate rights-of-way set aside, and we thought that the best mode for this community would be driver-operated buses, rather than some automated, indifferent kind of machine that goes around when you

push a button. Ideally the driver would live in the community and would say
"Hi" when passengers boarded: "Hi, Jim, where are you going today, everything
all right, are you on your way home?" He would provide the human contact and
would be a part of the communications network. However, the economics didn't
work out. One can't hire part-time bus drivers; union problems and the overall
cost prevented that.

We then tried to design a system that would reduce the requirement for operators. We conceived an automated system without a driver, as that would eliminate
a major part of the operational cost. Capital cost is no problem. That solution did
not succeed in part because there weren't enough people in the area at that time
to support it. In spite of these troubles, I, for one, am confident that we will have
an effective rapid-transit system in Columbia before it reaches its mature development stage.

There is an interesting phenomenon that is taking place right now in the community, and this addresses the second part of your question. The fact that we recognize community development as a process means that we have built into the
community an evaluation–planning–development capability as an entity in the
Columbia Parks and Recreation Association. This association owns and operates
all of the public systems, including the transportation routes. There is a transportation system in effect right now in Columbia. Those who do not have a car can
still get from any point in Columbia to any other point through a "call-a-ride"
system. There is also a peak-hour bus system. Its ridership is increasing, partly because it is part of a group of several facilities we packaged together. One fee of
$200 a year allows for free access to the Colum-bus, as it is called, free use of the
indoor skating rink, the golf club, the tennis courts, the boats on the lake, and
several other user-paid activities. So the community seems to recognize that transportation is one of the most important amenities and will probably make it a
freely accessible community facility, as are the parks, lakes, and walkways.

There is more to say about the second part of your question, which deals with
how we can avoid having a new city deteriorate into an old one. The answer is you
don't. Cities are continually changing, as do people, and parts of cities grow old and
die. The solution is to make the change simply a transformation into something new
and better, and that is how the process phenomena I've described operates.

GIFFORD: The topic that I prepared myself for was the role of transportation
in urban design and the actors involved, and I come with a specified bias against
gasoline-powered vehicles. I come with a specified bias in that I don't think that
normally transportation planners have taken into account the dynamics of gasoline-
powered vehicles in the plans and alternatives that must be developed in order to
limit their use.

With respect to Columbia, I don't think that it can be treated as an isolated entity. I think it has to be integrated with Washington; Washington is the economic
hub of that particular area, and I would rather ask some questions, assuming for
the moment that I am a Washingtonian. I would ask the people at Columbia what
they are doing to limit the use of gasoline-powered vehicles for travel between
Washington and Columbia. Have they actually tried car pools on an organized
basis? Have they tried to encourage the building of double-decker freeways? Have

they talked about leased minicars? Have they talked about banning certain vehicle types during certain times of the day? Have they talked about certain types of parking rights, park-and-ride systems? I am very interested in what kind of mechanisms have been established to look at the transportation system on a regional basis rather than on an intra-Columbia basis. To me, the regional problem is the real problem.

HOPPENFELD: Of course it is a real problem, and one of the most frustrating things that happens is the question you just raised, the "What have you done for me lately?" question.

Columbia is a wholly private approach at building a better community, and we recognize that most of the ideas you expressed are good ideas and are worthy of an experimental effort. None of them are economically feasible for a private developer in the process of building a community. There are very real constraints as we approach our three goals: serving the purposes of the people, enhancing the land, and making a profit. We simply were unable to venture risk capital in many of the areas that you have discussed. We could only work on the internal aspects of the problem related to the rights-of-way and bus routes in Columbia. The problem we face is the fact that Columbia is a single development approach, and there are very few community development entities with stated goals such as ours. There has been very little external response, although we discussed the problems of routing, the Metroliner, and others with state road commissioners and with the Department of Transportation.

We hear frequently, "There is a fantastic parking lot just outside of Silver Spring where the Metroliner is routed. What a site for a city; what values that stop creates. With that increased value you could pay for the whole superstructure of that city." However, there are many jurisdictions involved. These are regional responsibilities, and they are not being met.

While we did not do many of the things you mentioned, there are car pools; some who commute to Washington and Baltimore have chartered buses, and there are several buses that serve Columbia, even though Trailways has been on strike a year.

MERTZ: As Mr. Hoppenfeld made his presentation, I jotted down the key words, and I underlined those that I agreed with and I agree with a great deal of what he has to say.

First of all, I would like to compliment him on the product, Columbia; my family very nearly located there in 1969. I wholly agree with the thesis that transportation ought to be brought along as a derivative of social aspirations, public values, and not as the leading force. For some 15 years now we have gone a long way toward the notion that land development should come first and that transportation systems should follow. We have, over time, learned a great deal about the supply of transportation facilities and about what mixes of different modes are required to support different levels of activity. As Mr. Hoppenfeld points out, in Columbia they were able to plan their internal transportation system from the beginning as they planned their city. They were then in control of that supply.

To a large extent, our local governments, our municipalities, and, to some extent, our counties, are in control of that local supply, that is, the roads that are necessary for internal circulation. Generally, they do an excellent job of balancing development with the supply of the local access roads. They actually make it a condition upon developers to bring in those kinds of roads along with their development. So that is fairly well balanced.

The loose end in the process involves the middle- and higher-class type facilities; municipalities don't have control over these. It is usually a state function, and we have invented all sorts of regional transportation planning bodies to try to plan our highways as a derivative of land-use development. There is some modest success along these lines.

I would like to say that development normally runs ahead of the transportation supply. That normally leads to the situation where radical surgery must be applied to attempt to restore the balance of development with transportation supply. These efforts have not worked very well. We have had quite a bit of experience in attempting to restore the balance of transportation supply after development has taken place. We don't think that is a viable approach for the future.

That leaves only one choice, and that is to develop the supply of transportation, not just highways, along with the development to keep them in balance.

So I very much agree with Mr. Hoppenfeld that the development of new communities is going to be on the rise, but I don't see it at this time as a large percentage of the development that is going to take place in the future.

We are caught with the lack of institutions to carry out this balanced development concept. We hear so much about "balanced transportation"; I would like to call it balanced development. Are we going to move toward regional governments; will we move ahead with special-purpose regional development corporations; or will there be even more special-purpose regional transportation corporations? When I say "regional," I am speaking of the metropolitan scale. That last possibility would be unfortunate, I believe, because we would again be committing the sin of transportation first, development second. It is not at all clear what lies on the horizon, but I regard the number one problem as being the institutional one.

KOZIC: Referring to what Mr. Hoppenfeld said concerning the classic argument about values versus perfect order: It has become increasingly clear that all the social theories that have been expounded here during the past few years have come into some disrepute. If, in fact, the social theories are in disrepute, it means that we have not been able to measure these theories in terms of some quantitative value. If we are going to use social values or social theories to develop transportational networks or systems or even build new cities, we ought to be able to measure or quantify what these values are.

If in fact we do need a data base to test out the theories, or at least to measure what the theories are supposed to accomplish, then we should have a large set of socioeconomic, demographic, and geographic data that can be used for those purposes.

My question is to Mr. Finger: In the Urban Information Systems Interagency Committee effort there is an attempt to build these data bases; is it possible then to connect these data bases in some way as a means of measuring the value of these social theories and of bringing a little more realism into applying these values to transportation systems within urban areas?

FINGER: I have some trouble understanding which values you feel are in disrepute, because I can list a few that are indicated by the development trends and that do represent a set of values that people exercise, for example, the desirability for homogenous community living. That trend we clearly see, and it is tied, perhaps, to status seeking and to the desire to move to a "higher-class" neighborhood that usually means a higher-income-level community. This appears to be a continuing desire. Although this factor seems to be softening somewhat, there is still the desire of whites to live with whites and to live in homogenous white communities. There is some feeling still on the part of the black community that there is an uncertainty in moving into a white community and being the isolated black or one of the few isolated blacks in that community. Those feelings are part of the social values.

One can look at data, see what has happened, say that it is reflected in the set of current social values, and that we don't like them. Now, are there ways of designing or planning or motivating people to work together than can begin to break down some of those divisions in our society that are the result of social values people have set up for themselves?

The point is that we do live in a society where freedom of choice has been the basis of our living. That freedom of choice has also been made possible by some of the development programs that have taken place. For example, Mr. Mertz made the point, I believe, that a good bit of the freedom of choice has been made possible by the fact that it was easy for some families to live in a suburban community and easily travel into the city with their own automobile. They could afford the automobile and they paid their taxes, so they were able to have the highway system come to their neighborhood. That was freedom of choice tied to the ability to pay. Once there, these people erect various barriers to make certain that they can maintain the homogeneity of their communities. As the County Manager of Fairfax County told me, "Everyone who moves into the county seems to want to be the last one in." That really seems to be the case. Those are all social values.

Yes, we do need a data base that indicates what is possible in trying to establish social values that meet more of the idealistic foundation of our nation. I am referring specifically to assuring an equal opportunity tied to the ability to exercise that equal opportunity and freedom of choice for all people. Now the Urban Information Systems Interagency Committee is not really a program aimed at simply compiling data. The important part is that it is a management system. A city has to carry out certain functions: sending out tax bills, providing human health services or educational services. The system is to help answer the question of how the information in each of those areas can be assembled to permit the city to carry out those functions better and to satisfy the needs of the individual families. There is a need to collect information, and a good bit of it happens to be information on individuals. As a by-product the data can help cities analyze what these social values are and what the trends are.

I think most of us are just not happy with the social values that exist, but it is not that they have been proven wrong or that the social theories are in disrepute. I don't know that I have answered you, but I have indicated to you some of the concerns that I have in this area.

D. David Brandon   **THE NEW YORK STATE URBAN DEVELOPMENT CORPORATION**

In any planning situation, we would ideally begin by determining what our our social relationships are—how we as human beings relate to one another. We would then design an economic system that would support those kinds of interactions. Of course, it would also be necessary to consider our natural physical environment to arrive at the best design for our social and economic systems. Unfortunately we don't seem to work that way. It is evidently easier to struggle with problems involving our physical environment—transportation, housing, or a government facility, than to deal effectively with social and economic relationships.

The New York State Urban Development Corporation (UDC) was, however, an outgrowth of concern for social and economic matters, as well as urban development problems. Historically, there has been a lack of governmental machinery that could deal with urban development problems in a broad way. The Urban Development Corporation is an attempt to meet that need.

The New York State Urban Development Corporation was created in 1968 by the state legislature upon recommendation of the governor. A look at the nine-member UDC Board of Directors indicates some of the interest and involvement that the group represents. The members are appointed by the governor and include four state officials: the State Planner, the Department of Commerce Commissioner, the Superintendent of Banking, and the Superintendent of Insurance.

The other five members are private individuals: Peter Brennan, newly appointed Secretary of Labor and formerly president, New York City Building and Construction Trades Council, AFL-CIO; George Williams, Counsel, Wisar, Shaw, Freeman, Van Graafeiland, Harter & Secrast;

George Woods, former president of the World Bank; Kenneth Clark, president, Metropolitan Applied Research Center; and Alton Marshall, president, Rockefeller Center, Inc. Ed Logue, president and chief executive officer of UDC, has an urban development background in New Haven and Boston that is hard to rival.

Basically the UDC is a statewide organization concerned with creating balanced growth and assisting the urban development patterns desired by the state and its communities. This means developing several different kinds of programs and using special powers as well. It also means recognizing that problems are not confined to center cities but involve the whole urban complex or metropolitan area.

Although the UDC can also provide educational, cultural, and civic facilities, it should be clearly understood that it is a development organization, not an operating social service agency. Neither is UDC a long-range planning organization; other machinery for that exists in the state. However, the UDC does try, as much as possible, to eliminate or cut red tape that often stymies effective planning progress and also to maximize the use of the private sector. For example, the private "risk system" in the United States operates so that the investor attempts to maximize profit while taking as little risk as possible. But someone does have to take risks, and that more and more seems to mean the government! The UDC works with private investors and tries to make them more willing to put their dollars into projects that are in the public interest.

There are downtown areas all over this country where revitalization attempts have been undertaken with urban renewal programs that have been able to clear land, write down the cost of land, and make it available to the private developer. However, the person with $50 million to invest looks at the proposal and says, "Well, what are the other options this year for me and my $50 million?" He looks out around the suburbs and finds open farm land with only limited public restraints, such as zoning and building codes, less chance for labor trouble, and probably a new road and an interchange. Therefore he invests in the lower-risk suburban area rather than helping the community keep its urban center dynamic and alive. The UDC is trying to prevent that by eliminating some of the investment drawbacks.

Another prime UDC goal is the development and financing of housing for low-, moderate-, and middle-income families. Free-enterprise efforts generally handle the middle- and upper-income housing needs, but the assurance of an adequate place to live for those of lesser incomes has continued to be a problem.

Moreover, the UDC assists in industrial and commercial development, recognizing that housing alone is not the answer and that jobs must be part of a total community effort. For example, there must be housing for public and private employees near their jobs. Between 1960 and 1970 over 70,000 new jobs were created in Westchester County. Yet over 75 percent of those jobs pay less than $12,000 per year. Assuming 25 percent of income goes for housing, these workers cannot find a place to rent or buy in Westchester County, creating a long-distance commuting problem. UDC has at least begun to provide a balanced housing mix by introducing small projects for low- and moderate-income families on scattered sites.

Because problems are interrelated throughout an urban area, the UDC has created subsidiary corporations that can assist in its efforts. The Greater Rochester subsidiary corporation is one local example. It will develop the kinds of programs that can effectively be carried out within that eight-county region. As a basic goal, the Rochester subsidiary Board of Directors set a target of 15,000 housing units in the next 5 years and promised to provide one housing unit in the suburbs for every one they put in the city. These projects include both elderly and family housing, and a general scattered-site policy has been adopted so no one community is affected unfairly.

UDC also attempts to recognize the special needs of large sections of cities. Thus, the Harlem Urban Development Corporation (HUDC), with its own board of directors and its own staff, was created. HUDC is responsible for developing projects in that area of New York City that are consistent with the interests of the Harlem community.

UDC also occasionally develops subsidiaries to deal with major projects: The Welfare Island Urban Development Corporation and the Audubon New Community Development Corporation are examples.

The UDC has a number of powers that enable it to work more efficiently and effectively. For example, it can acquire land and condemn sites, if necessary. One of the problems that faces the new community of Columbia is that its jurisdiction is pockmarked with private holdings. These may very well, as they develop independently over the coming decades, create difficulty with the overall functioning of the new community. However, condemnation is a controversial power, and the Corporation uses it judiciously: It has condemned only one piece of property in the 4 years of its existence.

UDC also has the power to waive local codes and ordinances if it is in the public interest. This is very alarming to both local officials and citizens. However, when UDC does not use the local building code, it must use the statewide building code. Therefore the buildings are not substandard but rather conform to a model code in use by about 1,000 of the municipalities in New York.

The UDC can override zoning. This too is very controversial, particularly in such suburbs as Westchester County, because the communities are very conscious of their ability to help control the number of school children, and thus taxes, by large acreage zoning. However, by not allowing efficient use of the land, which is usually necessary in trying to provide housing for moderate- and lower-income families, the communities resist their fair share of the housing load. Local zoning has, nevertheless, only been overruled against the formal wishes of local government on one occasion in 4 years. (UDC has overridden local zoning on a number of occasions without objection of local government because it was mutually desirable and convenient.) Also a variety of procedures exists to protect the public. Public hearings and formal opportunities for local government to object must be held, and citizen advisory committees must meet to evaluate the situation, before any local codes or ordinances can be overridden.

The UDC has a full range of development powers that enable it to keep projects going when they would bog down if in the hands of others. We can hire architects and engineers; choose builders and developers and put them to work; utilize state, federal, and other assitance programs; make mortgage loans; and, if it is necessary, own and operate our projects. In New York State, for example, some urban renewal programs were conceived as long as 18 years ago but were unable to move into redevelopment until the State Urban Development Corporation agreed to be the prime developer.

Finally, the state legislature has authorized up to a billion and a half dollars of UDC bonds. These are tax-exempt but are not backed by the full faith and credit of the state of New York. Instead the UDC projects stand behind the bonds with an arrangement that enables the state legislature to appropriate money if it is desirable.

Following are illustrations of the types of projects UDC works out in partnership with local governments.

1. In Rochester, the Outer Loop Industrial Park was developed to provide for industrial expansion within the city limits.

2. In the Rochester suburbs the New York Central Railroad abandoned their railroad car building and maintenance facilities. UDC has purchased and rehabilitated the property for several new industries.

3. In Niagara Falls UDC is constructing the convention center that the city started but then found was more than it could handle. UDC is also the prime developer for the Rainbow Commercial Center in downtown Niagara Falls.

4. In New York City UDC is assisting with an industrial condomin-

ium, which is a new approach to industrial building ownership. In recent years housing condominiums have become more common and include personal ownership of the apartment one lives in. Using a similar concept in older, multistory industrial buildings, the industries will own their piece of the building, rather than owning a share of all the building through a cooperative.

5. Also in New York City UDC is helping to build a new fire training center, because we have the ability to do it rapidly.

6. UDC is also working on schools and day-care centers for the city of New York, again because of our ability to move rapidly.

UDC has housing projects in all the major cities and urban areas in the state of New York, covering a wide spectrum of size, type, and location. After only 4 years of existence, over 30,000 housing units have been either completed and occupied or are under construction or design. This leads to other problems, however. A diversity of public and highway transportation systems are then needed, ranging from internal systems for moving people and goods to appropriate links with the larger world beyond the project. The UDC is involved with many transportation-related projects: On the West Side of Manhattan the Miller Highway is in extremely bad shape. Manhattan also has a shortage of park and recreation facilities in that area (Figure 1).

The docks, so essential a few years ago, are now mostly unused and falling into disrepair. Large rail yards also exist that have potential for development under the right circumstances (Figure 2).

A unique study program is now under way that includes the UDC but, more importantly, federal, state, city, and neighborhood interests. The program will try to determine what can be done as part of an overall redevelopment program dealing not only with the transportation needs, but with the whole social and urban fabric of the West Side of Manhattan.

By using a system of piling and decking additional space can possibly be created and used for urban development, transportation, and open space (Figure 3). The best solution, from an urban development standpoint, would be to place the highway at the outer end of the existing piers. This would create 700–800 acres of additional developable space along the western edge of lower and midtown Manhattan (Figure 4).

The land-use potential includes the linkage of Riverside Park with Battery Park as a continuous open-space system along the Hudson River and provides an opportunity to once again open the Hudson River to the residents and the employees of lower and midtown Manhattan (Figure 5).

There are a number of special problem areas, as might be expected,

FIGURE 1   Old elevated section of Miller Highway along the docks.

FIGURE 2   Looking south along the little used docks on Manhattan's West Side.

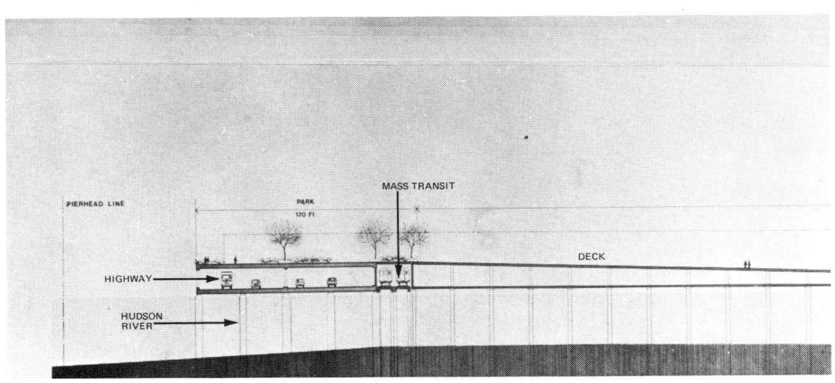

FIGURE 3   Piling and decking system with highway and mass transit.

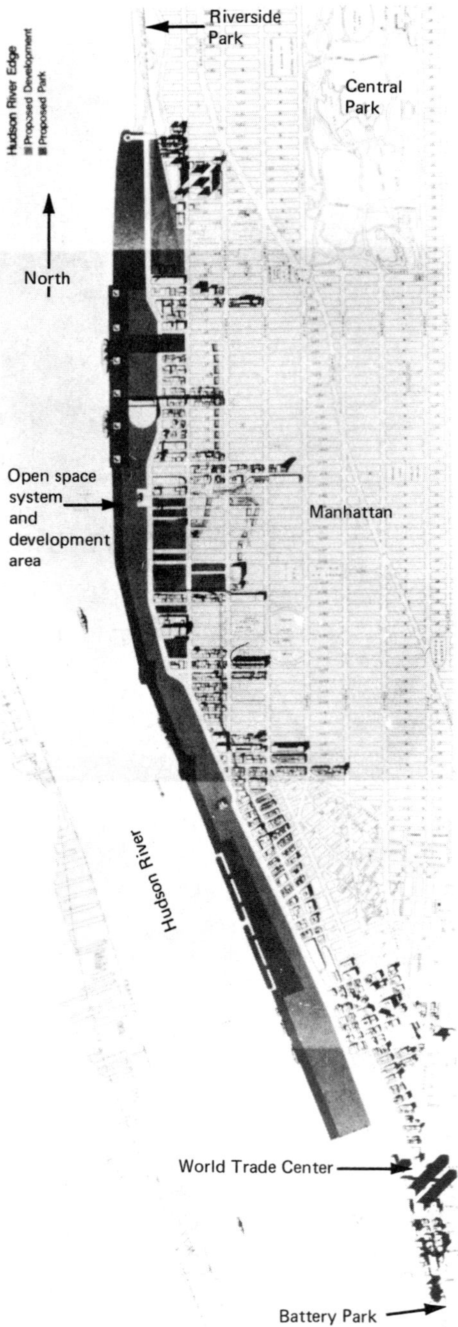

FIGURE 4   New developable space along
the Hudson River.

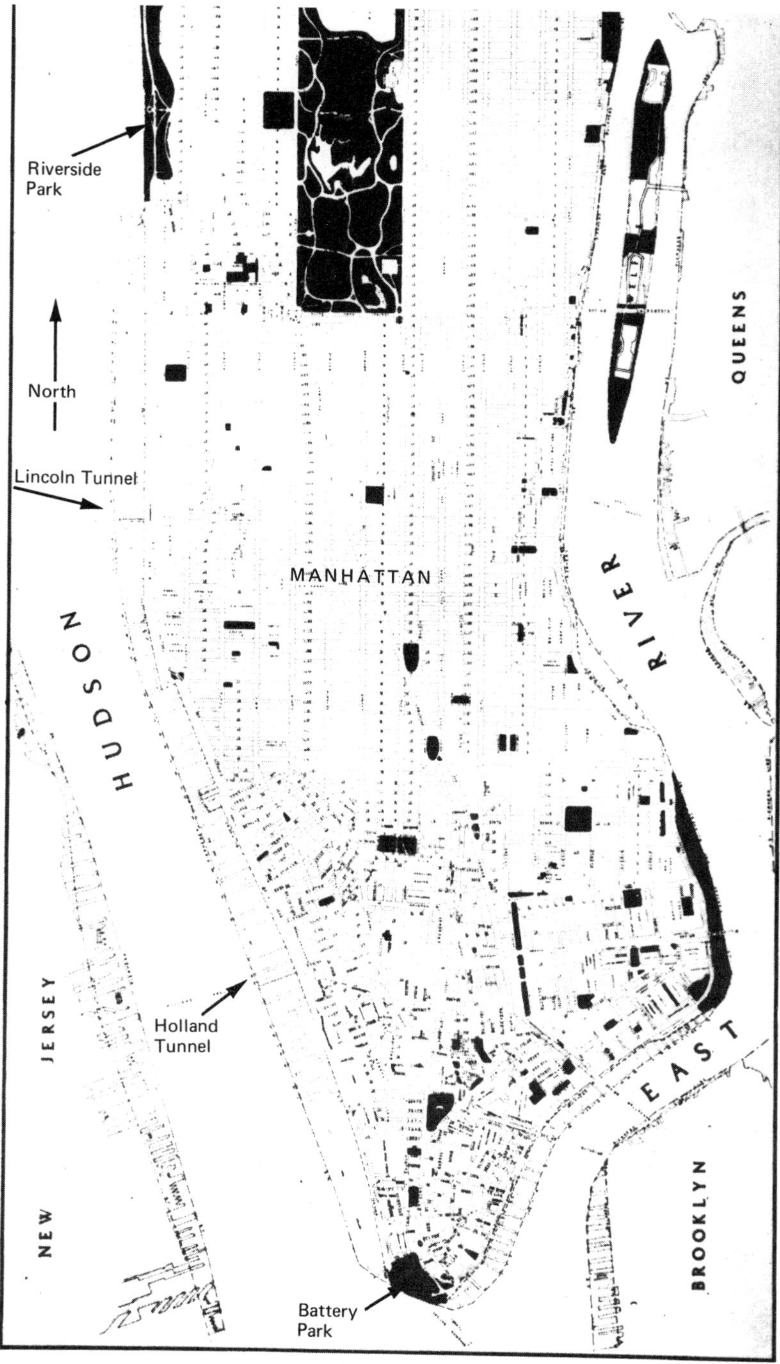

FIGURE 5 Existing parks (in black) showing the shortage of open space along the Hudson River.

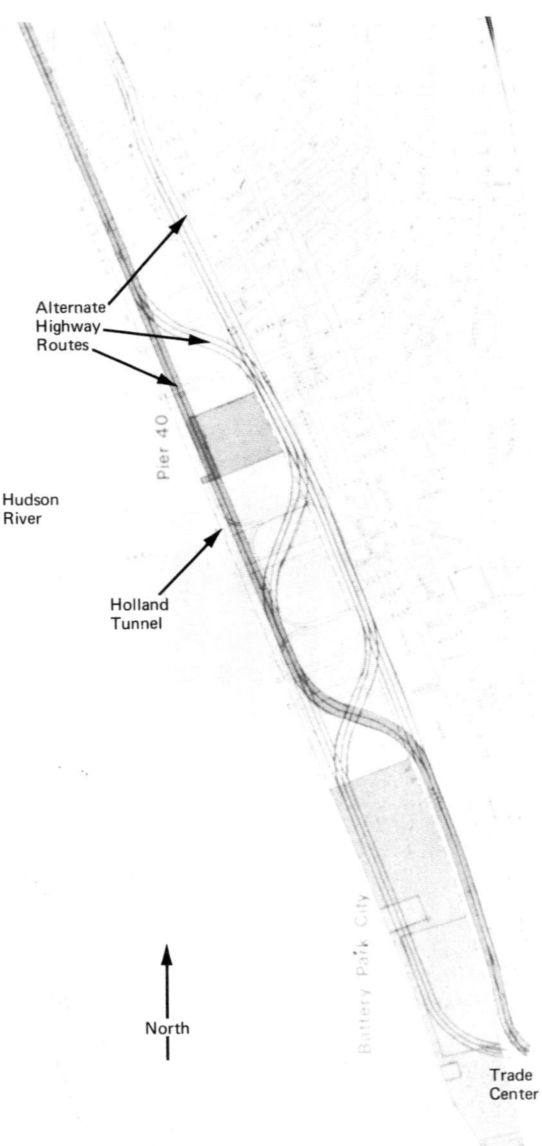

FIGURE 6   Alternate alignment possibilities: Battery Park City and Pier 40 area.

and the alignments of the highway routing can take various forms, depending upon need. Battery Park City, which is now under construction at the tip of Manhattan, and Pier 40, which continues to be active for shipping, are cases in point (Figure 6).

Farther to the north, in midtown, the convention center and superliner pier are similar problem areas (Figure 7), but these can be dealt with. The use of parallel or quay-docking, rather than finger piers, may meet continued cargo demands (Figure 8).

Also redevelopment can provide for integration of subway, people-mover, or busway systems into the sandwich deck. This will take care of the West Side of Manhattan, which, when current planned expansion of the New York City transit system is completed, will become the most underserved area of the city, particularly if additional urban development takes place (Figure 9).

Additional development area in Manhattan will enable a new town-in-town concept, with a mix of commercial, industrial, residential, civic, and openspace facilities arranged in an environmentally compatible fashion. The convention center area and the new superliner terminal are very much a part of this effort (Figure 10).

The detailed planning and development of individual parts of the area will take place over the next several decades as the projects are needed (Figure 11).

The current study effort provides a supreme test of whether or not the complex relationships involved with social, economic, governmental, land-use, and environmental interests can really be brought together to make use of this once-in-50 years opportunity. The study work is under way; the Steering Committee involves not only state, local, and federal officials but includes representatives of community planning boards as well.

Let me now turn to two large-scale projects—first, the Welfare Island new community. The site is a long, slender island in the East River, with its southern tip near the United Nations complex (Figure 12). It is called Welfare Island because, for the past century, New York City has handled many of its social service activities there. Private developers had hoped for an opportunity to develop the island, but for the most part they proposed development at an overwhelming density.

With the creation of the UDC, an agreement was reached between the city and the state to create a subsidiary development corporation to take Welfare Island and develop it (Figure 13).

The island will lose all sense of human scale if the density is too great (Figure 14). This model, if you are from suburbia or a smaller U.S. city,

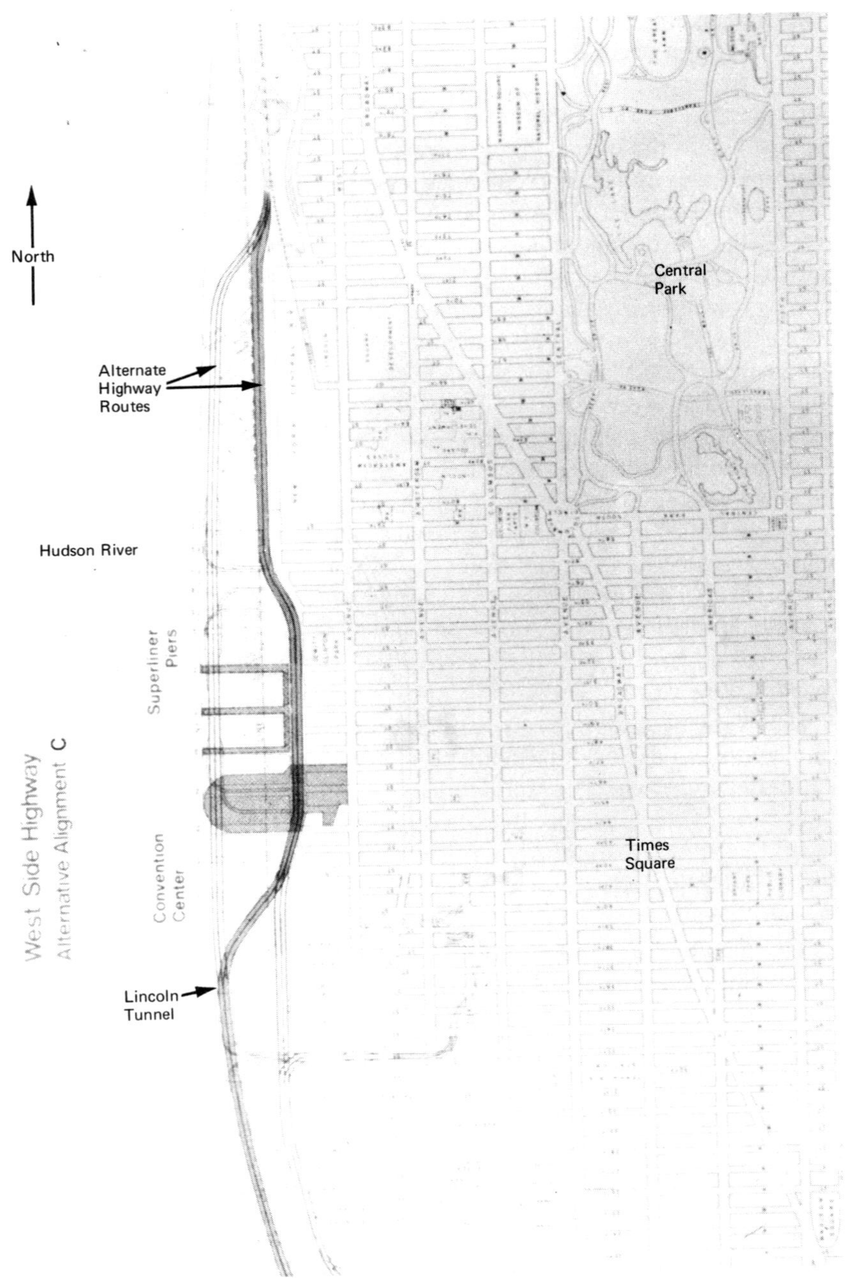

FIGURE 7   Alternate alignment possibilities: convention center and superliner pier area.

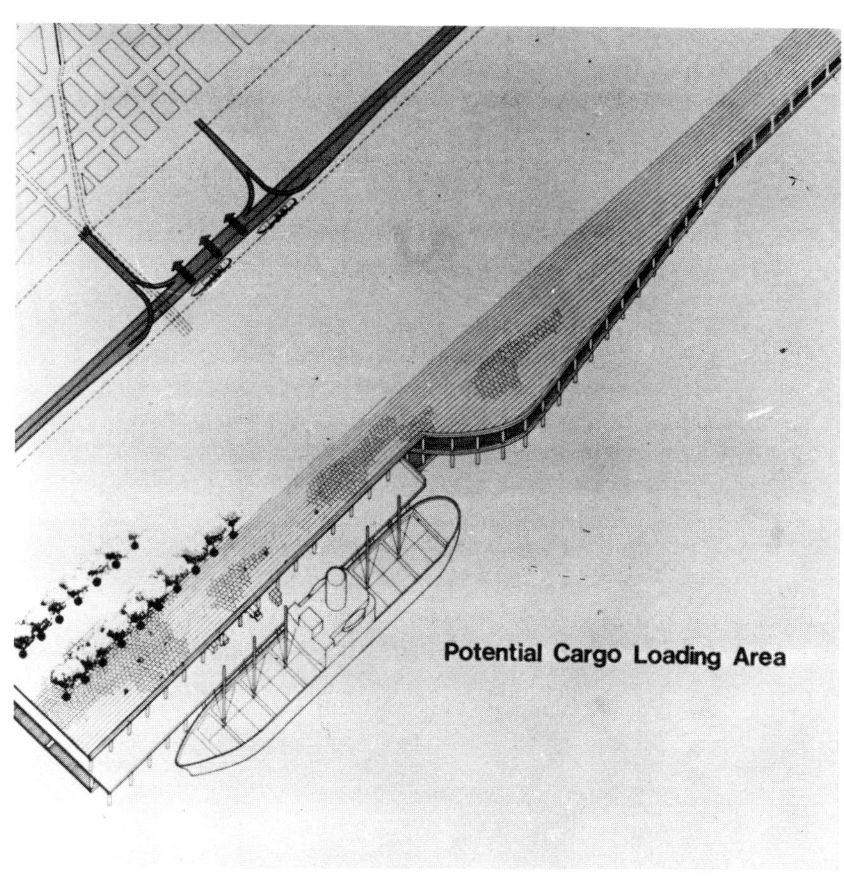

FIGURE 8   Use of quay-docking and deck system.

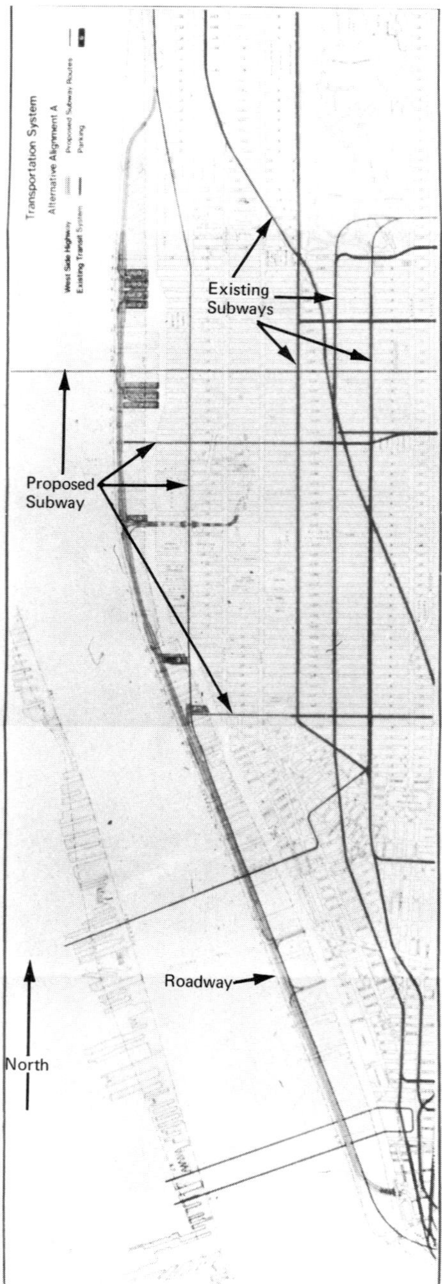

FIGURE 9 Existing and proposed subway routes.

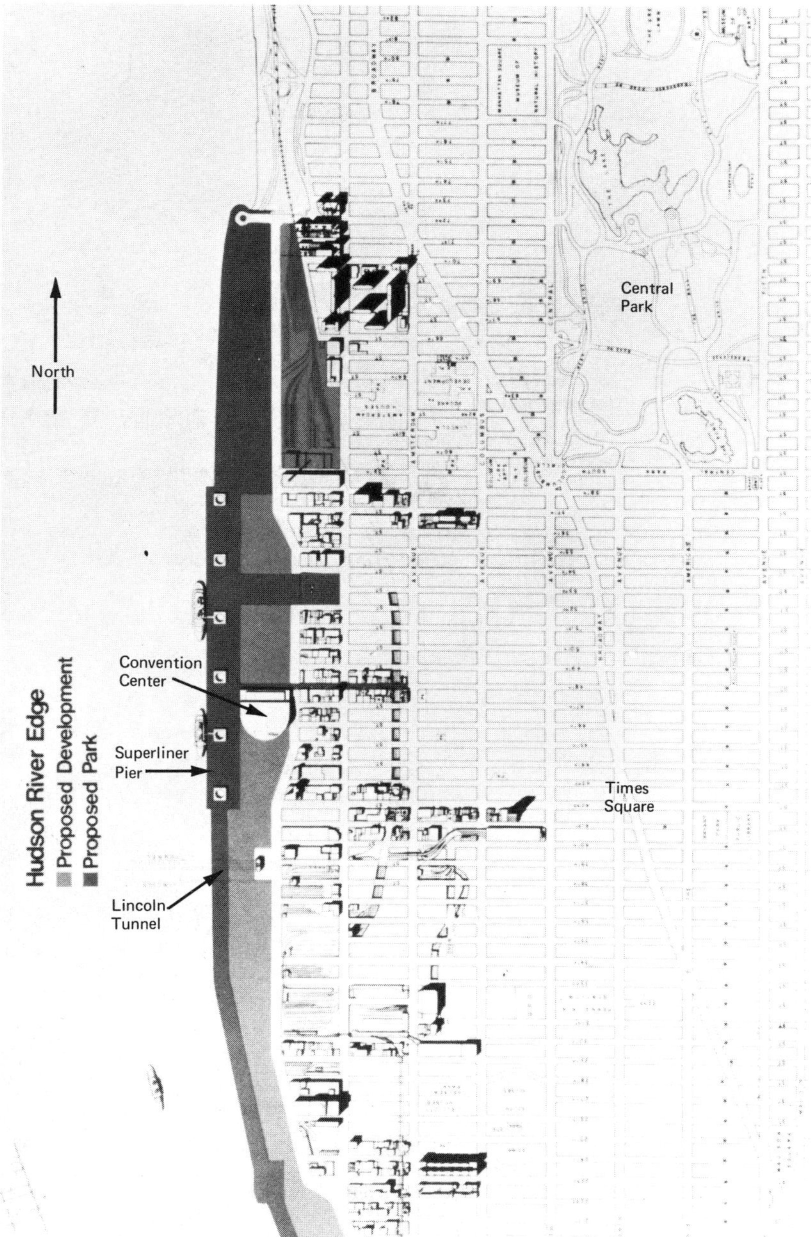

FIGURE 10 Mix of commercial, residential, park, and other land-uses possible in the convention center area.

FIGURE 11 Detailed project planning timed as needed.

FIGURE 12 Looking south on the East River with Welfare Island on the left and Manhattan on the right.

FIGURE 13   Model of the new community for Welfare Island.

may still look crowded, but by New York standards Welfare Island will be a low-density place to live. The plan calls for two villages and several major parks. There will be 5,000 dwelling units, with a total population under 20,000.

Although the island is 2 miles long, it is only about 800 ft wide and requires careful grouping of people and land uses (Figure 15). A major concern is that if automobiles are allowed on the island, its community environment will be destroyed. Therefore, we hope to terminate all automobiles at the edge of the island; transportation on the island will be handled by a nonpolluting bus system.

The automobile terminal (Figure 16) also will serve other purposes: A vacuum refuse system is being constructed that will carry all refuse to this terminal point.

The Welfare Island new community is being built: Figures 17 and 18 illustrate garage and housing construction.

My second example of large-scale UDC activity is in the Syracuse area (Figure 19). For many years planners there have discussed handling urban growth patterns by using new communities, but there had never been a method for doing that.

In 1969 a large site became available that had formerly been a military ordinance depot during World War II. Private interests had attempted for 20 years to develop it but never could. The UDC took that property (Figure 20), which is bounded on the east by the Seneca River and on the north by a large state game management area, for its Lysander new community (Figure 21). New limited-access highways now exist to the east and to the west of the site. The plan calls for a connection between those two facilities to serve the new community.

Transportation-related problems of Lysander really hinge on the ability of the transportation planners to maintain a planning and construction schedule that is consistent with the development of the new community (Figure 22).

FIGURE 14   Model of the new community showing the main street spine down the center of the island.

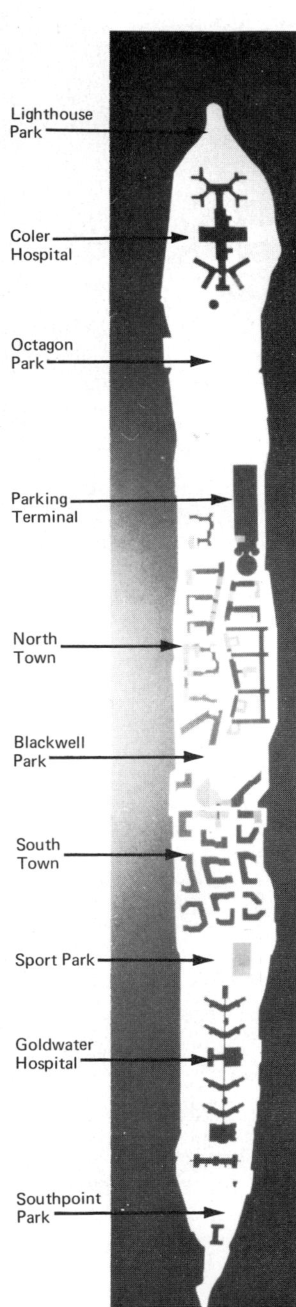

FIGURE 15 New community plan showing the two villages and two hospitals.

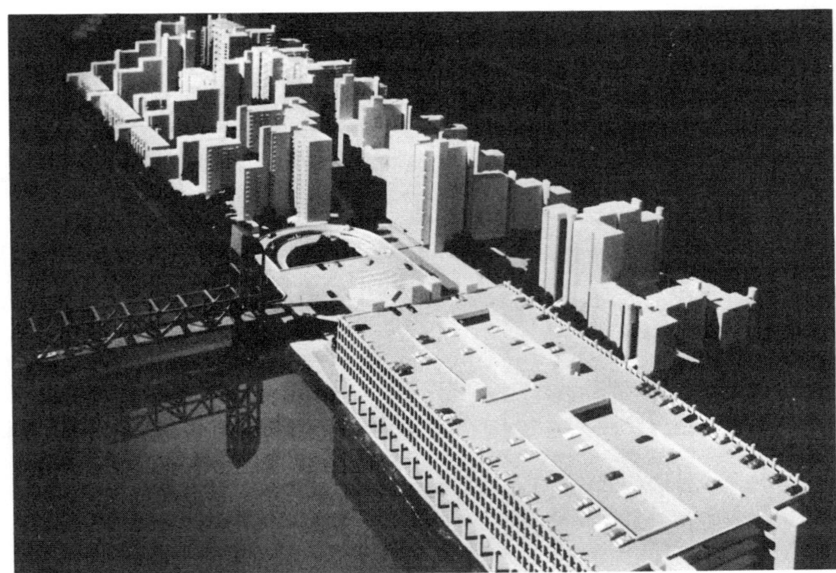

FIGURE 16   Highway bridge to the island and parking terminal.

FIGURE 17   Parking terminal ramps under construction.

FIGURE 18   Residential construction at the Chapel of Good Shepherd (1889) plaza in North Town.

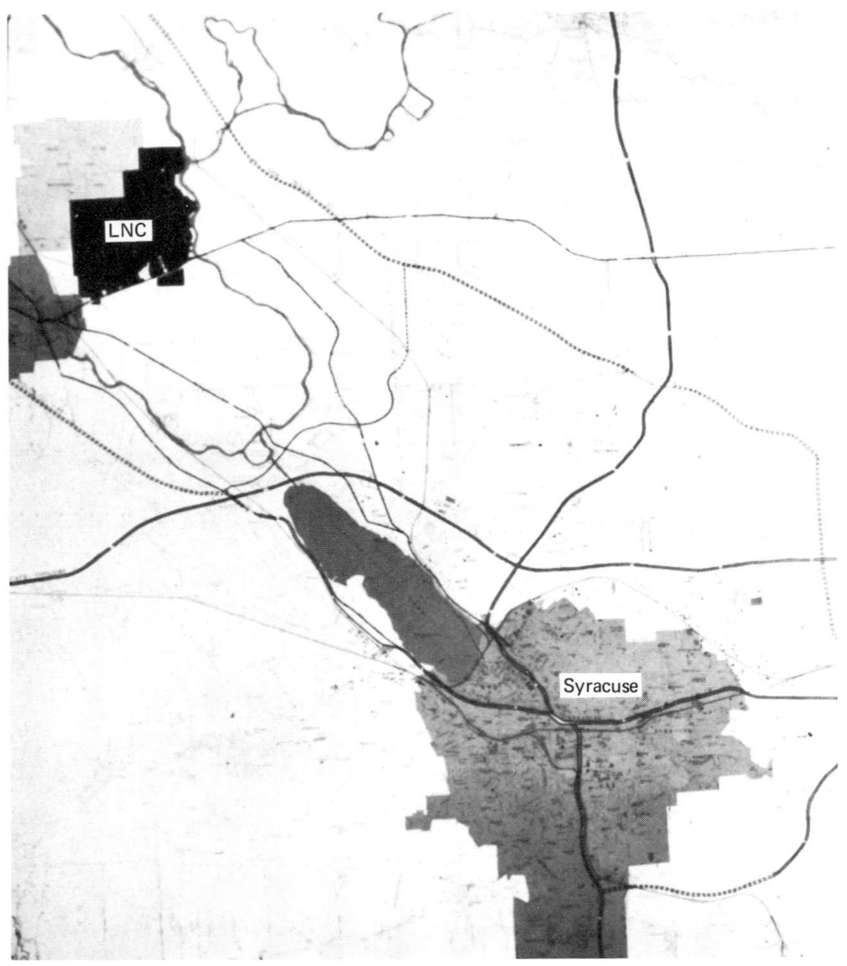

FIGURE 19   Lysander new community located northwest of Syracuse, New York

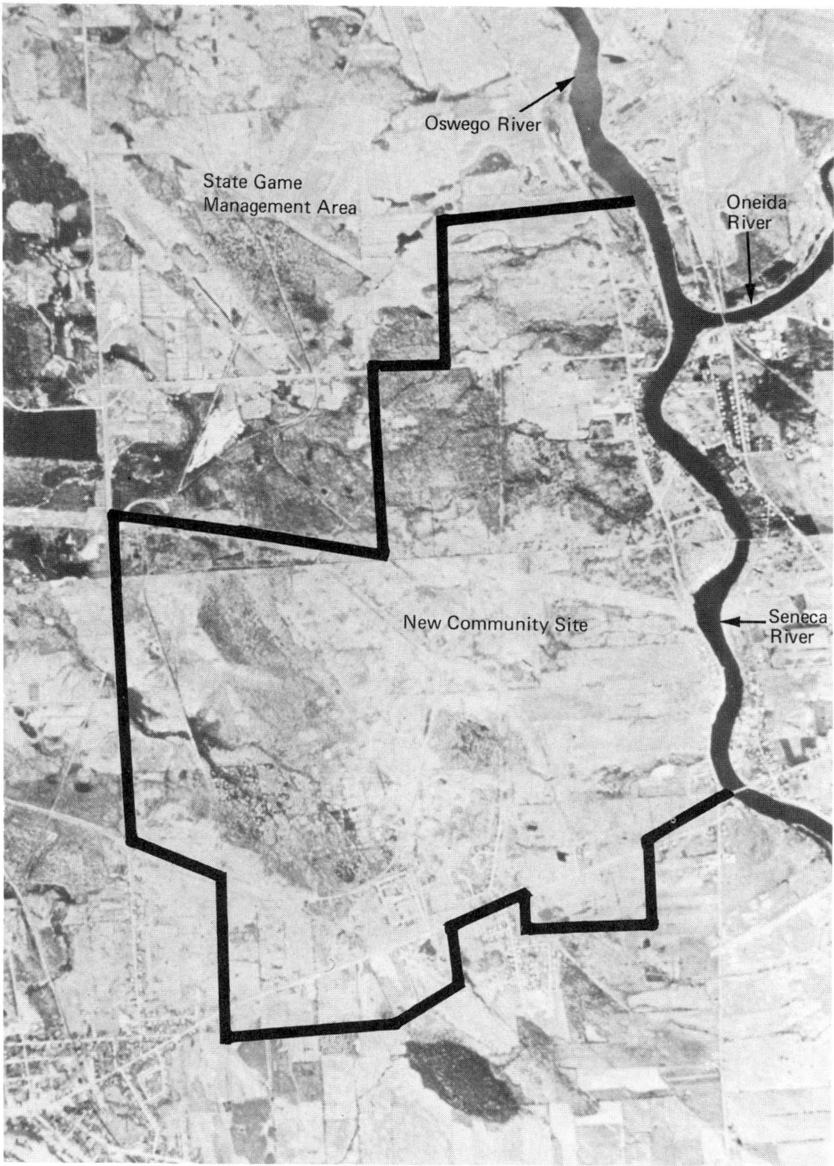

FIGURE 20 Lysander new community site, once a military ordinance depot.

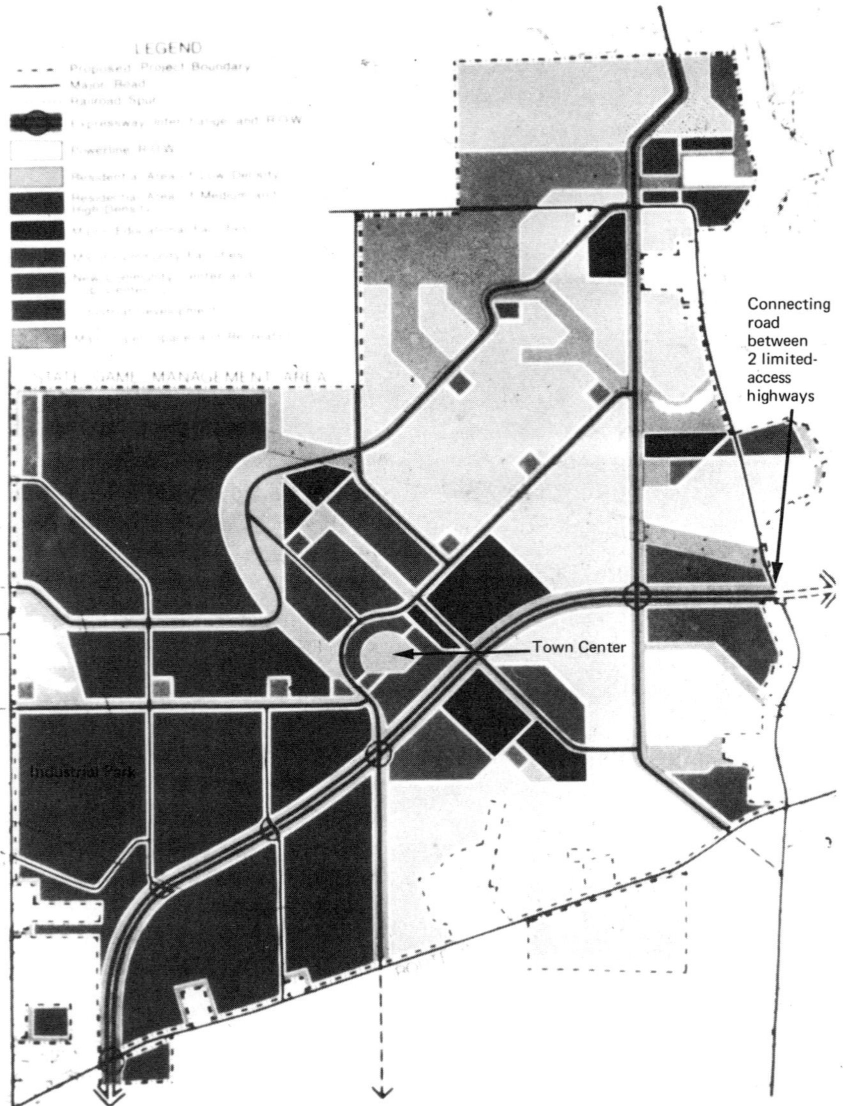

FIGURE 21 Lysander new community development plan.

FIGURE 22   Lysander town center.

DISCUSSION

GIFFORD: As a founding and original member of the UDC Board in Greater Rochester, I agree with the speaker; I think that Board was a very progressive one. As a supporter of UDC, I think it could serve as a model for the rest of the country, although it does have severe limitations.

Among those limitations are its inability to build low-incoming housing. For instance, UDC is currently involved in constructing middle-income housing in New York City, in a program that will subsidize rents for people with incomes up to $62,000 a year. I am curious as to the type plans UDC has made in the past year or so that will enable it to build subsidized housing for people in the below $7,500-a-year category?

BRANDON: The comment you make on New York City says something about the construction costs there. New York State has a program known as the Mitchell Lama Program, which provides tax abatement on housing built under certain circumstances. The rents are set as a percentage of the individual's income. If he happens to have a large-enough family and if the costs of constructing and operating the housing are expensive enough, it may be possible that families with a fairly high income could become eligible.

For the most part, UDC does not build Mitchell Lama; that is being done by others. In a standard UDC project, about 30 percent of the units would be reserved for low-income families and elderly, and the remaining units are used for moderate-income families. Both of these groups fall below the Mitchell Lama middle-income market level.

UDC is very dependent upon other state and federal programs as a means of writing down project costs to the point where the rentals really do reach the low- and moderate-income levels.

UDC uses various techniques to try to hold down costs, including system building, modular units, improved construction techniques, and product innovations.

One of the biggest costs carried forward as part of the rent is the interest. At this time the Federal 236 Program provides some relief, by a write-down of the interest to as low as 1 percent. It is very difficult to reach the lowest income level, but we do by using existing federal and state programs.

GIFFORD: Just a point of clarification—in order to understand the limitations of UDC, I think it is fair to say that the UDC has not displayed a capacity for building housing units for people who make $7,500 a year.* Many of our cities, including New York, have more than one third of the working populations falling within this income category of $7,500 a year or less.

It is an important point, because I think there will be long-range problems facing UDC, where UDC will find itself building moderate-income housing to the same degree that Mitchell Lama builds moderate-income housing.

One other point I did want to make—I am pleased that UDC is deploying the kind of transportation planning that I think can serve as a model for the rest of the country with respect to comprehensive planning.

MERTZ: I really enjoyed this excellent description of the Urban Development Corporation; it was just getting under way when I left New York in 1969, so this brings me up to date. I am really fascinated by the fact that you can exercise the right of eminent domain and override local zoning laws. That is really a tribute to statesmanship.

I had one question. Within the charter of UDC, could you build and operate a transportation system?

---

*Mr. Brandon disagrees and offers an average project as an example: UDC is now beginning to rent various projects around the state, and Unity Park in Niagara Falls would appear to be a reasonable example of the general approach. This project includes studio, one, two, three and four-bedroom apartments. Rents to the resident range from a minimum of $31 a month for one person with minimum income ($1,488 per year) under rent supplement in an efficiency apartment to a maximum of $204 a month for a family of eight with a maximum allowable income ($10,650 per year) in a four-bedroom apartment (see Table A). The first few months of rental availability resulted in 111 of the 204 units occupied, including 13 of the 20 studios, 26 of the 40 one-bedroom, 46 of the 76 two-bedroom, 17 of the 50 three-bedroom, and 9 of the 18 four-bedroom apartments. Fifty-five of the families in occupancy at that time were under the low-income program, and 56 of them under the moderate-income one. Breaking the information down in a different fashion, 3 families housed were the result of housing relocation, 25 were under welfare, 22 were elderly, 18 were nonelderly single individuals, and the remainder were other eligible families.

This clearly illustrates both UDC's interest and ability to assist in housing those of lower income. However, it is impossible to produce housing that can rent for $31 a month without some type of federal or state assistance. A greater commitment at the federal and state levels would enable UDC to accelerate its construction program.

interests found it difficult to put together the pieces that would permit the terminal construction.

UDC could build a transportation system if there were a means of showing how the revenue would balance expenses. As UDC has no taxing power, it is essential that the project show a positive cash flow.

In New York State there are metropolitan transportation authorities in most of the urban regions of the state, and those authorities are attempting to deal with specific transportation needs. UDC is working with them in a number of cases and looks forward to doing much more.

FINGER: We believe that a model of the UDC is something that we would like to see reproduced. There are small attempts at this, attempts that are functioning

BRANDON: Yes, we have the capacity to do that, if it is appropriate. We can do civic projects, and, for instance, in some cases we are building parking garages. Although this type of project is not our primary mission, we do respond to community needs in the transportation area if found desirable.

In Albany, UDC is building a new bus terminal because the city and private

TABLE A Unity Park, Niagara Falls

Type of Apartment		Low Income: Rent Supplement				Moderate Income: 236 Interest Reduction				Middle Income: Fair Market Example, None Rented as Middle Income	
		Min. Rent	Max. Rent	Min. Income	Max. Income	Min. Rent	Max. Rent	Min. Income	Max. Income	Rent	Max. Income
Eff.	1 per.	31	83	1488	4000	103	113	4944	5400 5700[a]	192	13,824
	2 per.	31	100	1488	4800	103	135	4944	6480 7000[a]		
1 Br.	1 per.	37	83	1776	4000	123		Not feasible		230	16,560
	2 per.	37	100	1776	4800	123	135	5904	6480 7000[a]		
2 Br.	2 per.	45	100	2160	4800	149		Not feasible		278	20,016
	3 per.	45	113	2160	5400	149	152	7152	7290 8200[a]		
	4 per.	45	121	2160	5800	149	163	7152	7830 8200[a]	278	22,518
3 Br.	4 per.	51	121	2448	5800	170		Not feasible		317	25,677
	5 per.	51	129	2448	6200	170	174	8160	8370 9400[a]		
	6 per.	51	138	2448	6600	170	186	8160	8910		
4 Br.	6 per.	57	138	2736	6600	188		Not feasible		350	28,350
	7 per.	57	146	2736	7000	188	197	9024	9450 10,650[a]		
	8 per.	57	146	2736	7000	188	204	9024	9800 10,650[a]		

[a]New higher maximum income.

but don't have the full authorities of UDC. For example, Michigan has a small group approaching it, and New Jersey has a state finance organization.

Let me emphasize that the UDC legislation was created during the emotional aftermath of Martin Luther King's death. It has had to tread very lightly in the use of all the authorities that were mentioned. The fact that UDC has not used their powers very extensively is a display of statesmanship. It may also reflect the tenuous nature of those authorities, recognizing that the state legislature could withdraw those authorities at any point if enough pressure developed. That legislature comes from the local communities, and if the local communities sense a home-rule threat, that can happen.

Let me discuss a problem that is reflected in the Welfare Island development where there is real consideration for the transportation system within the island community.

First the housing being built on that island is for subsidized families. I don't know if they are the $60,000–income families or not, but subsidized families at any rate.

I expect that a substantial number of people will be living on that island within a couple of years. The only way to get to that island now is by automobile, by a bridge that goes from Manhattan to Long Island City and then back over a small bridge, and the cars go into a garage.

The burden on the surrounding area is the question that I am raising in terms of talking about a regional transportation system. The subway won't be in operation, probably, until 1980; the suggestion is that maybe people will be able to get to Manhattan Island using a ferry, which involves using the internal circulation system and transferring to the ferry. When you arrive at the other side in Manhattan you transfer to another system and go into the Manhattan route. I maintain that is not good regional transportation planning.

BRANDON: There has been a great amount of work done on this. A new subway line is being build under Welfare Island, and a subway stop is a part of the design. Unfortunately, the speed at which the subway line can be built, equipped, and placed into operation does not match our development schedule.

UDC has been working with the city, the Transportation Authority, and others in transportation for several years in designing a secondary transportation link. An aerial tramway system, which could tie directly into Manhattan, is actively under consideration.

FINGER: I think this is another example of the kind of problem you can get into and represents one of the few cases where development is actually preceding transportation. In most other situations, transportation was first and development followed.

Harmer E. Davis

TRANSPORTATION AND URBAN PLANNING

What has to be done with urban transportation planning to make transportation more effectively contribute to improvement in the quality of urban life? It is convenient to regard transportation planning as a technology. As such, it is a part of the production process that starts with inventories and demands and ends up with facilities and services that presumably meet objectives and fulfill needs.

There has been considerable progress in developing the concepts, the methodology, and the analytic techniques that are required to produce system plans. What is needed now are the decision- or people-oriented practices and the institutional arrangements to make a very complex process effective.

I will mainly address these latter problems, although improvement in technical methodology, can, by no means, be neglected.

Planning for transportation improvement seems to be a very popular exercise these days; nearly every governmental unit—federal, state, and local—engages in some aspect of it. Federal laws require that a transportation planning process be carried on in every urban region as a condition for receiving federal aid for transportation purposes, and millions of dollars are spent in this area every year. Small armies of people are involved. Yet a widespread uneasiness about transportation planning seems to be developing, especially in the urban metropolitan regions.

This is not to say that these efforts are not productive; on the contrary there are numerous examples of transportation planning efforts that have resulted in highly successful transport facilities and services. But, at the same time, the results of many long-range transportation plans lie moldering on the shelves.

General urban planning is also a pervasive effort, conducted in nearly every town and city, many counties, and numerous urban regions. The federal government and many state governments devote considerable resources to it, and a whole new profession has come into being to engage in it. Yet, here too, we find undercurrents of dissatisfaction and frustration over the acceptance and implementation of plans for improved organization and function of the urban complex, and for viable urban development. There are allegations, even among planners, of too much planning for the sake of planning.

Again, this is not to say that some urban plans have not resulted in improved urban form and functioning. But the fact remains that, in our urban regions especially, two important things are lacking: (a) the development of truly multimodal transportation planning that together with other functional planning, supports and strengthens overall urban regional development and is supported in turn; and (b), that these activities be structured and positioned to produce tangible results that can ameliorate some of the problems now making our urban areas less than the most desirable places in which to work, play, or just live.

What then, we may well ask, has gone wrong here? Why hasn't all this planning resulted in easy mobility and better cities for all?

Aside from the passing observation that as a society we really do not agree on what we want our cities to be like, nor how much we are willing to pay for their improvement, I submit that these questions are neither the most useful nor germane to the resolution of the problem.

Rather, the issue is, where do we now stand in the arduous process of forging a planning process, a new technology, that can be useful in shaping the urban environment in which we must live? And what next must be done?

I think we should recognize that planning, especially transportation-system planning, is in an evolutionary state; and as a modern technology, it isn't very old. Transportation and urban planning, moreover, are on the verge of moving into the next stage in this evolutionary process, where we will see, among other things, an integration of the plan preparation and the plan-implementation processes. These are the features I would like to emphasize. I interpret the uneasiness and dissatisfaction with the present state of the art of the transportation planning process as a symptom that we are ready to move on.

HISTORICAL ANTECEDENTS

Before examining the concepts now emerging, a brief historical view of transportation planning may be helpful. Although some of these ideas will be known to many of you, I will mention a few of the key features.

One of the early landmarks in the development of modern transportation planning was the initiation, in the mid-1930s, of the highway-planning surveys. These were made possible by the Federal Aid Highway Act of 1934, which allotted 1.5 percent of the federal aid funds for this purpose. These highway-planning surveys were a landmark, not so much for the immediate results, but rather because they marked the beginning of the accumulation of information that laid a basis for some significant new concepts and provided comprehensive, quantitative information for practical programming.

One concept that emerged was the view of the highway network as a composite interacting system made up of a hierarchy of functional subsystems: feeder routes, major through routes, etc. This led also to recognition that the routes in urban areas were a part of the total system; and the federal and state highway programs began to shift from a completely rural focus to one that increasingly involved the urban areas, although there were, of course, other compelling reasons for this shift.

From the origin-distribution and home interview portions of the highway-planning surveys there emerged another new concept—the interrelationship between land use and transport usage. (Here the term "land use" refers to the kind and the spatial distribution of socioeconomic activities throughout a land area.) Of course, the dependence of land use on accessibility had been well recognized, but new planning data showed that different patterns, and combination of patterns, cause different transport usages. It became possible to predict, at least on an empirical basis, transport usage or demand from land-use characteristics. Generally acceptable transportation demand models are still not widely applicable to all transport modes and conditions, but these are a marked departure from the earlier practice of using linear projections from past and current trends.

In the early 1950s a new pattern of urban transportation planning studies developed; those of the Detroit and Chicago areas were pioneering examples. These studies and numerous successors required various cooperative arrangements, although usually on an *ad hoc* basis, and the timely advent of the high-speed electronic digital computer made possible the handling of the enormous amounts of data necessary to this kind of planning. The studies were keyed to the concept that future travel patterns and transport usage could be predicted from estimated future land use, setting the stage for closer coordination of the elements of urban planning. Over the succeeding two decades important analytical techniques and models were devised that greatly amplified the methodology of the process. The earliest studies of this sort were largely highway-oriented, although crude modal-split models were used to estimate transit usage. More recent studies have come to include more specific and extensive treatment of the transit element in regional transportation plans.

One weakness of the present transportation planning process is that it depends on the *predicted* future land use for the planning of transport facilities and services. While there has been increasing communication between transportation and land-use planners, most long-range land-use plans represent a *desired* state by the general planning body; the actual land-use patterns that emerge may diverge considerably from those envisioned by the professional urban planners as a result of economic forces.

I might point out here that it has been characteristic of urban planning within the urban regional infrastructure to have the various planning elements working independently. The various functional planning agencies, dealing with water, waste disposal, utilities, transportation, etc., largely have been concerned with their own systems only. Even within the field of transportation, planning has mostly been done separately by mode. More serious in the long run, however, has been the continued separation of general urban planning (including land use) and functional planning, such as transportation.

During the 1950s, and even more so in the 1960s, a trend—toward localized opposition to freeway routings—became apparent. Freeways not only affect land values, but in some cases, by cutting through neighborhoods, they cause marked changes in the daily habits of the local residents. It was obvious that changes in design policies, location practices, and planning guidelines were due.

A notable first step toward conciliation of urban and highway planners took place in 1958 at the Sagamore Conference in New York State. At this meeting, under the sponsorship of the American Municipal Association, the American Association of State Highway Officials, and the Highway Research Board, some influential agreements concerning roles and responsibilities of the parties concerned were hammered out. One general effect was to increase the attention of the highway agencies towards reducing or avoiding detrimental impacts of route location and facility design on neighbrohood integrity and other community environmental factors.

Another result of the gradual recognition of the interaction between transportation and local urban needs was the incorporation into the Federal Aid Highway Act of 1962 of the requirement that after July 1, 1965, federal aid for projects would be denied unless there existed, in any given urban region of more than 50,000, "a continuing comprehensive transportation planning process carried on cooperatively by the states and local communities." The implementing Bureau of Public Roads memorandum specified that, in addition to economic land-use and transportation issues, "social and community value factors, such as preservation of open space, parks and recreational facilities, preservation of historic sites and buildings, environmental amenities, and aesthetics" must also be considered.

The development of these requirements gave rise to a need for a new understanding among an even broader range of participants in urban and transportation planning affairs. It also led to a notable conference initiated by the National League of Cities, the National Association of Counties, and the American Association of State Highway Officials, with the support of the Bureau of Public Roads and the Automotive Safety Foundation, held at Williamsburg, Virginia, in 1965. The "Williamsburg Resolves," as they were called, indicated increasing concurrence among various urban and transportation planning groups on questions such as organization for regional planning, identification of urban-development goals, multiple use of land for transportation and other purposes, and increased participation of local decision-making entities at appropriate points in the planning processes.

CURRENT TRENDS

I should like next to estimate present views about the condition of urban transportation planning and its possible future course. To a considerable extent, I will draw upon views expressed at a conference held in November 1971 at Mt. Pocono, Pennsylvania, conducted by the Highway Research Board under the sponsorship of the Federal Highway Administration, the Urban Mass Transportation Administration, the Office of Environment and Urban Systems of the United States Department of Transportation (DOT), and the Highway Users Federation for Safety and Mobility (Automotive Safety Foundation). While I will try to reflect the general tenor of the conclusions reached at the Pocono Conference, what follows is really my interpretation of what occurred. The conference and its sponsors should not be blamed for any misinterpretations I may make.

It may be of interest to note in passing that consensual viewpoints very similar to those of the Pocono Conference were arrived at through a series of transportation planning seminars held in six metropolitan areas of the United States during 1970–1971, by the American Institute of Planners under the sponsorship of the Office of Environment and Urban Systems of DOT.

It is now generally agreed that the key unit or scale for urban transportation planning is the urban region. While planning goes on in various degrees within the various governmental entities comprising the urban region, the social and economic interactions of an urban region are not limited to the geographical boundaries of municipalities. Certainly for much of *transportation* planning, the urbanized *region* is a logical entity.

Planning at the urban regional scale is difficult because most regional agencies do not have elected governing bodies with authority to make decisions on land use or on facility location. There is generally no general governmental authority at a regional level to which a planning unit can be tied. According to a tabulation prepared by the DOT in 1970, transportation planning was conducted under *ad hoc* cooperative arrangements in 64 percent of 211 urban areas surveyed. Twenty-seven percent had formally established regional planning commissions. Nine percent had voluntarily established councils of government. Some of the *ad hoc* arrangements, however, were associated with centralized state transportation planning.

To overcome the "sometime" nature of this situation, the Pocono Conference recommended that metropolitan planning be a "statutorily constituted process for area-wide planning, carried out by an official body established by state legislation, assuring adequate and equitable representation of the various decision-making bodies in the metropolitan area."

A trend toward better coordination of general urban and regional transportation planning has been in the making for some time, but the participants in the Pocono deliberations went practically all the way; the conference recommended that "metropolitan planning agencies should integrate or coordinate comprehensive planning with all functional planning, including transportation planning."

The key word here is *comprehensive planning*, not just *land-use planning*. The discussions indicated a recognition of the interrelationships not only of land use, transportation, water supply, and other functional elements but also housing and relocation, urban renewal, environmental protection, etc. The participants also felt that the area-wide planning agency should be staffed and supported by local and state funds sufficient to actually program comprehensive planning in addition to performing review and clearinghouse services.

The question of the intimate relation between land use and transportation deserves special attention. While recognizing the political realities of land-use control, the conferees called for legislative authority to impose a cooling-off period when efforts to change either land use or transportation plans were initiated:

Areawide planning agencies should be empowered by legislation to suspend temporarily, pending reconciliation, significant proposed changes in local land use controls that could clearly impair the integrity of legally adopted areawide land use and transportation plans, or which would require modification of such plans. . . . Areawide planning agencies should be empowered by legislation to suspend the execution of transportation or other facility projects which are inconsistent with legally adopted land use and transportation plans.

The conferees also urged that such planning agencies include in their functions a continuous monitoring of land-use and transportation developments, to more effectively provide informed comment, under their review function, regarding the effects of land-use controls and the impact of transportation and other functional projects on the regional economy and other urban activities. It was also felt that the strengthening of this advisory role would help provide decision-making bodies and public officials with better information on the consequences of proposals to change land use controls.

The conferees also recognized the relation between transportation planning and such activities as housing, urban renewal, and relocation:

Metropolitan housing policies and transportation plans must be related in order that transportation may foster the achievement of metropolitan goals. The housing element in the regional comprehensive planning process should anticipate the needs of those who will be displaced in the development of transportation and other facilities. . . . Areawide relocation planning should be integrated at the metropolitan level with comprehensive planning. Relocation policies and priorities should be consistent for all public works programs.

The importance of gauging the environmental effects of transport developments and the need to minimize or avoid detrimental impacts have recently received increasing emphasis. The Environmental Protection Act of 1969 required detailed evaluation of transport system impacts by the planning agencies. Participants in the Pocono Conference commented: "Environmental considerations, and the formulation of goals concerning them, are important elements of the comprehensive planning process. Planning agencies should develop capabilities for evaluating environmental effects to a degree comparable to their capabilities in other areas."

FROM PLANNING TO IMPLEMENTATION

A major thrust of the discussions at the Pocono Conference dealt with procedures and arrangements directed toward implementation of plans.

In recommending that planning move closer to implementation, the conference took several tacks.

Urban, regional transportation planning now deals with a rather long-range time scale and the general, rather than detailed, features of proposed development policies and systems. Participants of the conference commented:

Continuing refinement of the long-range regional plan at the sub-area or corridor scale is needed to make areawide planning more relevant to programming and project implementation. Planning at this intermediate level should also focus on an intermediate time frame ranging from 5 to 15 years into the future.

This intermediate planning scale may also be necessary to permit adequate consideration of social and environmental impacts.

On another tack, the conferees recognized that practical barriers to implementation may be lack of funds over an indefinite period, for the planning and construction of expensive facilities, or the lack of community willingness to undergo the changes and disruption a proposed facility or system might cause. It was suggested that: "To achieve the level of transportation service consistent with the overall planning and development goals of an urban community, the transportation planning process should conceive and evaluate a wide range of alternative strategies."

The conferees pointed out that such alternative planning strategies as increasing the efficiency of utilization of existing facilities rather than constructing new facilities should be considered in the *planning* process. They also suggested consideration of nontransportation strategies that would reduce the need for transportation facilities, i.e., land-use policies. Other suggestions included flexible design standards (e.g., partial-access control), or the integration of transportation facilities programs with housing or other programs, and the joint use of right-of-way for segregated auto and bus traffic, etc.

The conferees also recognized that implementation may be blocked by blind, uninformed opposition of alarmed citizens and considered the problems of citizen participation in the planning process. Such participation provides a means of discerning community goals and values that are of local importance. The conferees, while recognizing that some citizen opposition has almost become a professional discipline in itself, felt that providing information to citizens early in the planning process could aid in reducing disruptive activity. There are a number of kinds of citizen participation and a number of points in the planning process where participation could be more or less effective. Citizen participation is not a substitute for decision making by elected officials, but it may make a useful contribution. However, it was also noted that meaningful citizen participation costs money.

ROLE OF LEVELS OF GOVERNMENT

While the Pocono Conference addressed itself mainly to improving transportation and urban planning on a regional basis, it also recognized that *all* levels of government have roles to play in making such a planning process possible, workable, and effective.

The need for consistency among the policies and requirements imposed by the various agencies of the federal government was stressed in a number of ways, although no sentiment toward centralizing all federal policies affecting local regional planning in one single agency was evident.

Differences in amount and availability of subventions from higher levels of government, both for planning and for facilities, can greatly distort planning priorities. Funding schemes that would have a neutral effect on planning priorities are needed.

Finally, the Conference considered the role of the states, which are taking a new and stronger role in transportation planning. About one third of the states have already established a state department of transportation involving planning functions of some sort. My own view is that state involvement as an equal partner in the regional planning effort would have merits, including better coordination of statewide plans.

CONCLUSION

As far as the direction in which urban transportation planning seems to be developing, I must say that I tend to be optimistic. From what I now see, substantial improvements in planning will occur in this decade, and a planning process that is much more powerful and effective will emerge. I would guess, however, that the improvements in effectiveness that occur will be due as much to institutional-type changes as to changes in planning methodology per se.

It is likely that the urban region will continue to emerge as the focal and natural unit for urban transportation planning, but the basis for functioning on this scale will be considerably strengthened. While we may not see the emergence of metropolitan governments in this decade, changing attitudes and policies of the federal and state governments will enhance the effectiveness of regional-scale planning. In particular, the states may take a new part in transportation planning, greatly strengthened and broadened in scope; one possibility is state transportation district organization that is coterminous with regional planning boundaries.

An accomplishment of the coming decade will be transportation planning on a multimodal basis, although new techniques as well as new policy attitudes and practices at all levels of government will have to be devised if this is to be truly effective. Conditions for this are ripe. For one thing, the attitudes and conditions that fostered separatism in transportation planning are changing.

The decline of separatism as a planning style will also result in a greater coordination between general urban regional planning efforts and planning efforts relating to the various functional planning activities, such as transport. Although the need for regional planning is urgent, making comprehensive urban regional planning effective will be difficult. The concept of comprehensive urban planning at the regional level is relatively new and, as yet, has no real constituency. Failure to resolve the incompatibilities between land-use policies and transport development policies can only lead to frustration of both.

The growing need for useful and visible end products from transportation planning efforts will force an expansion in the scope and detail of the regional planning. This will come about partly because of the need for closer coupling between the plan preparation, programming, and project implementation stages of system development and partly because the estimation of social and environmental impacts requires a finer degree of system delineation than is now available from current regional planning practice.

Finally, we will probably see the development of improved techniques for relating planning technology to the decision-making process. These will range from inputs from affected communities ("citizen participation," for want of a better description), to outputs that can be better utilized in political decision processes.

Archibald C. Rogers **URBAN DEVELOPMENT
CONCEPTS IN RELATION TO
TRANSPORTATION DESIGN**

Because process and product are inseparable, an analysis of the total urban design process is fundamental to any understanding of development concepts.

From my experience as an architect involved in urban planning, urban design, and transportation planning, I see a new kind of "ball game" emerging. Perhaps the area of transportation planning, because of its high visibility and impact on physical change, illustrates this best. The new "game" or process can be likened to a three-legged stool. First, a new designer—in the form of a multidisciplinary team—has replaced the conventional, separated roles of the highway engineer, the architect, and the urban planner. The team is carefully tailored to fit the particular scale and kind of project and therefore may involve other disciplines, such as ecology or behavioral science.

Second, replacing the traditional Renaissance patron who individually or institutionally paid the bills, is the decision-making team. I quite agree with Mr. Davis that in our society you cannot expect decision makers not to make decisions. Whether they are elected or appointed officials, whether they are public or private sponsors, that is what they are there for. These men have the resources and the legal authority, and they make their decisions incrementally committing their resources as they go along.

The third leg of the stool, for better or for worse (and though many of us regard it as for worse, it is here to stay), is the community. Citizen participation is essentially negative today. Mayor Wagner, when he stepped down as mayor of New York, commented, "The city is no longer governable." I think most people misunderstood that statement.

I don't think Mayor Wagner was referring to too many problems on too great a scale. What he meant was that the individual communities that made up the five boroughs of New York had become so "turned off," so cynical, so well advised, and so well heeled that they could, and, in fact, did veto anything that City Hall proposed. This veto power is the essential power of the electorate today.

Moreover, these communities do not have the resources to substitute anything positive; the result is stalemate. I submit to you that stalemate is the condition of our society today, and the problem is not unique in New York City.

The design process is an *open* trialogue among three teams, then: the multidisciplinary design team, the decision-making team, and the community team (if "team" is *le mot juste*). Starting from the very beginning, there must be an understanding of the "givens," an understanding of the limitations, and an understanding of the objectives. But openness has not characterized our design and decision-making process. It is not very comfortable for a designer to step out of his ivory tower and expose his tender ideas to public scrutiny. Nor are officials accustomed to exposing their decision-making processes to open view.

The trialogue will consist primarily of posing realistic alternatives, but also, I would hope, highly imaginative alternatives. One should examine the design problem, whether it is primarily in architecture, urban design, or engineering, in context. One should determine what limits are imposed by its context, and within these limits, the spectrum of directions or actions that can be taken. These, then, will provide the basis for identifying strategic and tactical alternatives as the process goes up the decisions ladder. At each rung some alternatives are discarded, and those that remain are refined. This design process is basically one of synthesis, and there are two ways to go about it that I call, "Synthesis I" and "Super Synthesis."

Synthesis I is a systematic approach to the problem and its solution and, I believe, very much in the current fashion of systems analysis and systems design. It is not a new technology or a new methodology as much as a new attitude. All parts of the problem are perceived and synthesized into the optimum solution. Most of us, I am afraid, will be content with this, but it is not enough.

From the well-solved problem—from Synthesis I—we must go on to the next step, as great societies in the past have done. Super Synthesis means to synthesize the solution with the human user, to relate man to his physical surroundings in all its facets. Again this is perhaps not methodology as much as it is an attitude—and one I commend to all of the design disciplines.

The next point I want to make relates to the abandonment of experimentation. I know the academies are oriented toward research and rightly so. Yet not the least tragedy of our times has been the withering away of a very important tradition in our quite youthful nation, the tradition of the trial and error experiment.

In a sense, each design alternative, as part of this trialogue or design process, is no more than an experiment. It is put down on paper, tested in various ways, including computer modeling, and evaluated comparatively to find its errors and successes.

Today there is a crying need for experiment, but to experiment one must accept the risk of failure. In the private sector we can no longer accept such a risk. Instead there is heavy investment in product-oriented research.

The public sector does have the resources for this kind of experiment. But it is understandingly hesitant and so afraid of failure that it does not truly experiment. It tries to preprove everything to be sure of success, and in the process this very valid American tradition of experimentation is sometimes lost.

Once in a philosophical discussion with Jacquelin Robertson, Director of Mid-Manhattan Development in New York, I spoke in favor of the idea of a grand strategy from which could come a tactical plan, beautifully designed and pure. Robertson got quite angry and said:

You sound like DeGaulle. That is the French system. The American system is quite different.

We see a tree to be cut down, and we pick up an axe and hack away at it. And we break the axe. Then we try another axe, and finally one works. And out of this experimental approach we then build up a grand strategy.

I think he was quite right. We must make room for error, because we will learn from error. We need not apologize for failure; on the contrary, we should accept it. Thus, we will rediscover one of the basic attributes of our society—experimentation.

All of this relates directly to transportation design. There are four basic transportation, planning, design, and development concepts I would like to summarize.

First, the completed trip has not been given proper priority in transportation planning so far. The concept suggests that every trip starts and ends on the feet, that many trips should involve different modes, with modal interchanges. A garage, for example, should not be the termination of a transportation system—in this case a highway or streetway system—but should be an interchange point at which the driver, passenger, or rider changes from one mode to another. Thus the garage should be very beautiful and well designed in terms of pedestrian scale. It should, in fact, be a portal to a pedestrian system.

The idea of the completed trip affects all modes of transportation, and it should be financed from a single fund without reference to mode. Moreover, we have found from experience that the methodology of automotive transportation planning is absolutely transferable to pedestrian planning. There are desire lines, peak hours, and all the other considerations. The only difference is shoe leather instead of wheels.

Planning to minimize transportation is a second concept. Here we are on a collision course with our antiseptic approach to land-use planning in this country, generally expressed as a two-dimensional and widely separated categorization of uses: One lives in "yellow," plays in "green," and works in "purple." Getting to and from these different uses is quite costly, in time, in money, and in ecological deprivation.

We can overcome this. There is no reason that we cannot incorporate all uses in the same building or the same community. Shopping, recreation, and residence *do* go together and have done so throughout history. Certain kinds of manufacturing are perfectly acceptable, cheek by jowl, with residential facilities.

There is no reason that one should not have offices *and* apartments in a single high-rise building, with shopping below and schools above. Such an arrangement would minimize the basic need for transportation, and it would seem to me that a fundamental objective in all planning, whether we call it transportation planning or not, should be to reduce the need for travel.

Immediately over the horizon is the impact of cable TV and two-way telecommunications. To me this holds out one of the greatest hopes for minimizing transportation. Indeed, it seems conceivable that it could revive something that is now quite old-fashioned and obsolete; the idea of cottage industry, of the person performing a production task in his home under some coordinated control system made possible by two-way telecommunications.

Third, the transportation system has a more important function than just solving traffic problems; as part of a total corridor system it serves as the skeleton for and determines urban form throughout Western society. The total corridor should be developed first, as part of implementing an overall development or land-use plan. I think it is the most important lever for implementing such a plan. And with this kind of program we could safely discard zoning.

The public skeleton not only moves people, goods, ideas, sewage and water, and power, it is also the locus of the public's capital investment. And such investment should be made according to a strategy; it should be aimed at bringing about an optimum physical development, and the monetary values created in private properties by the public investment should be recaptured by the public.

Finally, let us consider amenity. We do not design for buses, railroad cars, or automobiles. We design for people. I remember getting into an argument when I proposed that the traffic engineers should be employed in designing a pedestrian system and that the resulting pedestrian system might include an area where no cars were permitted. The local representative of the American Automobile Association quite angrily replied that his constituency would never accept such an idea. When asked what his constituency was, he said it was cars. I suggested that actually his constituency was the people who owned and therefore rode in cars. He shouted me down and contended I was wrong. I didn't argue the point further.

But we do have to consider the person, whether he is overlooking a pathway, moving on a pathway, or moving in a vehicle. I do not wish to argue for bringing architects into the field of transportation planning, except where they may be helpful and desirable. I *do* make the point, however, that one of the very best and earliest of our Pullman cars was, indeed, designed by an architect, H. H. Richardson.

I see no reason why the kinds of values that the architect tries to consider, not always successfully, in designing individual buildings or projects should not also be recognized in designing vehicles and the pathways along which they run. These values are not generic to architects; they should be considered by all who design.

There are five new criteria, I think, by which we will test design in the future.

First, we will use a criterion of *competence* in lieu of efficiency. Competence goes beyond efficiency. No doubt the building must work, but it must work as part of a larger system. That is the interrelationship that, if properly solved through design, will be judged as being competent.

Second, *economic viability* will be measured by a new and broader matrix of costs and benefits. The consumer will have to pay to diminish ecological damage for example, or to ameliorate the trauma of social disruption, in addition to absorbing conventional user costs.

Third, consideration of *aesthetics* is fundamental to all design, including the architecture of our cities, and has been since man came out of caves. (Réné Dubos suggests this was so even when man lived in caves.) A post-Renaissance view of aesthetics, however, will take it out of the ivory tower, out of the hands of the elite, and put it into the hands of a sophisticated society that hungers for recognition and for art.

Fourth, a new and urgently needed criterion is that everything we design should be in *equilibrium with its natural setting.* This may not be completely attainable, but we can approach it. In everything we design— vehicles, pathways, buildings, or communities—we should seek to minimize the use of irreplaceable resources and the production of harmful effluents.

The last, and perhaps most important, criterion is community architecture—an architecture whose elements are in *sympathy with the users,* those who live in it and those who are touched by it.

Of all five criteria, this is the most difficult to satisfy. Ironic and tragic illustrations of this fact are not difficult to find. Some time ago, a large and very beautiful, public housing project in St. Louis, designed by a very fine architect, was honored with a design award. Under the criteria obtaining then and now, it deserved this acclamation. Yet this summer it was torn down because it was a social tragedy, partly a failure of the architects, but, more importantly, I think, a failure of social attitude, of understanding what the end purpose of this project was to be.

We don't know very much about the concept of community architecture, but we have some hints from the field of behavioral science. Edward Hall (*The Hidden Dimension*) suggests that all of us do have a sort of halo, an aura that influences our interactions with others and with our physical shell.

I would like to turn now, in my role as chairman of the National Policy Task Force of the American Institute of Architects (AIA), to the broader issue of a national growth policy. The Task Force has called for the early establishment of a national growth policy. In January 1972 we published our first report, *A Strategy for Building a Better America,* recommending the elements we believe must be included in such a plan. The study was approved in May by the 1972 Convention of the AIA.

Today, with the added help of the Ford Foundation, we are developing a second report detailing the new public and private mechanisms required to carry out our recommendations, and we expect to present it in May 1973 to the convention. This, too, we believe, will receive the same enthusiastic endorsement by our membership.

Against this background, the American Institute of Architects notes with grave concern the recent report of the National Academy of Sciences–National Academy of Engineering entitled *Urban Growth and Land Development,* which flatly recommends against any national growth policy.

By timing my criticism to a symposium sponsored by the National

Academy of Engineering and held within the precincts of the National Academy of Sciences, I may appear to be less than grateful for the hospitality of these two prestigious institutions. I must accept the risk of possible misunderstanding, however, since I feel that the issue between the architects, on the one hand, and the engineers and scientists, on the other, might most clearly be drawn at precisely this time and in precisely these circumstances.

The negative recommendation contained in the report of the two academies is based on three premises.

1. We do not know enough about the impact of the present processes of land development.

2. There is a lack of agreement on national goals.

3. Because of the foregoing two premises, no such policy is possible. But even if it were possible, its establishment would not be "wise and proper."

We take exception to each of these premises. First, we do support the report's call for additional research programs and for demonstration projects, but these should constitute a positive program to add to our knowledge base, not a negative excuse for delaying the urgently needed establishment of a national growth policy.

No doubt the availability of enough knowledge is a matter of judgment on which individuals and institutions may disagree. Yet it seems probable that there never really will be enough knowledge about the problems of growth and urbanization to satisfy all, despite the decades of study and the billions of dollars that have been spent to date.

Under these circumstances it seems clear that the adverse effect of our present land-use and development processes can be demonstrated not only by the massive volumes of studies but by the evidence of the world around us. We see in our alienated society, in our polluted environment, and in our chaotic communities all that we really need to know about the problems that beset us. What is needed now is not more study but the will to address these problems as an urgent national priority and the competence in our public and private institutions to carry out programs that will solve them. It is the lack of will and the lack of competence to give effect to our national will that is missing today. Accumulating more knowledge about our present development processes will not solve that problem.

Second, we do not accept that there is a lack of agreement on national goals. These stem from our Constitution and, by and large, are accepted by most of our citizens. All of us, regardless of race, creed, or economic standing, want decent communities with decent housing; we want high-quality education for our children, safety and security within our neighborhoods, and the freedom to live in communities that express in their design our great variety of life-styles.

We do agree that there is no consensus in the nation on the means to achieve these goals. But this disagreement is precisely why it is so important that a national policy be established through the democratic processes, as we have established many other kinds of national programs.

It should be clear that we, the American Institute of Architects, are not recommending the dismantling of our defense establishment or other external efforts as a condition of correcting our domestic problems. On the contrary, it is our belief that with the resources at hand we can build and rebuild this nation during the next 30 years to a far higher level of quality than has yet been achieved.

We have no lack of resources or talent to do the job, providing there is a policy that will provide the necessary incentives and remove the present obstacles to building a high-quality environment in equilibrium with nature and in sympathy with society.

Third, we take particular exception to the final statement, namely, that the establishment of a national policy under any circumstances would not be "wise and proper." This premise negates the prior two. It stands by itself, regardless of the knowledge that has been accumulated and regardless of a consensus on national goals or on the means of achieving these.

The third premise appears to defend the status quo, and given the urgent problems facing our nation, we do not believe it is defensible. I find it hard to believe that two great institutions, such as the National Academy of Sciences and the National Academy of Engineering, are really denying the existence of these problems and proposing to support the present situation in this nation.

The American Institute of Architects, therefore, urges the academies, through their institutional mechanisms, *urgently* to review their statement as it appears in the *Urban Growth and Land Development* report. Though we do not ask that they support our specific recommendations, we would like that. We do ask for an endorsement of the need for a national policy as a matter of great urgency.

Finally, we urge that the academies work with the AIA in any way that is appropriate in developing their recommendations for such a policy and, more particularly, in carrying out the research programs and demonstration projects the Academy report recommends.

FINGER: First, I would agree in the main with both of the last two addresses. However after Mr. Rogers added this last statement pertaining to a national growth policy, I would say that it is a subject that requires far greater clarification and discussion, including comment from the people who were on the subcommittee that wrote the report. He referred to it as a National Academy report because it is a report prepared by a subcommittee of an NAS-NAE Advisory Committee to HUD, although it has been reviewed by another group of scientists within the Academy. I don't believe there is an operation in the Academy similar to the AIA approach of trying to get an agreement from the entire membership. The report is an expression of the people who wrote it, and the subcommittee was chaired by Robert Wood, President of the University of Massachusetts.

Let me give you one example of a basic difference that might exist. There is uncertainty in the minds of many people on what is even meant by a growth policy. For example, there are some who believe that a growth policy implies a control and predetermination on the part of "somebody" as to how growth will take place and how development will take place.

I myself doubt that such a policy would be acceptable in our society in light of our accepted freedom of choices, freedom of opportunity, and a variety of lifestyles that have to be available in order for our people to exercise that freedom of choice.

I once enunciated a growth policy that was to maximize the opportunities of people to express their choices by making available the broadest range of living opportunities. That could be a growth policy.

ROGERS: That is ours, sir.

FINGER: I have read yours, Mr. Rogers, and I am not certain that it is, but all I am saying is that there is a wide range of understanding of what is meant and that we would need a much longer meeting than this, and I would suggest that the subject may be an appropriate area of discussion for the academies.

GIFFORD: I am going to say "ditto" also.

MERTZ: I was taken by two points in Mr. Rogers' presentation. First was his three-legged stool of the designer, the decision-making team, and the community. I sketched those out on my notepad, and I drew some arrows between them, and I twisted his words around to fit my old-fashioned view of representative government. With my arrows I have shown the designer and the community both being advisory to the decision-making body.

In my arrows I find the linkages of communication between the designer and the community as a kind of an information-gathering and communication process that provides a greater level of information to the decision-making body. I am

171

able to square that with my view of representative government, and that is what I think he said.

I am also very interested in his point on equilibrium. This struck me as being particularly appropriate. Two things occurred to me as he said this. I grew up in the West, and on every hand we heard about our vanishing timber supply. If what I now read is correct, we have established an equilibrium now. We grow as much timber as we use. The other point I remember is the great controversy over the fact that the lumber people didn't want to change their practices and become farmers—that is, farm the forests. Now they do it and are proud of it.

I think that we are faced with the need for balance in many areas today in order that we can become able systematically to manage our resources to prevent a systematic drift toward a deteriorating position.

For Mr. Davis and his presentation, I can only say that he speaks for me. I am very much involved in all of this process that he described; he has been involved ever since the beginning he mentioned, in 1934, and he neglected to say that he was the Co-Chairman of the Pocono Conference. I think very highly of his presentation.

LOGAN: Mr. Rogers, representing the American Institute of Architects, took exception to some of the statements made by the Land Use Subcommittee of the Advisory Committee to the Department of Housing and Urban Development of the National Academy of Sciences and the National Academy of Engineering regarding the subcommittee statement concerning a policy on national urban growth.

Marshall Kaplan, who was staff consultant to the subcommittee that drafted the report, is in the audience and would like to have a few minutes to give his views on the Land Use Subcommittee report.

KAPLAN: First of all, I want to thank the chairman, the audience and the panel, for the opportunity. I also want to thank Mr. Rogers for stating a viewpoint on the Land Use Subcommittee's report, because I think it will, hopefully, persuade some of you to read it.

It is difficult to write reports about land use, and I think most of you realize that not too many people, even the professionals, will read it.

I don't think I am going to rebut, as I believe that Mr. Rogers and the Land Use Subcommittee are in agreement on principles and general needs. If we disagree, it is on how you operationalize these, and I would like to talk about that in terms of our committee's function.

First of all, most of the members of our Land Use Subcommittee were members of previous task forces that concerned themselves with the problem of land conversion, and I think they were involved in the development of a number of the conventional wisdoms that some of you have heard and in effect accepted concerning how we solve our land-use problems. It is to their credit and to the Academy's credit that a committee could be structured to criticize the past, the assumptions of the past, and hopefully to—in Mr. Rogers' words—move forward so we can define an operationally successful urban land-use policy.

Let me explain what I mean in terms of some of our assumptions. For the past 15 years we have assumed that the population growth in America will exceed, from the 1960s through the year 2000, 100 million. Now I understand that we will probably see a smaller population growth—using 1960 as a base—of approximately 80 million. That is still a lot of people.

They will consume less than 20 million acres of raw land, but that, too, is quite a bit of land. However, it isn't of the proportion that we thought it would be in the sixties and will constitute only about 2 percent of the land mass that is America.

This will set patterns, and certainly we all are trying to achieve a better quality of life, but it is important, first, that we begin to state the general parameters for the problem so that our rhetoric and our polemics and our debate about land-use policy, whether it is with the administration, the professional, or the layman, can be based on a factual set of premises.

Secondly, we have talked for a long time about the tremendous increase in land values around the country, particularly in our SMSA. However, as a whole, the land-value increment on an aggregate is far less than we had anticipated.

The evils of speculation are there, but they are limited to a far smaller sector of our metropolitan areas than we had once anticipated. The latest studies indicate that, on an aggregate, landowners have seen an appreciation in land value of from 6 to 8 percent a year during the 1960s. What that means is that holding costs and taxes are what one would expect.

In specific sectors of high demand, we have examples of annual increments far in excess of those figures, but I suggest that when one begins to create national land policy, he should include the actual base during consideration of what the policy is really trying to accomplish. In effect, that is what the Land Use Subcommittee tried to do. It didn't try to debunk land policy or the need for land policy; but it did try, in terms of the conversion process, to go back and reassess some of the assumptions of the past. We all began with the commitment to work toward improvement and with a concern as to why we haven't some improvement. I believe a reason for lack of improvement is that some of the past task forces premised their goals and their assumptions on mistakes, and the subcommittee does point that out.

What did the subcommittee propose? When we said land-use policy is unwise and improper at the present time, it was included in a long paragraph that said a "federally defined master plan," and a prescribed coordinated federal policy at the present time is unwise and improper. As professionals committed to progress, we were concerned that we did not have enough information, that there was not a consensus as to means and objectives in tangible operational terms, and that the harm in having a federally prescribed master plan at the present time outweighed the benefits.

All of us on the subcommittee are federalists, but we said at this time the subcommittee supports a set of criteria that, in effect, is our definition of a policy. I think that goes far beyond the AIA's present statement, which I think a lot of us would support on its own premises.

We further suggested that from now on, no federal funds be distributed unless there are state and local plans available concerning growth that reflect low-income housing needs of some of the people who are trapped in our center cities and that no federal funds be distributed unless there are a set of environmental and other locally defined priorities consistent with the accepted national objectives.

We say a consensus could be reached now on a set of criteria that would lead to improvements in the land distribution pattern and that would be a substitute for a global master plan or coordinated federal policy. We would be within nationally stated objectives; we would be relying on state and local plans.

We then defined a set of demonstrations containing some of the conventional wisdoms coming from programs that have been prescribed but not tested in the past.

We thought these were sufficiently valid that they could be proposed as limited demonstrations around which evaluation could take place. If successful they could then be escalated to national policy.

These demonstrations proposed were:

- Presently, there are over 20 federal categorical planning aids for growth purposes, related to software as well as physical planning. We suggest a single management planning grant from the federal government concerned with growth that would test the validity of that type of process.
- Second, we suggest that the problems in the suburban areas are not so much race as they are ones of revenue when low-income families are accepted. After all, mayors can add and subtract, and the costs of services do increase when a low-income population moves in. In order to test what would happen if we eliminated that extra burden in a few select suburban areas, we have suggested that the federal government fund a services grant that would make up the gap between the level of services provided before and after the addition of low-income families.
- Third, we have also suggested land-bank demonstrations, but we recognize there are problems associated with land banks. For example, when land is taken off the market, the price builds up in other areas. There has been much discussion about land banks and of European experiences that may not be relevant to the American experience. We suggest, however, that there is sufficient validity in the land-bank concept to start experiments now so that we can find, if it is possible, a workable, operational, "land-bank" in this country.
- Fourth, we have suggested demonstrations involving extraterritorial land acquisition that would allow cities to acquire land outside their boundaries for future growth.

The report discussed the federal land disposition policy; since one of the biggest owners of raw land in this country is the federal government. Such land isn't always in the right location, and we asked the federal government to begin a massive inventory of what might be called "urban" land.

To avoid such difficulties as occurred with Washington, D.C.'s, Fort Lincoln, started in 1967 or 1968 and still in 1972 more of a promise than a reality, we suggest work on appraisal and residual pricing of the land so that a federal land-disposition policy can become a meaningful part of a set of pro-grams.

The report suggests that the public sector should be able to recoup the land values it creates by highway systems, zoning, and so on. There is some empirical data in the report but far more data is needed.

We do know that highways can increase the value of contiguous land by a factor of two to fifty, zoning by a factor two to four or more.

There are constitutional and economic problems with a recoupment policy, but we suggest that the federal government move into several metropolitan areas in concert with local government and begin to try out a recoupment policy.

• Finally, the report gives a critical analysis of the new-towns program. Of all the people we expect will be added to the population, newborn and immi-grants, before the year 2000, only about a quarter could be housed in 100 new towns that are projected by the most fanciful observations of those who support such programs. That is a large number still, some 10 percent of the total popu-lation. We suggested to HUD that they initiate a new-towns type of program in concert with a series of real demonstrations.

The report also suggests a set of research projects that would help define a viable policy with respect to growth at the national level.

ROGERS: I would just like to express my personal thanks to Marshall Kaplan for taking the time to come here to clarify the issue, the apparent division between us on a national policy.

We do support his call for research and demonstration projects and would certainly like to assist the academies in any way possible in order to get these projects funded and implemented.

Beyond that, and I am sure Mr. Kaplan would agree, we are in a political arena, and even though we may do scholarly papers off in our ivory tower, we are going to be dragged kicking and screaming before the political bar. I think we should accept this and welcome it, and I would hope, toward that end, that perhaps the subcommittee could take the next step beyond this present paper and start forming their own recommendations for a national policy. We do not mean a national master plan or a 5-year economic plan. Again, we would just welcome any opportunity to help you in this. We believe strongly in multi-disciplinarianism.

Panelists:
Kurt W. Bauer
Donald S. Berry
and
Archibald C. Rogers

SESSION III:
URBAN INSTITUTIONAL BARRIERS INCLUDING MODAL ASPECTS

Paul C. Watt

TRANSPORTATION PLANNING IN THE SAN FRANCISCO BAY AREA — A HISTORY OF INSTITUTIONAL FRUSTRATION

It must indeed be mysterious, if not downright frustrating, to citizens who have more than a casual interest in transportation—particularly in the major metropolitan areas—that progress toward a well-coordinated solution has been so slow. We have seen technological advances that put men on the moon and opened new dimensions of knowledge in many fields. Obviously we have the technological know-how. Are we as a nation committing sufficient resources to accomplish the mission? Probably not—but there has been an ever-increasing funding base for planning, research, construction, and capital facilities. What then is the real problem? What are its dimensions? What can be done to solve it?

To answer these questions, we must examine where we are today in our attempt to solve the urban transportation problem. Let is use the Bay Area as our laboratory in looking at where we are today and the course that was taken in getting there. We could just as easily look at Los Angeles, Chicago, Washington, D.C., or the New York metropolitan area—or even a single county region, such as San Diego or Miami–Dade. The urban transportation problem exists, no matter what size or scale the area may be.

The Bay Area contains 4.5 million people spread over a 7,000 square mile region surrounding the bay. There are coastal plains, rolling hills, and mountains, interspersed with beautiful valleys that give unusual structural elements to shape the land settlement pattern of the region. However, there are also nine counties and 96 municipalities within the region. There are 562 local units of government (i.e., special districts for schools, transit, parks, sewage, water, etc.) in addition to the cities and counties; 520 of these levy property taxes. The philosophy of "home rule" permeates the region.

Before the 1950s transportation planning in this diverse region was primarily done through the Division of Highways at the state level. The cities and counties were doing the traditional city and county planning studies, which included a transportation plan mostly for highways and freeways. Transit planning, such as it was, was handled separately by private and public operating agencies that existed.

It wasn't until the 1950s, when the Bay Area Rapid Transit (BART) Commission was formed to prepare a plan for a mass transit system for the Bay Area, that any attempt at coordinated planning was made. A private consulting firm was retained to undertake the preparation of a regional plan as a basis for the development of a regional transportation plan. Ten years later, the Association of Bay Area Governments (ABAG) was formed by a joint powers agreement with the local counties and cities administrations to provide overall regional planning coordination. The creation of ABAG was, to a considerable degree, a response to the ever-increasing requirements of the federal establishment.

It is important to recognize the role of the federal government during this period. Metropolitan or regional planning became a requirement for the granting of federal funds for local categorical grant programs, whether for open space, sewage and water, or transit and highway projects. More and more federal rules specified consistency with regional planning across local jurisdictional lines.

This approach really led to the next stage of the transportation planning process in the Bay Area. The BART Commission Study, begun in the early 1950s, led to the development of a rapid transit system within a transport plan for the Bay Area. The study initially provided a nine-county transit system. However, by the time the plans had been reviewed, the problems of financial implementation weighed, and voter approval of the bonds for construction obtained, only a three-county (Alameda, Contra Costa, and San Francisco) system remained. In 1962 these three counties voted a $792 million bond issue to begin the 75-mile system, which recently opened its first leg. However, with only a three-county trunk transit system and a highway and freeway system that was being challenged (San Francisco had earlier stopped the planning, development, and construction of the Embarcadero Freeway with its "freeway revolt"), it was felt, with the prodding of the federal and state government, that an overall transportation study was needed.

In response, the legislature created in 1963 the Bay Area Transportation Study Commission (BATSC), with a 5-year life, to undertake this study and report back to the legislature. This effort followed the pattern of the Chicago Area Transportation Study (CATS), Pittsburgh Area Transportation Study (PATS), Los Angeles Area Transportation Study

(LARTS), Penn-Jersey Transportation Study (PJ), Tri-State Transportation Commission, and a number of others across the land that were spawned primarily by the Highway Acts of 1956 and 1962. These acts strengthened the requirements for coordinated, comprehensive, cooperative planning with emphasis on regional land-use planning as a basis for multimodal transportation planning.

Even with its emphasis on comprehensive and multimodal planning, the BATSC program was viewed in the Bay Area as basically a highway-oriented study for two significant reasons: First, the transit element of the program was not developed in a close working relationship with the transit planning and operating people. This does not mean that a valid attempt was not made to have a transit element properly coordinated with the freeway element. However, secondly, the problem developed because of the way the program was funded, staffed, and administered.

I might add, parenthetically, that this particular point was not unique to the Bay Area, but in one way or another applied to most of the metropolitan transportation planning programs. These study programs were funded basically from three major sources: (1) *local*, representing state funds and city and county funds (usually from the dues collected by the local Council of Governments (COGs); (2) Department of Housing and Urban Development (HUD) *701 metropolitan planning funds* (usually used to match the local city- and county-collected COG funds); and (3) Federal Highway Administration or Bureau of Public Roads (BPR) *1½ percent funds*, which also include state money, since the state put up its funds and then was reimbursed for most of them during the program period.

This arrangement, created explicit to meet the intent of coordinated, comprehensive, and cooperative regional and multimodel transportation planning, worked more often than not to the contrary. HUD and local funds were used to acquire staff needed for the work, along with staff people who were provided by the state highway department as their in-kind contribution. Fitting these diverse staff elements together was difficult at best.

Instead of a central coordinated staff, a bifurcated one tended to develop, particularly since in most cases the state–FHWA monies were three times the HUD–local impact. Since the state–FHWA participation was primarily in-kind staff from the highway department (this preceded the departments of transportation that are now being created by many states), the modal imbalance was felt, and the transit planners, particularly, felt left out. This arrangement also made it awkward to develop and fill special job specifications.

When you add to this situation the problems inherent in developing computer models, the assembly of a suitable data base, and the assimilation of data and prediction of viable results, suitable for transportation planning, then BATSC and many of the regional planning studies have come of age. The only problem was that BATSC failed to produce a transportation plan that was understood and accepted by the officials and citizens of the region. At best, there was a feeling that the state highway and freeway plan, which had existed previously, had been given a clean bill of health. The transit element was still seemingly an issue, and the problem of how transportation and land-use planning were related was still hazy. To further complicate this situation, the BATSC Commission went out of existence; its 5 years were up. The commission completed its report as best it could and recommended that a continuing, official regional transportation planning agency be created, and, although a bill to create a Metropolitan Transportation Commission was introduced, it failed to pass the 1969 session of the legislature.

In the meantime, to assure that federal aid was not cut off, in 1969 an *ad hoc* Regional Transportation Planning Committee (RTPC) was created by a memorandum of understanding between ABAG and the Business and Transportation Agency of the state. This committee carried with it the same funding, staffing, and administrative problems as BATSC, but was weaker. Subsequently, the RTPC attempted to relate the transportation planning program to ABAG's new regional plan, which was adopted in July 1970. As the Urban Mass Transportation Administration (UMTA) programs began to provide increasing funds for transit, RTPC stepped up its activity to bring the transit agencies into the transportation planning game as equal participants. Its real contribution was developing the basis for this continuing coordination, which ultimately led to the regions eligibility for two thirds, rather than only 50 percent, funding for capital grants.

Legislation establishing the Metropolitan Transportation Commission (MTC) was introduced into the legislature again and, to the surprise of many in the Bay Area, was adopted in September 1970, to become effective in November. While it was a statutory agency, it still had some problems in providing the answer to the Bay Area's transportation planning problems. First, the legislation provided no source of funding—only a hunting license. Secondly, it did not clarify the role between MTC and the regional planning agency.

To remedy the *first* problem, MTC, once it was appointed, had to begin a search for funding, establishing the policy that it would retain its own objective staff to develop the Regional Transportation Plan by June 30, 1973, as mandated by the legislation. It further stated that its work program would be oriented toward the preparation of a balanced multimodal transport system. This policy represented a change in the funding approaches of BATSC and RTPC. In a sense, MTC asked the state and FHWA to put cash into the pot to support overall staff. UMTA and other sources were approached on the same basis. UMTA and limited state funds were acquired, and the planned program was initiated. After long negotiation, the state committed its share of the state–FHWA funding as a part of the unified work program. In this case, MTC signed a memorandum of understanding to ensure that the planning requirements be met within the MTC work program.

To solve the *second* problem—the relationship to the regional planning function—MTC also signed a memorandum of understanding with ABAG in July 1971 to ensure that transportation planning would be related to the land-use and travel models. The agreement also delegates to MTC the review of transportation projects under Office of Management and Budget Circular A-95 relating to federal grants.

The commission is moving toward a June 30 completion date for its plan, which is not to be just a map depicting transit lines and freeways. More importantly, it must include a 10-year capital improvement program and a financial plan indicating the sources of funding and recommendations for innovative ways of securing new funding and the development of spending priorities for the monies that become available.

A few words are in order as to the nature of this plan. We feel that the approach that is being taken is an important move away from the traditional transportation planning efforts. We are calling the plan an "issue-oriented" plan. Instead of proposing a number of alternative transportation plans that relate to the overall regional plan, we are saying that the basic plan is determined by the available transit and highway facilities. MTC must then decide—based on the staff work presented— what elements the final plan will include, i.e., will there be a southern crossing of the bay, will there be a BART extension to Livermore or a bus solution, etc. The staff is attempting to present these issues and the assumptions behind them to MTC to set the policy direction. The commission meets twice monthly, with the public invited to listen and participate as it wrestles with these issues. Finally, there will be a structured mechanism for review and amendment of the plan following the same approach.

This Regional Transportation Plan, once adopted, carries some clout. No transit extension, no freeway, no transbay crossing may be built that is not in the plan. New legislation was recently signed into law—the Transit Development Act of 1971—that places gasoline under the sales tax. This tax creates a public transit fund for the nine Bay Area counties

and designates that M TC shall allocate the funds based on the plan, thus
ensuring a more coordinated public transit system in the Bay Area.

This is where transportation planning for the Bay Area is today. Until
we have found solutions to the complex institutional, intergovernmental,
multijurisdictional cross currents that impact our metropolitan area governments, which, of course, affect their ability to develop coherent financial programs, we will continue to see the same slow progress in the implementation of more innovative regional transportation solutions.

For example, in the Bay Area we have the three-county B A R T District, a two-county (and only parts of these two counties) Alemeda-
Contra Costa (A C) Transit District, a two-county service area within
the six-county Golden Gate Bridge and Highway Transportation District
(three of the counties are outside the region), and the San Francisco
Municipal Railway, which is entirely within that city–county. All are
dependent on jurisdictional and funding relationships that make it very
difficult to operate in a coordinated manner, much less enter into a
program that might be able to develop and introduce some more innovative systemwide approaches.

In contrast, highway-system construction over a period of time has
been very effective because of the basically simple institutional system
Thomas McDonald, the first B P R administrator, put together in 1916
to simplify governmental decision and create the funding mechanism.
The federal–state partnership is characterized by a passthrough of federal funds to the state construction authority requiring only minimal
processing. It was a tremendously innovative program. Ironically, this
ability to build only highways quickly and effectively has led to the
present public dissatisfaction with the national highway program. It is
unfortunate that a regional planning program with a mandate for multimodal planning and construction was not the charge to B P R at that
time.

Another reason that we have not seen rapid innovative steps to improve metropolitan transportation is that monies to be invested are
made available, in most instances, by locally elected officials, in some
cases sitting as members of regional bodies. These officials tend to become confused by the varying ways in which glamorous new concepts
are presented to them and what these concepts might mean to their
constituency. They do not know how to judge the viability, the stage
of development (experimental or operational) or the availability of
these new concepts. In addition, they are, quite naturally, hesitant to
support advanced concepts in transportation, due to the inherent risks
involved. For example, B A R T's basic design was generally conventional,
with several innovative concepts that had to be tested. Yet these officials

have observed the problems the suppliers have in implementing these innovative concepts. When industry talks to these officials, there is too much emphasis on new hardware proposals without equal concern for ways to incorporate the new technology.

In closing, lest I paint too dark a picture, let me say that there are many indicators that point to a rosier future. All levels of government—federal, state, regional, and local—should, within a reasonable time, start to bring innovative institutional approaches into existence in our urban areas. At the federal level there is increased funding for new hardware and systems. Equally important is an indication of federal willingness to urge the strengthening of state, regional, and local institutions that can implement such programs. The state, through the creation of an increasing number of departments of transportation that demonstrate concern for transit, airports, and goods movement, as well as highways, is doing much to create a better environment for new approaches and solutions. Finally, at the local level, cities and counties in increasing numbers are recognizing the efficiency of a regional approach, since their problems, and solutions often go beyond local borders. Also, regional agencies such as the Metropolitan Transportation Commission in the Bay Area, with its increased power, should be increasingly responsible for aiding in the development of innovative programs.

Walter A. Scheiber

MEETING URBAN TRANSPORTATION DEMANDS: PROBLEMS AND PROGRESS IN THE WASHINGTON METROPOLITAN AREA

In today's society, impediments to urban transportation progress and an improved quality of life have a habit of changing with some degree of rapidity. Five years ago the list I would have provided would have been a very different one. Perhaps our best course of action is to direct our primary attention to the "here-and-now problems" and at the same time try to anticipate new impediments that may occur and affect our daily lives.

Each urban area has its own unique characteristics that influence its approach to impediments to urban transportation progress. The Washington area contains about 2,400 square miles and includes not only the District of Columbia but portions of Virginia and Maryland as well. Transportation problems involving the whole area, therefore, may require legislative approval by two state legislatures, the Congress of the United States, and, frequently, various of the 15 major counties and cities within our region.

In addition to this governmental hodgepodge, we are, of course, subject to the traditional problems that are associated with life in any fast-growing urban area anywhere in the country.

One of the major factors in the development of our region has been an immense increase in population over the past two decades: From a population base of slightly more than one million people in 1950, our area grew to slightly more than two million in 1960 and now has passed three million.

In order to deal with this growth, our area's local governments' operating budgets have increased by more than 80 percent in the past 4 years, and within the past decade, 50,000 acres of raw land have been converted to urban uses.

These are just a few of the indicators of our area's recent dramatic growth. In an effort to deal with both the traditional and the special problems of this kind of rapid growth and change, the local governments in the Washington area, in 1957, joined together to form the organization with which I am associated, the Metropolitan Washington Council of Governments. COG, as it is called, is one of about 200 voluntary, multipurpose areawide associations of local elected officials in urban areas throughout the United States. Most of these organizations are concerned with, among other things, alleviating the regional transportation problems that cross the municipal boundaries of their urban communities. Like a good many other COG's, ours coordinates a wide variety of interjurisdictional and areawide programs, not only in the field of transportation, but in such fields as community development, health and environmental protection, human resource problems, and public safety. In addition to acting as a vehicle for coordination, COG provides land-use, transportation, and comprehensive planning studies for metropolitan Washington. Thus, we have under one umbrella a variety of areawide activities, which considerably reduces the problems of institutional interaction and provides further opportunities for coordination. Basically, we offer a forum for the development of areawide policy and plans, a mechanism for improved intergovernmental cooperation and coordination, and a voice for the local governments of our metropolitan region.

Our organization is funded jointly by our local governments and various state agencies, including the two states and the District of Columbia highway departments and through a variety of federal grants and contracts, at an annual level of approximately $4 million. This budget supports a multidisciplinary staff of about 160 people, half of whom are professionals and of whom about 30 or 35 concern themselves primarily with transportation matters.

Regional transportation planning for our area was initiated with the establishment of the National Capital Region Transportation Planning Board (TPB) in July 1965. This new organization was formed in order to comply with the requirements of the Federal Aid Highway Act of 1962 and was initially independent of the Council of Governments. In 1966, however, both organizations adopted resolutions associating the TPB with the COG and bringing staffing responsibilities for the transportation process under the COG.

The resolution that was jointly adopted provided that the TPB would serve as COG's transportation policy arm and would advise on all matters concerning transportation or transportation-related items within the context of COG's comprehensive planning program. At the same time, however, the TPB itself retained the responsibility for developing and maintaining a regional transportational planning process that would meet the requirements of the Federal Aid Highway Act of 1962. The most important aspect of this affiliation was the establishment of a cooperative working relationship between the two organizations without changing the basic responsibilities of the TPB, which was required to carry out its legislative mandate under the Highway Act. With this kind of close association of policy and technical levels, we have been able to achieve substantial assurance that urban transportation planning programs in the Washington area are brought together with a variety of other functional planning programs as part of a total and relatively comprehensive planning effort. Since both COG and the TPB are made up predominantly of local government representatives, comprehensive transportation planning and comprehensive regional planning are both, to a large extent, politically responsive to the community, acting through its elected officials. This differentiates our program from transportation planning in other areas.

Major policy decisions on highways and mass transit in Washington have a way of reverberating throughout the country. As a result, powerful political and lobbying forces are focused on proposed transportation improvements here to an unusual extent, and each member of the Congress brings the views of his constituents and, of course, his personal feelings to bear on transportation decisions for this city. The President, too, is concerned with the effect of transportation decisions made here, and he has repeatedly expressed his desire to see the transportation system within our community serve as a national and international model.

In addition to the personal interest of both the White House and Secretary Volpe in our regional transportation problems, we also feel the full weight of the executive, legislative, and, more recently, the judicial branches of the federal establishment, as indicated by the recent court decisions regarding the construction of the Three Sisters Bridge over the Potomac and portions of Interstate-66 in Northern Virginia.

Of course, this interest has provided us with some unique opportunities to take advantage of available federal grant programs to test and demonstrate innovative and action-oriented transportation improvements: a two-way express bus program, providing rush-hour service for both inner-city residents and suburbanites; express buses operating on reserved middle lanes of a major interstate highway in Northern Virginia; new types of hardware—not only vehicles but bus shelters—in connection with an Urban Corridor Demonstration Program that we are conducting here.

Although these grant programs have strengthened our transportation planning process by attracting and maintaining the interest and the involvement of the many local elected officials who are participating in the process, we are, nonetheless, faced with the complex and politically sensitive problems of local versus federal roles, responsibilities, and decision-making powers. This is a dilemma that is not peculiar to Washington but perhaps is felt more keenly here than in other areas.

Another problem with which we must deal is the reconciliation of center-city and suburban goals and objectives. In the District of Columbia the most pressing needs are for adequate housing and for an economic revitalization of the core city. Major surburban concerns, on the other hand, relate primarily to the control of growth and to the provision of adequate transportation. There is an obvious need to reconcile these divergent concerns. One of the greatest challenges of metropolitan organizations, such as the COG, is to identify tradeoffs between center-city and suburban needs that are compatible with overall regional goals and objectives.

Another barrier to metropolitan progress is the diffusion of responsibilities at all levels of government. Even within federal departments, different program offices have different policies, procedures, and guidelines, and all federal departments and agencies are struggling with such new factors as the National Environmental Policy Act and its requirements for environmental impact statements, criteria, and standards. Clearly, improved coordination and simplification of federal requirements would help greatly to reduce impediments to progress.

Considerable diffusion of responsibilities also exists at the state, local, and regional levels. Broad general mandates and descriptions of responsibilities at these levels too frequently prompt these agencies to spend more time protecting their respective jurisdictions and arguing about who is in charge of what than in addressing the real-world problems for which they are responsible. Surely progress would be facilitated if each agency more clearly defined its responsibilities and developed specific cooperative working relationships with other agencies, particularly in the field of transportation planning.

Transportation facilities are not and never have been ends in themselves. They are a means of serving travel demands generated by the distribution of population and land-use activities. Land development has generated travel demand, which is served by transportation facilities; these facilities, in turn, influence land development, which generates new travel demands, requiring additional facilities, and so on.

However, with the rapid change in human values and environmental concerns over the past several years, it has become obvious that we can no longer afford an unlimited supply of new transportation facilities to meet growing urban travel demands and that other alternatives must be considered such as reduction of travel or better utilization of existing facilities.

In addition, the transportation implications of a proposed zoning and rezoning of an area must be understood in terms of additional transportation facility costs and potential environmental impact before the zoning decision is made. Decision makers should either refuse the requested zoning because of the possible adverse effects or should be prepared, at the time of the zoning, to commit themselves to the necessary transportation facilities. State and local elected officials, with the support of their land-use and transportation planners, must improve their understanding of the interaction between transportation and land use and as well as their ability to control and restrain land development patterns that create adverse transportation impacts. Otherwise, decisions on transportation and particularly highway proposals that affect the environment will become increasingly controversial and difficult to implement.

Now to accentuate the positive. From our Washington perspective, there are a number of encouraging developments on the transportation front. Secretary of Transportation Volpe inaugurated a program of intermodal planning in the field last August. This has led to establishment of a multimodal task force that is attempting to provide more coordination than ever before at the working level toward the reduction of our national and regional transportation problems. A unified transportation planning program has resulted in the preparation of a single annual planning program of work for the area. Comprehensive short-term transportation capital improvement programs, consistent with long-range development goals, have been prepared. Joint funding of comprehensive planning, including transportation planning by the modal administrations, is now a reality—and a very welcome reality.

Another encouraging development is the emphasis being placed by the Departments of Transportation (DOT) and Housing and Urban Development (HUD) on consistent criteria for certification of areas eligible for planning and implementation programs. This should streamline the development of a uniform transportation certification system meeting both DOT and HUD policies and standards.

There are also signs of improved coordination at the state, regional, and local levels. Much credit is due the Urban Mass Transportation Administration (UMTA) for fostering and encouraging clear definitions of agency roles and responsibilities as a condition for transportation technical study grants. As a result, for example, COG and the Washington Metropolitan Area Transit Authority, the regional agency responsible for the construction and operation of our METRO rapid-rail system, have adopted a written policy statement on their respective roles in transit planning. The statement is specific in identifying each agency's own long-range and short-range transit planning responsibilities, and it has served as a basis for strong cooperative working relationships in addressing the area's transportation needs.

Under a technical studies grant from UMTA, COG is now coordinating the preparation of a $4.7 million, 33-month unified, comprehensive, short-range transit development program for the Washington area. Eleven agencies with transportation planning and implementation responsibilities, including some whose primary responsibilities may be in both land use and in transit, are participating in this study.

As the grant recipient on behalf of all the participating agencies, COG is responsible for overall program coordination. Each agency, on the other hand, is responsible for the direction, management, and conduct of its respective project activities. We are tremendously pleased with the response of these agencies, and we hope that this program will set a pattern for future efforts in this and other areas as well.

We are also making progress, we think, in improving center-city–suburban relationships. For example, under a grant from UMTA, we have developed a successful two-way express-bus demonstration project, much of which has been taken over by private transit firms. The project has provided relatively inexpensive transportation to suburban jobs for center-city residents and quick return service for suburbanites who work downtown.

We have negotiated a series of mutual assistance arrangements in various fields, such as public safety, that have been of direct benefit to both our center-city and our suburban governments.

Most recently we have completed negotiations on the implementation of a "fair-share" housing formula, by which subsidized low- and moderate-cost housing will be allocated equitably throughout Metropolitan Washington so that the central city will not have to carry the entire burden of this kind of housing. Secretary Romney acknowledged this achievement by allotting to our area a bonus of subsidized housing units for the current year, some 40 percent higher than that for Fiscal Year 1972.

These encouraging developments are indicators that our center-city and our suburban officials are learning to work cooperatively and effectively together toward common goals.

Implementation of these programs, of course, depends on the participation, understanding and commitment, of the decision makers. As a staff, we strive to gain the interest and the participation of our local officials in our planning programs. Special projects, we think, contribute heavily to the participation and understanding of the decision makers, and we have made a special effort to build these types of projects, which provide officials with the opportunity to participate in nonplanning programs and studies, into the planning framework. We frequently find that these programs are easier to understand, more vivid, and more interesting to local officials, and by involving them in projects of this type, we are able to help them educate themselves in the techniques and the arts of planning, in planning issues, and ultimately in uniting the short and long-term goals. Special projects have fostered an awareness of the planning process as well as of the TPB's capacity and potential to assist in solving regional and local transportation problems. They have led to a working understanding of data and findings and have helped local officials provide sound policy leadership. Moreover these projects have provided publicity to insure that the constituents of our local officials—our citizens—know of these efforts and begin to understand their implications.

One of the most successful action projects is the Shirley Highway Express Bus Demonstration Project. This work began through COG in 1968, with a study to determine the potential for using one of the reversible lanes on Shirley Highway in northern Virginia for express buses on an exclusive or preferential basis. The contract was awarded by DOT to the COG because of the regional character of the project and because of its multimodal implications; it involved not only automobiles and buses but also future connections to our METRO rapid-rail system. A steering committee was established that included representatives of the Highway Department, the Regional Transit Commission and Authority, private bus companies, and DOT itself. The steering committee functioned as a special committee of the TPB and reported regularly to the board in order to keep the steering committee's efforts within the framework of the total planning process.

The Shirley Highway Project has served as a powerful magnet in drawing local elected officials, and particularly those in northern Virginia, into deliberations. They were among the first to suggest that the Shirley Highway experience be applied on other highways. The use of separate bus roadways has also been suggested. The influence on the Shirley Highway Project is already being felt in the consideration of alternative long-range transportation networks for our area. The project, we think, is an outstanding example of how experience from a short-range activity can begin to shape long-range decisions.

I believe that the future will bring to us not only an increase in this kind of integration of short- and long-range activity, but a growing determination at all levels to improve working relationships and to simplify and cut through institutional and administrative impediments to progress. Over the next few years this determination to produce innovative, concerted attacks on transportation problems on an areawide scale will have progressed to such an extent that the word "comprehensive"—a much misused word—will take on a more positive meaning.

I see encouraging achievements through more and more of our transportation planning agencies, such as those described by other symposium speakers, and, I hope, through our own topnotch Transportation Planning Department in COG, under its director, Al Grant, and its deputy director, George Wickstrom. And I see professional administrators, planners, and engineers increasingly adopting broader viewpoints, more flexible attitudes, and concerns for planning and implementation in the real political world.

This combination can work; it has got to be made to work. We simply have no choice. On the largest question of all, whether planning can be effective, there are, frankly, no transportation alternatives.

DISCUSSION OF ADDRESSES BY PAUL C. WATT AND WALTER A. SCHEIBER

BERRY: I feel that successful metropolitan area transportation-systems development can best be achieved through planning and implementing combined land-use and transportation plans, rather than through efforts in transportation alone or land use alone. An essential feature in the implementation, in my opinion, would be for land-use planners and the others in other metropolitan agencies to try together to develop transportation corridors in some of these outlying growth areas. These corridors could then be protected from development until needed for transportation, whether by highway, transit pneumatic tube, or other mode.

If transportation and land-use development are to proceed together, it is apparent that there are some new governmental institutions and enabling legislation—map acts and zoning changes, for instance—that would be needed covering combined transportation and land-use planning. Authority is needed for establishing and protecting transportation corridors, flood plains, recreation areas, and related aspects aimed at achieving a better quality of life. Planning is needed to permit more effective development of suburban areas, perhaps along the lines of Columbia.

The implementation stage should provide, perhaps, pass-through legislation that would give funds directly to metropolitan areas where they have set up a consortium of governments. Such metropolitan institutions are needed to handle the funding problems.

There is consideration at the federal level of a Department of Community Development that may be pushed, depending of course on who is elected President this next year.

My question for the first two speakers is, first, what powers do they now have for combined land-use–transportation planning as compared with those for transportation planning?

Second, do these powers include that of corridor reservation? Finally, are they able to receive funds on a pass-through basis and to portion them out with some autonomy to where they are needed?

WATT: I believe Mr. Scheiber might be in a better position to discuss the first point, land-use and transportation planning, since in Washington they are both together. In the Bay Area we are still struggling to get them together. I think I can say this: There is no group working harder than the Metropolitan Transportation Commission (MTC) to insure that the planning is done in the right place, that is, by the regional planning people, and that transportation planning provide support in determining what the land-use pattern should be.

As to the second point, at the present time in the Bay Area there is really no legal mechanism within either ABAG, or in COG involved in the regional planning, or in the MTC, to purchase land, or to acquire rights-of-way in a corridor. However, the Metropolitan Transportation Commission may well include proposals for legislative changes that would allow the MTC to include this type of acquisition in its implementation of programs.

As to the third point, funding, the MTC has the legislative authority to serve as a pass-through agency and has done a fairly effective job. However, additional authority that would relate to federal funding programs as well might be included in the legislative proposals in the plan.

I am optimistic that, at least on the second two parts of your question, we will be able to do something positive, and I am very hopeful that we will be able to combine the land-use and transportation planning to help solve that institutional problem.

SCHEIBER: I think that with respect to the first part of Professor Berry's question, the laws pertaining to mapping, reservation of land, and so forth may well be on the books in a good many states.

I believe the problems are essentially political and fiscal, rather than legislative. The big question in most communities is not whether there should be a transportation corridor in a given area, but where to put it, how to satisfy the people who will be impacted by its selection, and how to pay for it.

One of the things that elected officials concerned with areawide development are learning is how better to make the political decisions. I think officials and citizens of our region are learning to isolate issues, to involve those people who will be impacted by major decisions of the type implied here, and to go through the give-and-take process that will permit us to alleviate the political aspects of the problem.

When it comes to the financial aspects, I do not have an answer. The reservation of transportation corridors substantially in advance of development nonetheless takes a lot of money, even though the area around it may not be developed. Some communities are enacting land-banking ordinances; some state legislatures are providing this type of state legislation. They are buying up land to the extent that they can for future needs. But this is at best a haphazard process at the present time and still is not fully worked out.

As far as the integration of land-use and transportation planning is concerned, we have tried, and I think with a substantial degree of success in our particular organization, to carry out both of these activities under a common umbrella so that both disciplines impact constantly—and I mean every hour in every day— upon each other. Hopefully, decisions about both land use and transportation will be better for the fact that they are combined in this agency.

With respect to the matter of pass through of funds, I think this is something that increasingly will come to characterize regional organizations such as ours and will strengthen them.

I mentioned the short-range UMTA grant given us, which is passing through us to a large extent to other agencies who are doing detailed planning. You mentioned the consortium idea, that is contained in the Senate version of the Federal Aid Highway Act, by which local governments can get together and create an entity through which to pass funds not only to state highway departments but local governments as well.

The bill now on President Nixon's desk to provide for new legislation concerning water quality also contains an interesting variant on that, with a proposal not only for a regional plan but for a mandatory regional program of implementation. That program must be created cooperatively by agencies working together and will serve as a framework for all grant activities, once the plan and program implementation have been worked out.

These are some of the things which I see.

ROGERS: I see a sort of theme in both Mr. Watt's and Mr. Scheiber's talks, in terms of identification of barriers; I just have a couple of minor points.

I don't know, Mr. Watt, whether California is first at tapping the highway taxes for mass transportation. If so, Maryland is second.

Also, I think one of the aspects behind the talk that Mr. Scheiber gave involves a unique situation. The Washington metropolitan area adjoins the Baltimore metropolitan area, so that the Maryland financial plan for financing its suburban share of the METRO subway system in Washington is also able to fund a comparable subway system for metropolitan Baltimore.

I see land banking, the last point that was made, as really not so much dependent on massive new funding, but as a means of creating the opportunity for this funding, because private developers do bank land and finance out of the appreciating values of that land.

If indeed the legislation is there to permit the reservation of corridors, it should also permit the acquisition, if not of abutting private property, at least of those values created in that property by the public investment in corridors. From this feature, I think, could come a vast new source of revenues to help fill what is now a rather limited purse.

My final points are these. It seems to me that the barriers that have been identified by the first two speakers are essentially these. First, there is the jurisdictional chaos, or balkanization, on the one hand, in terms of geographic areas and, on the other hand, in terms of programs. The shorthand for the geographic situation is "home rule," and the shorthand for the categorical programs is simply the different kinds of hardware.

At the level of the geographic localities, this comes in its most pernicious form in terms of zoning as it relates to property taxes. This is what Jack Paterson, in *Business Week*, calls: "The game of beggar-thy-neighbor." And I think, speaking as an architect, one of the most glaring examples of the categorical program is the Highway Trust Fund, not so much that it isn't necessary to build highways, but that in many states—and one of these is Maryland—the highways are being built for no real purpose any more. If states don't use their share of the fund, some other state will get it. I would view the future of the Highway Trust Fund as part of a community development corridor fund.

The next comment is: Who synthesizes a corridor? Who makes all of the plans; studies all of the impact areas? These questions apply at the level of what I mentioned yesterday as Synthesis I—which is just solving the problem in a physical sense—and at the level of Super Synthesis—which includes the relationship to the society.

These are very important questions. Planners do not synthesize; in my view there is virtually no planning agency, whether it is transportation or land use, that synthesize in a real sense, because they do not program the expenditures.

I see basically four alternatives to solving what I regard as a serious institutional crisis in this country, in order to remove the constraints of the barriers. Two alternatives are too radical to be accepted—one is simply to preserve the present institutions, protect them, wrap the flag around them, and put down the change that threatens them. I don't think that will work. The second alternative is simply to destroy these institutions out of hand; you hear some mighty respectable people saying that. The third alternative, and the one that has worked, is the adaptation of our present institutions. Yet I don't know that this will work today, because the pace and scale of change is so great that even with adaptation we will always be a few laps behind.

I seriously recommend to you the fourth alternative of the parallel-institution concept, the experimental design of new institutions that are comprehensive, that cut across all sorts of jurisdictional lines. Some of these will fail; some will not, even though they may be charged with doing jobs that are now not being done by the old institutions.

Let us see who wins; if the new institutions win, there are fairly graceful lifeboats for those of us—and that includes all of us—who are trapped in the old institutions.

BAUER: I think that Paul Watt's and Walter Scheiber's presentations described somewhat, though perhaps not totally, different approaches that are being taken to solve the transportation problems of two of the largest urban regions of the United States.

I think the presentations illustrate once again that each of our large metropolitan areas is really a unique entity and that each must develop its institutional structure for planning and plan implementation in its own way.

I personally believe that the approach being taken in the Washington area has some important advantages over the approach being taken in the Bay Area, advantages that I think will become more important with the passage of time. These involve the fact that land use and transportation are inextricably interrelated. If progress is to be made toward the solution of both land-use and transportation problems, those problems must be addressed within the framework of a comprehensive planning effort, an effort that really integrates—doesn't just coordinate but really integrates—transportation planning with all other types of functional planning—sewer, water, parking, open space, housing, and so on—with land-use planning.

Consequently it seems to me that transportation planning should not be carried out by special-purpose agencies, such as transportation commissions, but should be carried out by official, comprehensive areawide planning agencies.

I think separating transportation from land-use planning and plan implementation is bad conceptually, as is separating highway from transit or from other forms of transportation planning, and that such separation will, in the long run, defeat the objectives of both the transportation and land-use planning processes.

I would like to ask Paul if he concurs in these observations and, if he does, what the reasons were why an institutional structure that would truly integrate rather than try to coordinate comprehensive transportation planning was not either selected or possible in the Bay Area as opposed, let us say, to the Washington area.

WATT: First, I agree wholeheartedly that we are having to *ad hoc* this relationship. I am not sure that I can completely trace the reasons this has occurred, but part of it gets back to the role of planning.

You will have to forgive me, I guess; I supposedly am a planner, but I think part of the problem has been that planning, particularly at the regional level, has not yet received the stature and the support that it really needs. We all know the place we are today with the COG's. Mr. Scheiber has a very excellent program in the Washington COG, but ABAG's program is not as excellent, even though it is doing the best that it possibly can under some very trying conditions. These are still voluntary institutions.

One county in the Bay Area recently tried to withdraw from the association, but they were pushed back in by the state. I think that indicates that some counties are still not serious about regional planning, and until they are it is very difficult to bring effective implementation into the transportation planning program. As a result, in California, the legislature has created a whole series of single-purpose implementing agencies and, in a sense, has charged them with the responsibility of participating in regional planning, even though collectively we haven't been able to figure a way to do it.

John Knox, for instance, has introduced three bills that would create overall umbrella regional governments, with land-use, transportation, and other planning aspects included as part of it. It has passed one house of the legislature on three occasions and came within two votes of passing in the other.

I think all of this is indicative of the next step in the evolutionary process. ABAG in our area is doing the best job that it can, but the local elected officials didn't create ABAG to be a strong agency; they wanted to be sure that it didn't rock the boat, in some instances. I believe this is a problem we face.

KEMP: Paul Watt mentioned that there are at least four major transit operators working within the area of MTC jurisdiction. I would be interested to learn what, if any, levers the commission has to attempt to encourage things like coordinated schedules, joint fares, through services, and so on.

WATT: Again I have to refer to something that is yet to be tested, but I am very, very hopeful. Within the implementation phase of our planning program we will program the sort of device that you mentioned that will attempt to set up a regional coordinating mechanism.

Our commission chairman takes the position that such a step is needed, but right now it is not there. We have some of the more traditional incentives, I think, for bringing it about right now. As in the Washington COG, we are the pass-through agency for UMTA projects, about 21 in our case, that go out into the local operating communities. We try to relate how BART and AC, BART and MUNI, BART, MUNI and Golden Gate Bridge coordinate, and we—the commission in this case—sit on each of these groups.

UMTA says to them, through us, "No more of our capital facilities monies are going to come until you all are working together, and we see this so-called transit development program coming into being."

We are far from saying that we have an integrated set of routes, headways, fares, this sort of thing, but I think that there is a very healthy attitude developing among these operators in the Bay Area. For the first time they see that their destiny will be much rosier if they work together than if each should try to obtain the maximum amount of whatever is available in the region.

I think the final key is going to be SB-325, the law providing for allocation of sales tax on gasoline money for transit programming, that for the first time provides a substantial source of funds at the local level to match the already available federal funds.

The state bill goes one step further and allows up to 25 percent of these funds to be used for operating subsidies. MTC in this case has to indicate how all of these things tie together before their claims are approved, and that is going to provide a much better program of overall coordination.

TOTTEN: I think we are all aware that planning is important and are all aware of what planning is all about, but my concern is the need for a little more attention on the "how" plan. If we get into the "how" complex, we need a matrix, and since it is an integrated problem we need an integrated matrix.

My question to the panelists is: What are we doing about developing live, real-time integrated interfaces so we can convert the "what" in the plan to the "how" to do it?

SCHEIBER: In our organization we are attempting to develop an automated real-time data base, at least real-time in the sense it is updated at least annually. We started with the collection and synthesis of data concerning land use throughout the Washington area; we are adding other elements to the system, as funding and time permit.

However, I cannot in all honesty say we have a system that fully satisfies our needs, nor a system of the type, I think, which you feel to be appropriate and necessary for a relatively scientific planning process to proceed.

WATT: I would only add to what Mr. Scheiber said. I think we are all trying to put together the right data base, but I hope in our case that we are profiting by BATS's past mistakes in data gathering and in the types of data that are needed.

We are trying to locate our data users, to better determine what they need data for, and to package it in the way that they can use it. Now we are far from a perfect match in this area, but we are aimed in that direction.

BENTLEY: I can't understand how the transportation planning process can ever be properly achieved unless it is integrated with the land-use planning process as well as with the utility or community facilities planning and other programs, so that there is a total planning entity. My comment would also apply to the funding and implementation planning part of the program. My question relates to the suggestion for a land-bank including the reservation of transportation corridors.

Are you not, in attempting to do this, departing somewhat from what we classify as a planning process? Do you not then become more involved in terms of a rigid plan, rather than a planning process, since you are establishing definite corridors through either reservation or land banking and then are moving into the project planning area rather than the planning process?

SCHEIBER: If I understand Mr. Bentley correctly, he raises a basic question that perhaps was implied by Professor Berry, although I did not choose to address it at that point. It seems to me that that is the question of whether transportation is there to serve land used or to cause land uses by its presence in the given area.

Theoretically, we say that transportation is to be the servant of the total community need. However, in reality, if we do not do some advance planning, if we do not delineate some transportation corridors in advance of development, we sentence ourselves to a sprawl throughout our communities that all of us would acknowledge is an undesirable situation. Therefore, I do not see what Mr. Bentley may be implying as an inconsistency in the suggestion that it is necessary to delineate transportation corridors as part of the planning process.

BAUER: I personally feel very strongly that the planning process has to produce plans. It can't just be an endless process. I think that at the regional or metropolitan scale, those plans do have to be of sufficient precision and accuracy to permit the state and local units of government to act to reserve land in advance of need for various essential public facilities and services.

If we don't do that, we will be repeating all of the mistakes of the past. For example, in my own region we believe there is a need for the development of a belt transportation facility; as Professor Berry said, at the present time we see this as a freeway facility, a freeway facility on which some special form of bus rapid-transit would operate. But there is nothing to say that in the far-distant future that could not be some other form of transportation facility.

If the land for that 34 miles of facility is reserved now, there would be about 85 structures displaced, and the land could be acquired at the cost of about $300,000 per mile for the 34 route miles. I contrast that to a piece of urban freeway that is being developed within our region, where the right-of-way costs alone are $9 million per mile, and where there are about 10,000 structures being displaced for that mile of facility.

Unless we carry the plans to a sufficient level of detail and precision to permit this land reservation, I don't think we will have helped in the areawide planning process, either with the state or local units of government.

Milton Pikarsky

CHICAGO PLANNING AND DEVELOPMENT

The impact of transportation on the needs and aspirations of all Americans is incredibly complex when we view it in its broadest involvement of the public. Patterns and style of urban growth; environmental change; economic, social, and recreational stimulus; a share in the grim death and injury statistics from the highways and streets—all of these factors contribute to the broad spectrum of the quality of life across the nation. How well we solve our transportation problems is the key to determining whether our cities will survive and prosper.

The understanding of how public transportation arrived at the desperate straits it is in today and how the attendant delays, inconveniences, disruptions, and congestion have come to threaten the urban economy leads us to consider some of the salient events in contemporary transportation history that have produced the existing imbalance in transportation modes.

The automobile age is generally considered to have begun in 1903, the year of the organization of the Ford Motor Company. By 1916 there were more than 3.6 million registered vehicles, but paved roads were sadly lacking. To meet this deficiency the federal government inaugurated a highway program, on a 50–50 funding basis. In 1956, in what we all can agree has been the initiation of the greatest public works project ever undertaken, Congress passed the Federal Aid Highway Act, which initiated the Federal Interstate Highway System with its 90–10 matching ratio. This federal sharing percentage was decided upon for the pragmatic reason that the 90 percent federal share was the smallest amount capable of involving all 48 states.

A 4-cents-per-gallon gas tax was imposed to pay for these highways to assure a continuous and adequate source of funding. The results have been the rapid construction of many highways that, in turn, encouraged automobile travel and buying thus increasing the Highway Trust Fund, which could only be spent for highway construction.

An unfortunate, but little appreciated, result was the decline in use of public transportation. It is worth noting that until 1926 the revenue passengers on the nation's public transportation facilities increased in direct proportion to the population. By 1926 the ratio of people to registered vehicles was 11 to 1, and since that year, as the ratio declined, the number of public transportation riders has also declined. The one exception was during World War II, when gasoline rationing contributed to an increase in the nation's transit riders.

Today we find that the quality of life in our urban centers is suffering from a variety of ills. Sixty percent of air pollution is caused by the automobile. Urban noise, congestion, and overcrowding are in no small measure attributable to the hundreds of acres of city land utilized for highways and parking lots—land that could be utilized for more desirable social purposes. While it is true that nearly half of the population own automobiles, a full 25 percent of our population lacks access to a car. For these people—especially the poor, the aged, the very young, and the handicapped—adequate public transportation is the only means of contact with the outside world, and in most areas adequate public transportation just does not exist.

What is needed, and what the public seems to want but does not yet adequately support, is a highly coordinated, integrated system of road, rail, and air travel to keep Americans moving and to generate new life in the nation's declining urban centers. Such a system should include links within the city to get people from place to place rapidly and inexpensively, direct service to outlying airports, convenient transportation to suburbs and recreational areas, and fast intercity and interurban links.

The massive technological capability of this nation provides the means for achieving this balanced, responsive transportation system that is so desperately needed. Such a system requires not only the innovation of new techniques and ideas but the optimum utilization of existing equipment and facilities, using a variety of the diverse and many-faceted areas of engineering competence from hardware development to systems analysis concepts.

Figures 1 and 2 show a particularly successful innovation that was pioneered in Chicago: the placing of rail transit in the expressway median strip. The first expressway rapid transit in service was initiated on the Eisenhower Expressway, and, because of the success of this rapid transit

FIGURE 1　Rapid transit in median strip of the Eisenhower Expressway.

FIGURE 2   Traffic exodus on the Dan Ryan Expressway.

line, the concept was used in the construction of both the Dan Ryan
and Kennedy expressways, where one fourth of the Kennedy expressway
extension is in subway. The rail service is an addition to the conventional
subway system and the famous elevated (Figure 3) from which the central business district, The Loop, is named. In all, the Chicago Transit
Authority (CTA) operates over 1,200 rapid-transit cars on approximately
90 miles of subway, elevated, and surface rights-of-way.

A unique characteristic of CTA rapid-transit service is that most lines
are of an "express" nature. Under this plan, stations with heavy traffic
are designated "AB" stations; more lightly used stations are successively
designated "A" or "B" stations. On one line, the Kennedy extension,
the plan has resulted in doubling the average distance between stops and
decreasing travel time 20 percent.

This pseudo-express service operates during the day and through the
evening rush hour. After 7 p.m., in the interests of security, all four and
six-car trains are cut to two cars, and all trains stop at all stations. This
increases security in essentially three ways: First, this arrangement
makes for shorter headway between stations; second, more people are
in each car; and third, each car now contains a CTA trainman, since all
trains normally carry two transit personnel. This service is relatively new,
and no data are yet available as to its effect as a crime deterrent. It is

FIGURE 3 A portion of the Chicago elevated system for which The Loop is named.

FIGURE 4   Terminal located within median strip, the Dan Ryan 95th Street Station.

believed, however, that such steps will prove effective, because previous crime rates were highest in those cars that contained no trainman, carried few passengers, and occurred between stops having trains with largest headway.

In addition to these specific alterations, a total analysis of the whole transit operation as it relates to security is being carried out under a federally funded program. Hopefully, this study grant will define methods and techniques for effectively increasing transit security and will lead to funding for recommended techniques.

To encourage use of rapid-transit lines, extensive thought and effort have been directed toward the development of convenient and efficient intermodal transfer facilities. One unique and successful concept has involved the placing of interface terminals above the rail right-of-way, within the air rights of the median strip (Figure 4). With the lower level serving as the loading platform for the transit car, and the upper level bridging across to the surface streets, the passengers at some stations are able to transfer to connecting bus service without leaving the median terminal building. In the median terminal at Jefferson Park on the Kennedy Expressway, a pedestrian bridge connects by escalators to a suburban railway station and to a bus loading area that offers a cano-

FIGURE 5　Common loading bay, Jefferson Park Terminal, Kennedy Expressway.

pied, open plaza (Figure 5); the transit terminals house bus ticket offices and rental areas for commercial retail enterprises.

A variety of patron conveniences are incorporated in most terminal designs, including direct-access passageways with escalators (Figure 6), infrared heaters, translucent canopied interchange areas, and common loading bays that connect with feeder-bus service. High illumination and the absence of obstructing columns add to visual appearance and insure safety and security (Figure 7). Park-and-ride facilities and common loading bays are included at most terminals.

The addition of a new terminal complex helps generate new business in its immediate neighborhood. For example, within a few months after the Jefferson Terminal opened on the Kennedy Expressway, three new restaurants opened, and a number of business establishments in the adjacent area were extensively refurbished. This pattern of stimulating business development is typical of areas with improved transportation service.

Another technique that has also worked well in Chicago is the use of the bus system to complement the rapid transit lines. Chicago, like so many cities built on level terrain in the early 1800s, is platted on a rectangular grid system. Buses, following this street pattern, often ran parallel routes, sometimes duplicating portions of the rapid-transit service.

FIGURE 6   Northwest passage connecting suburban railway with city service.

A type of systems analysis was carried out to rearrange these routes to avoid duplication with rapid-transit lines and, more important, to develop a feeder-bus system for the rapid-transit stations. In this way the rapid-transit terminals become intermodal exchange points with the bus system, which, in turn, forms a neighborhood-orientated radial network converging on the rapid-transit terminals.

An immediate result of this newly formed "feeder" network service was an increase in new ridership of 26,000 per day with 140,000 riders changing their riding habits through new transfer issues and shortening their length-of-ride time. This last point is an important one, since it is known that the greatest source of rider loss occurs on long bus rides across town. By offering public transit patrons a convenient opportunity to transfer to the rapid-transit system, riders that otherwise would have been lost to the automobile have been won over to the public transit system.

All but 12 of the city's 135 bus routes pass within a block of a rapid-transit terminal, with approximately 25 percent of all buses converging directly on transit terminals. Less than 10 percent of the total number of bus lines are completely independent of rapid transit and in some cases, such as the Archer Avenue route, provide concentrated service in the absence of rapid transit. In all, the CTA operates a total of 2,700 buses over 2,000 miles of city and suburban streets; 99 percent of all Chicago residents live within 3/8 of a mile of rapid-transit or bus service.

Although the bus is a highly flexible vehicle, not bound to rails, it must compete on the street with the automobile; as more automobiles enter the streets, less roadway space is available for the bus. The smaller, more maneuverable automobile is most often the winner of this unequal competition. Yet the bus is a far more efficient user of roadway space. At average load factors, the bus takes up only 6 feet per passenger. If it were not for the automobile in its path (Figure 8), the bus could move passengers with speed, comfort, and economy over a smaller highway network and at a much lower total systems cost. In rush hour, which is the time when our existing highway system is most seriously overtaxed, these load factors are even more favorably tilted toward the bus.

To reduce traffic congestion and encourage use of high-capacity bus transit, several methods of preferential treatment for buses have been implemented in Chicago. Our efforts have been directed toward increasing the speed, convenience, and dependability of service. Two types of exclusive lane use are in operation: a "bus-only" lane located in the center of one-way, downtown, heavily utilized Washington Street (Figure 9) and two "reverse-only" lanes used at the Union and Northwestern

FIGURE 7   High illumination and removal of obstructions—free passage Logan Square Subway Station.

FIGURE 8   Midmorning congestion on Clark Street.

FIGURE 9   Exclusive bus-only lane on downtown Washington Street.

FIGURE 10   Exclusive reverse bus lane permitting passengers to exit at train loading platform.

railroad stations (Figure 10). The reverse lane gives the bus passenger the added convenience of direct access to the train platform, while the automobile passengers must exit from their cars on the opposite side of the street.

While the extent of usage of these preferential services is too small to have any great impact on the overall service, studies have shown that the localized time saving is substantial, depending on the time of day. Comparing travel times on two adjacent and similar streets for a trip across The Loop, the bus-only lanes have a 50 percent advantage in the early morning hours before 9 a.m., taking approximately 5 minutes as compared with 7 minutes on a conventional street over a timed area. However, in the afternoon, from 2 to 6 p.m., the bus-only lane ride takes just 6½ minutes, compared with 15 minutes in conventional traffic, giving the bus-only system an advantage of more than twice that over conventional traffic.

Another interesting factor now under study is the relationship of the bus stop–shelter location to ridership. Traditionally, bus riders seek protection in doorways and under canopies, thereby making use of the natural protection offered by buildings. As traffic on a street increases and commercial land values also increase, the buildings at busy intersections are frequently torn down and replaced by service stations, parking lots, or franchised drive-in establishments, just at the place where the bus stops. These offer no natural protection and expose the transit rider to the additional hazards of cars driving in and out. A solution to this problem involves the recognition that changes in land use can directly affect transit ridership and therefore urban traffic patterns. When natural patron shelters are destroyed by a change in land use, the new tenant should be required to provide an acceptable substitute. The entire question of bus shelters is in need of serious study and consideration, particularly with regard to its long-term effects on commuter patterns.

Generally speaking, the greatest single stimulus to travel in any form is fare reduction. Yet the hope of stabilizing fares to stimulate transit ridership and thereby decrease traffic congestion and pollution rests primarily on whether operating assistance is to be provided by the federal government. At the present time, most urban transit authorities have sizable operating deficits and cannot pay operating expenses out of the fare box. The last time the CTA balanced income with expenses was in 1962, when salaries of personnel accounted for only 62 percent of the income. Today, with inflationary pressures on salaries not reflected in increased fares, salaries consume 82 percent of the fare col-

FIGURE 11   Skokie Swift, a two-station commuter shuttle developed as a pilot project under a federally funded demonstration grant.

lection, and the projected operating deficit for the CTA this year is $21 million.

In order to improve transit service without attendant fare increases, the Department of Transportation provides demonstration grants as a means of encouraging new and innovative concepts in transportation service. Presumably, this federally funded demonstration grant should be ideally suited for finding solutions to our most challenging problems. However, one of the major drawbacks to these grants is that support is limited to the initial grant phase, typically 1 year. If the service demonstrated is not wholly self-supporting within this time period, the transit system operator has the choice of continuing service at a deficit or withdrawing service. Since every new service attracts some riders, a later withdrawal of this service imposes some hardships and gives rise to resentment by those affected. Consequently, the CTA and most public carriers only consider demonstration grants that are bound to succeed and avoid those demonstration projects that may fail. Both of the CTA demonstration grants—the only two applied for—fall into this safe category: the Skokie Swift rapid-transit line and the O'Hare Airport express bus.

The purpose of the Skokie Swift (Figure 11) was to develop and test a high-speed, two-station, commuter shuttle rapid-transit line. It runs on a 5-mile portion of an abandoned interurban railway through a light population density suburban area. The service pays its own way and has been continued, serving 8,000 passenger rides per weekday. Park-and-ride facilities and connecting suburban and Greyhound Bus loading zones are provided at the Skokie Terminal.

The O'Hare Airport express bus, operating between O'Hare International Airport and the Jefferson Park Terminal, shows how one mode can interrelate with several others. The express bus that operates on a 24-hour basis, 7 days a week can be reached by rapid transit, bus, automobile, and commuter railroad patrons, thus giving needed service to O'Hare International Airport for workers and travelers alike.

Since the inception of this service, the average number of passenger trips per day has increased gradually and is currently about 1,300. Within the airport, buses make stops at the various airline entrances to the passenger terminal buildings and also serve the cargo area east of the terminal buildings. The express route is served by special air-conditioned buses that are capable of maintaining highway speeds while operating nonstop on the Kennedy Expressway for a 15-minute running time to or from the airport.

Yet the Skokie Swift and O'Hare shuttle would not have been initiated had it not been expected that the service would pay its own way. It is unfortunate that truly innovative concepts cannot be examined without pragmatically anticipating the negative public opinion that would accompany an unsuccessful demonstration.

Given our tax system, only the federal government has sufficient revenue to undertake major projects of the type described here. Consequently, anyone deeply involved with mass transit today necessarily becomes equally deeply involved with the federal government and the transportation-grant process. He soon finds himself contending with a great variety of requirements and guidelines, assembling statistical data to meet specified criteria, and coping with the extensive matrix of agencies and officers that must be coordinated for a successful application.

For a major metropolitan area simply to accumulate the data needed to fulfill the grant application requirements sometimes takes nearly as much effort as the proposed work. According to most grant requirements, the project description must give details of each facility and accompanying equipment to be used. Each major item of the project must be isolated, explained in engineering terminology, and illustrated to show how it relates to the overall concept of the project. This must be accompanied by a detailed cost analysis of the various alternatives illustrating the most optimum choice, together with a detailed schedule. All of these tasks require highly skilled, professional engineering time. In this respect, a large city has an advantage because such professional skills are usually on the staff; in small communities, consultants must be hired. In either case the task is expensive, and where the grant request is small, the cost of processing a grant application occasionally deters a small community from pursuing desperately needed funding assistance.

Most projects proposed are of sufficient magnitude to require a comprehensive mass-transit study, involving social, economic, and environmental impacts, project benefits, preliminary engineering to confirm feasibility, and benefit–cost ratios. This undertaking not only adds significantly to the cost, but introduces large delay times and can absorb more time than the proposed project. It occasionally contributes to the abandonment of the grant application.

The United States Office of Management and Budget's A-95 Regulation relating to mandatory clearinghouse reviews is administratively required and constitutes another major delay and expense. In most areas, this review must be carried out by both state and regional agencies. At times, the examining criteria of one reviewing agency differs from another so significantly as to be basically incompatible. It took the city of Chicago considerable time and effort to persuade the state of Illinois, which has a competent, experienced, cooperative, and professionally able staff, to use the same criteria as the federal government in evaluating metropolitan area project grant applications. It should not be necessary to elaborate on how much additional time and effort would be expended in processing applications when there is no common ground for evaluation.

Another frustrating source of delay is the trend to let purely local disputes rise to the federal level for resolution. In any comprehensive transit program—particularly one that involves innovative change—it is to be expected that conflicts and unforeseen difficulties will arise. Any significant modification in the operation of an urban transit authority may effect commuting patterns in suburban and rural regions. Such changes could conceivably curtail or severely reduce ridership volume and fare collections of private operators, causing them to reduce their overall employment ratio and resulting in a displacement of transit carrier employees. Such matters are of legitimate federal concern. Yet such problems can clearly be resolved within the framework of the regional transportation planning agencies that include adequate representation of all governmental units and both private and public carriers. Concurrence by such planning agencies should be sufficient evidence of compliance with the requirements pertaining to the interests of all concerned. The existence of a regional agency or consortium of local agencies with specific authority and responsibility should preempt federal involvement in purely local matters.

Much is said these days about our nation becoming a government of advocacy. It is argued that when priorities and carefully defined commitments are not fully spelled out, an indecisive drift may set in and accomplishments decline. Hence the tendency to set priorities at the federal level to "get things moving." But the commitment and priority setting at the federal level should be consistent with the federal role. A commitment to rebalance transportation modes giving increased emphasis to public transit and giving priority to fund public transit programs promptly without impoundment of funds and similar delaying actions are examples of federal responsibilities. The setting of local priorities—which projects should be funded over others and which needs should be considered first—should be a purely local matter. Let us advocate "Home Rule" philosophy for resolution of local matters and work to distinguish between those concerns that are purely local and those properly belonging to the federal sphere.

To many scientists and engineers, these legislative and administrative considerations may seem arid subjects, more the province of dull clerks and stodgy mathematicians. Yet legislative, budgeting, and governmental administrative processes deal with the basic purposes of men, and ultimately with the course the nation will take. If the engineering community is to make the contributions of which it is capable, and if our purposes as professionals in our respective fields are to be realized, we must enter into the dialogue of legislative and administrative matters.

We have made tremendous progress in redirecting our national transportation policies during the last 2 years, progress that is daily being accelerated through the close cooperation of professionals working together in science, engineering, and government. Much is to the credit of Secretary Volpe and his able staff who have so aggressively pursued the legislative and administrative changes essential to increase the pace of mass transit development.

How well we, as working professionals in our respective fields, respond to these dynamic challenges and the decisions we make, will influence the quality of life for future generations. This is our challenge.

Vincent Ponte

A MULTILEVEL SYSTEM
FOR DOWNTOWN DALLAS

The word "transportation" has a specialized meaning when we speak of moving people and goods within the confines of a city, and especially when we focus not on the city as a whole but on its downtown center—the core (Figure 1).

The core is the heart of the city in more ways than merely geographically. It is the center of business activity and of public life, the storehouse of a city's real wealth and a major source of its tax revenue. Of the $80 million that Dallas collects from the full 300 square miles of its municipal area, almost $20 million comes from the small 150-acre plot in the middle of the Central Business District (CBD).

Keeping this patch of real estate active and thriving is of paramount concern to every city. It involves keeping the core accessible to the crowds of people and the tons of goods that move in and out of it every day. It involves keeping things moving within the core itself, but good circulation is no simple matter in a growing city where the small grid of downtown streets is practically unalterable. Highway engineers can trace their course in generous strokes across empty landscapes, airport designers may lay out their spacious terminals on several square miles of virgin meadow, but those concerned with circulation in downtown areas must operate in terrain already cluttered with massive structures and burdened with thick deposits of past history, often misspent history. And within the core, ease of mobility is not merely advantageous, it is essential to the core's survival. Whatever else keeps people from coming downtown unless they have to, congestion is certainly the most important factor (Figure 2).

One way to ease congestion is to banish trucks and cars from the core

FIGURE 1 Downtown Dallas from the air, looking north, 1970.

altogether and turn it into a pedestrian island. This notion goes back as far as Julius Caesar, who banned vehicles from the streets of ancient Rome during daylight hours. Another approach is to try to force the core to spread out and disperse, zoning it, for instance, so as to limit the height of future buildings. Either of these measures might work, and they are frequently proposed. But it would take no less than a Julius Caesar to enforce them, and we are not likely to see it happen in our time in North America. People want to be able to drive downtown if they choose to. Businesses have a legitimate need to be within a few blocks of each other, so that executives, bankers, lawyers, and clients can get together conveniently and quickly. This, incidentally, is the reason why the core is seldom larger than 200 acres, even in major cities.

But there is much to be said on social grounds as well for keeping the core compact. High density means liveliness, variety, interest—the essence of urban life. To spread out the core or choke off the flow of people would be self-defeating. It would vitiate the very excitement and vitality we wish to foster and preserve.

The task then becomes one of finding ways to combat congestion within the naturally existing boundaries and density of the core. This entails allowing automobiles the full and proper use of the local streets

FIGURE 2 Competition in the streets between vehicles and pedestrians.

by progressively removing trucks and pedestrians into special off-street facilities that are incorporated into new construction as it occurs. The result is a scheme familiar to all of us—the multilevel city.

The principle of separating cars, trucks, and pedestrians onto different levels is at least as old as the Renaissance. In 1912 Antonio St. Elia illustrated the concept in surprisingly sophisticated form (Figure 3). His plan included a pedestrian level (plus some fanciful and impractical sky-bridges), a vehicular level (minus, however, any separation of trucking as such), and a separate level for mass rail transit. He even included a visionary "people-mover" at pedestrian grade.

Only in our own times, however, has the concept been actually applied to any appreciable extent. The first significant multilevel system to be actually built was the 12-acre Rockefeller Center, with its underground trucking terminal and pedestrian concourse incorporated into a single structure. Rockefeller Center dates from the early 1930s; but since the war, and particularly in the last 10 or 15 years, multilevel systems, or fragments of such systems, have been introduced into core areas of a number of cities, usually in the form of pedestrian walkways extending for several blocks. The most extensive to date is in Montreal, whose pedestrian system now serves 45 acres—about 20 blocks—with continuous sheltered shopping promenades undergirded by parking and trucking terminals.

However logical and simple the multilevel system appears in concept it is difficult and complicated to bring to existence. A major problem that has to be confronted in the initial planning stage is to assure oneself that the system will integrate itself smoothly into the surrounding fabric of the core—in other words, that it will "take," as a grafted organ takes to the body of a host. This applies especially to the pedestrian network, which is the key element of any multilevel scheme. The chief danger with a pedestrian system, as in the one recently completed in Cincinnati, is that people may refuse to use it, preferring instead to keep to the sidewalks and clog the intersections as before. To attract people, a pedestrian system must have all the features that make the sidewalk interesting—shop frontages, restaurants, theaters, and so on. It must avoid bleak stretches of blank wall or dreary institutional frontages such as prestige office lobbies, airline offices and banking halls. Equally important, a pedestrian system must form the natural pathway between one point of dense concentration to another. It must connect parking garages, subway stations, railway stations, and bus terminals to the lobbies of office towers, hotels, convention centers, and department stores. It must also provide plentiful points of access to the surrounding streets. When properly planned a pedestrian system constitutes the terminal link in a hierarchy of transportation, from pedestrian system to a

FIGURE 3   1912 projection of a multilevel city center by Antonio St. Elia.

parking garage in a 5-minute walk; from garage by car to distributor road to freeway loop; from freeway loop to radial highway to carport at home in the suburbs.

The next major problem, that of actually constructing the multilevel system, is less daunting than it might seem. Obviously, it cannot be inserted into the core at one stroke. One cannot, for example, burrow under existing buildings to put in underground trucking. But redevelopment and self-renewal goes on continuously in every city center as old buildings are torn down and replaced by new ones; and there is no reason why fragments of a future multilevel system cannot be introduced into new buildings in the design stage itself.

In every city there are, in fact, already in existence many scattered fragments of pedestrian systems, at above-grade levels of department stores, for example, and in the concourses of office towers. As new buildings rise around them, these existing fragments can be extended into the new developments by underpasses or overpasses, depending on the level. A sequence of such linkages can cover a significant portion of the core in a surprisingly short time, with a dramatic relief to street traffic as a result.

Special opportunities arise when big land areas in the core or on its periphery undergo comprehensive redevelopment, whether through urban renewal or private assembly or through acquisition of railroad land. In such multiblock developments, like Rockefeller Center, Penn Center, or Presidential Center, major segments of a multilevel system can be inserted at a single stroke, including parking units and underground trucking. A multilevel system of this size is not only self-sustaining; it can stimulate similar developments in the surrounding blocks.

It was just such land opportunities that arose a few years ago in Dallas; and the evolution of a multilevel system in that city is an instructive example of the way a multilevel system can be created merely with the resources in land, money, and technology that are already available.

In Dallas the 150-acre core has grown upward rather than outward. This can be seen in matching photographs of the skyline taken in 1946 and 1966 from the same angle (Figures 4 and 5). During these two decades, downtown Dallas added eight new big office towers of 30 and 40 stories. Construction has proceeded since then at an accelerated rate. Four additional office towers are currently under construction, and another two are about to be announced. This dense concentration will add to the glamour and metropolitan sophistication of its skyline (Figure 6), but it also spells trouble down on the ground. The 7 to 10 million more square feet of office space that will go up by 1980 signify at least another 50,000 office workers and visitors moving in and out of the core daily. They signify more services like electricity, water, sewage, telephone lines, more trucks, cars, and buses crowding the streets. They signify 40,000 additional cars that have to be parked somewhere. Already, one step past the last proud office tower on the edge of the core, lies a wilderness of parking lots (Figures 7 and 8), an insult to the eye and a degradation of the whole downtown environment.

Trucking is the second related part of the circulation problem. Delivery trucks parked and double-parked at curb, pinch traffic into a thin trickle (Figure 9). Pedestrians crossing at intersections and blocking traf-

FIGURE 4   Dallas skyline, 1946.

FIGURE 5   Dallas skyline, 1966.

FIGURE 6   Dallas skyline.

FIGURE 7   Parking lots on outskirts of Dallas downtown area.

FIGURE 8   Parking lots on outskirts of Dallas downtown area.

FIGURE 9   Dallas traffic congested by trucks.

FIGURE 10 Main Place.

FIGURE 11   Pedestrian circulation system and sunken plaza, Main Place.

fic are the third part of the problem. To overcome this confusion, Dallas has undertaken to shift to a new model of circulation in the core—the multilevel system.

A start has already been made in a major private office tower complex known as Main Place (Figure 10). A pedestrian circulation system, level with the sunken plaza (Figure 11), extends deep into the substructure of the building and underneath the surrounding streets—a network of sheltered walkways lined with shops and thronged with people (Figure 12). Its walkways are connected to street level and offices above by elevators and escalators (Figure 13). This local pedestrian system is now extending itself into neighboring blocks. It connects to parking levels hidden below. Beneath the parking levels, trucks circulate in underground terminals that are planned to serve six and seven different blocks.

This particular development in downtown Dallas is only one of several in which the principles of the multilevel system are being introduced. To function successfully, they are being structured so that their individual circulation systems—parking and trucking—will dovetail effectively and naturally with future subway stations and with a simplified system of distributor roads that lead with minimum interference

FIGURE 12   Underground shops and walkways, Main Place.

FIGURE 13   Walkways and elevators, Main Place.

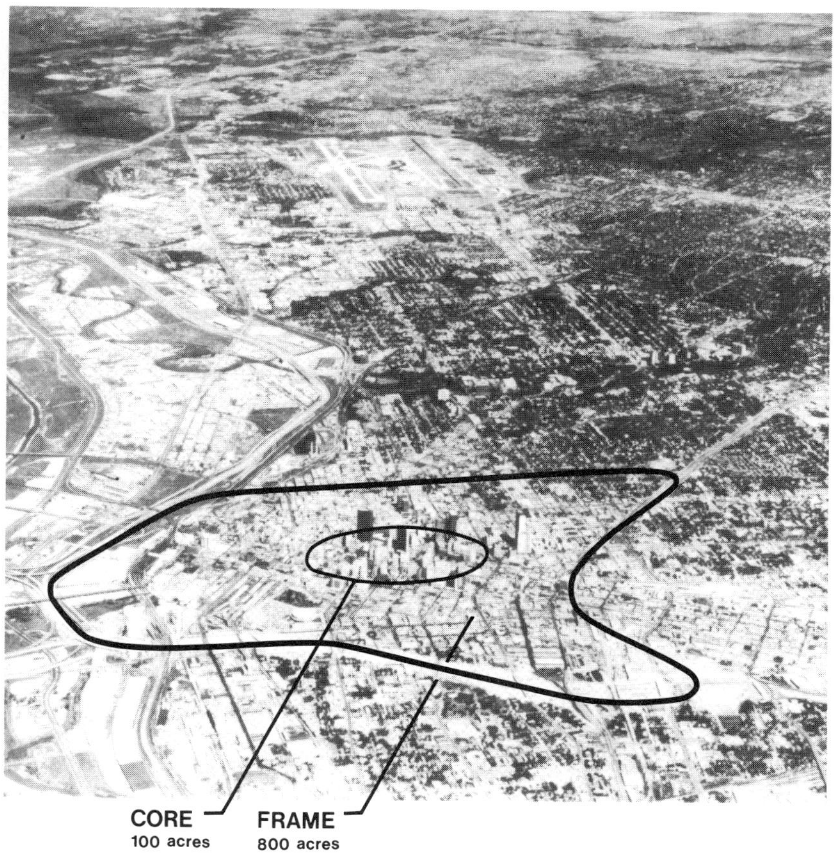

FIGURE 14   Freeway loop surrounding Dallas core.

out of the core to the freeway loop and into the surrounding region (Figure 14).

Within the CBD, accordingly, public and private multilevel developments are proceeding on a grand scale, with entire blocks being renewed at a stroke. The focus of this activity is, as always, the core, the roughly triangular dark patch in the aerial photograph (Figure 15). In a diagram (Figure 16) of the same area, it can be seen that the core is pinned down at its three corners by major new developments and pierced by a three-pronged street spine—Elm, Main, and Commerce, around which all major land uses are clustered. The area contains 14 million square feet of office space, three major department stores, and five hotels.

FIGURE 15   Aerial view of Dallas CBD and core.

Parking garages, dispersed through the core's 150 acres, occupy a total of 20 acres and provide 18,000 stalls. The demand however, for parking in a car-oriented city like Dallas cannot be met by the garages alone. Therefore, 27,000 additional spaces have spread into 140 acres of parking lots, located chiefly around the core's periphery (Figure 17).

Even to the most hardened urbanite it must come as a shock to learn that parking lots alone occupy over a fifth of all developable land in the CBD and that the pressures that produced this proliferation have by no means leveled off.

As Dallas grows so will the need for parking space. By 1980 the CBD will need 25,000 more stalls to accommodate the 170,000 automobiles expected downtown every day. The multilevel reorganization currently

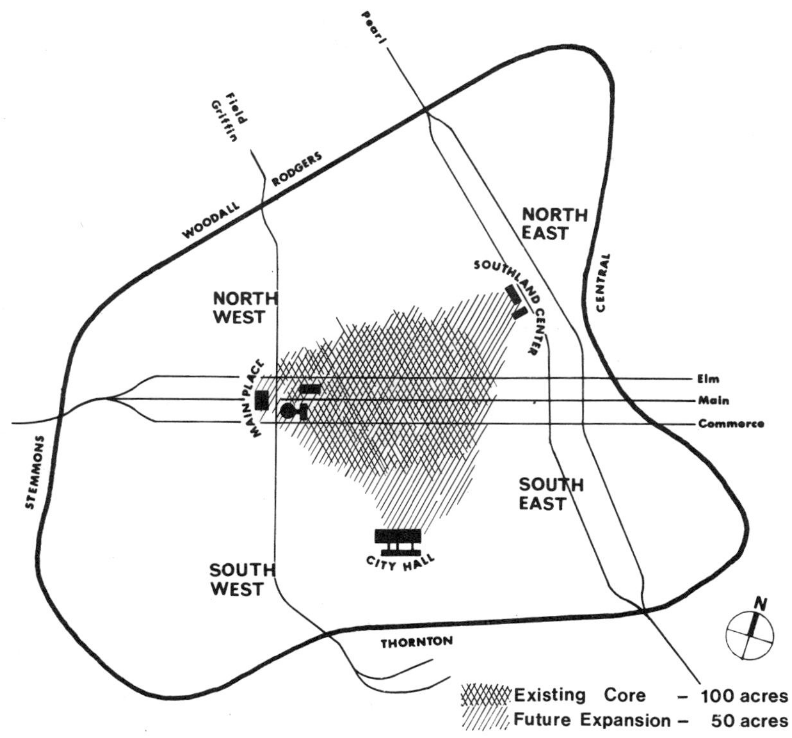

FIGURE 16   Schematic view of Dallas CBD and core.

under way in downtown Dallas will provide the necessary parking space
for the future and, at the same time, gradually eliminate the existing
wasteland of parking lots.

The land areas in which this multilevel reorganization has begun include 14 separate projects located in three general zones, all of them
lying in the southwest sector of the Dallas CBD (Figure 18). The southwest quadrant, consequently, offers the most immediate opportunity
for the establishment of a pedestrian system which will eventually extend itself to other areas of the core. Six fragments of a pedestrian system, isolated but close together in places (Figure 19), already existed
within the three designated zones.

By 1970 this fragmentary system was expanded at three points (dark,

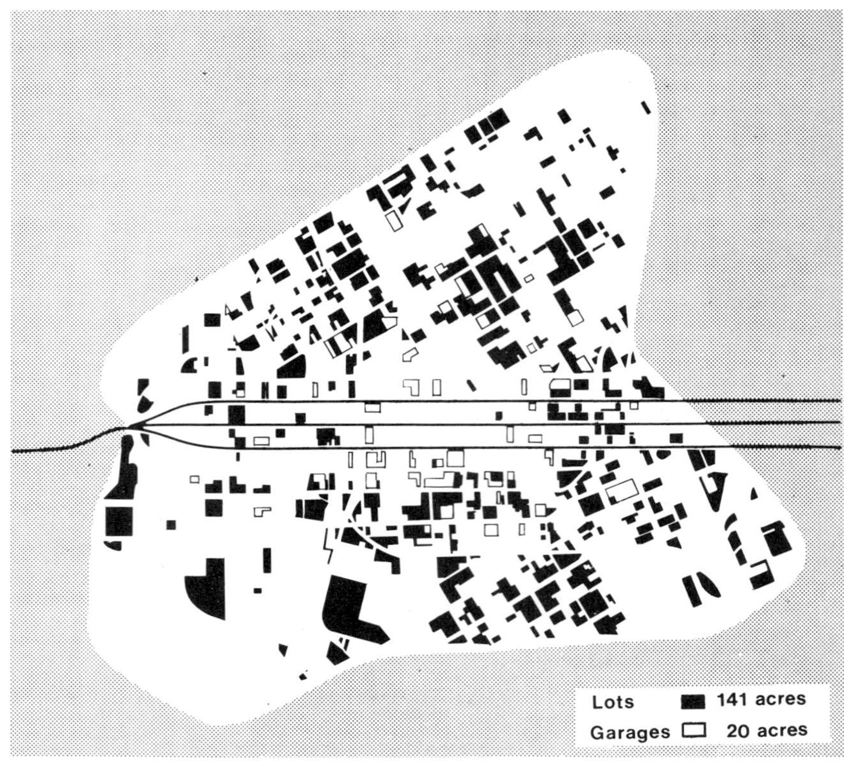

FIGURE 18   Southwest quadrant.

heavy lines in Figure 20), and the original six fragments had coalesced
into five.

By 1975 as a result of further developments already under construction for the most part, the pedestrian system will double itself (addi-
tions shown in dark, heavy lines in Figure 21). The five units of 1970
will have then coalesced into three.

The combined pedestrian networks will at that point service a land
area of 70 acres. It will contaiń 2 miles of cheerful, shoplined promenades, a sheltered world for pedestrians only. Into this system will be
routed 11 office towers (9 million square feet), 10 parking garages
(5,000 stalls), four banks, two hotels (700 rooms), a 1,000-seat movie
house, a new city hall, an expanded convention center and a new central

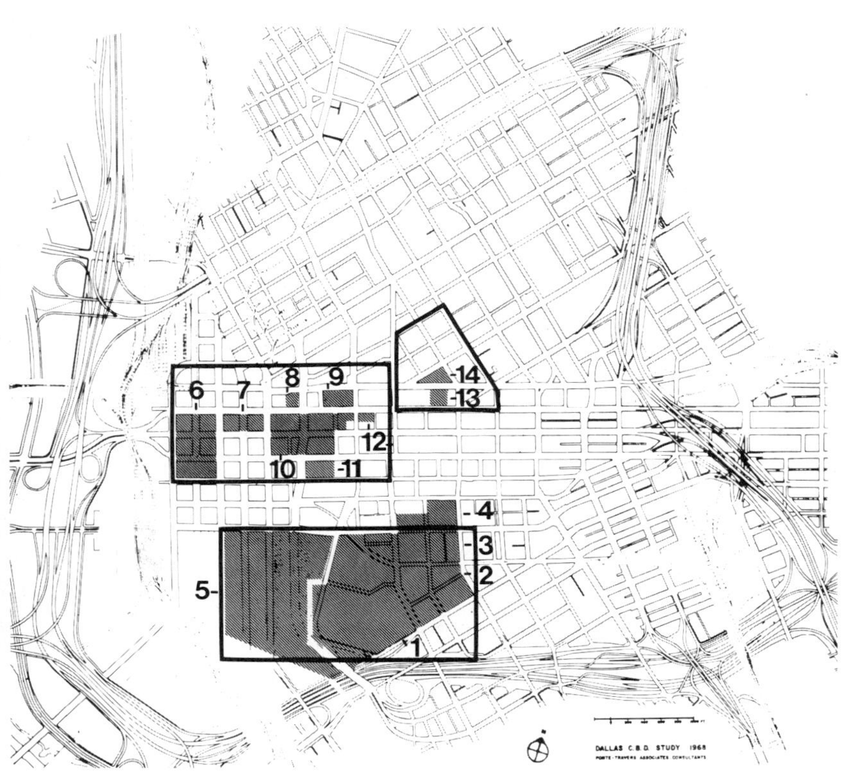

1	Convention Center	**8**	Elm Place
2	New City Hall	**9**	New LTV Tower
3	Park (& Garage)	**10**	Main Place
4	Cultural Area	**11**	Federal Office Bldg
5	Griffin Square	**12**	Metropolitan Garage
6	County Government	**13**	NBC Site
7	El Centro College	**14**	Thanks-Giving Square

FIGURE 17   1968 parking supply.

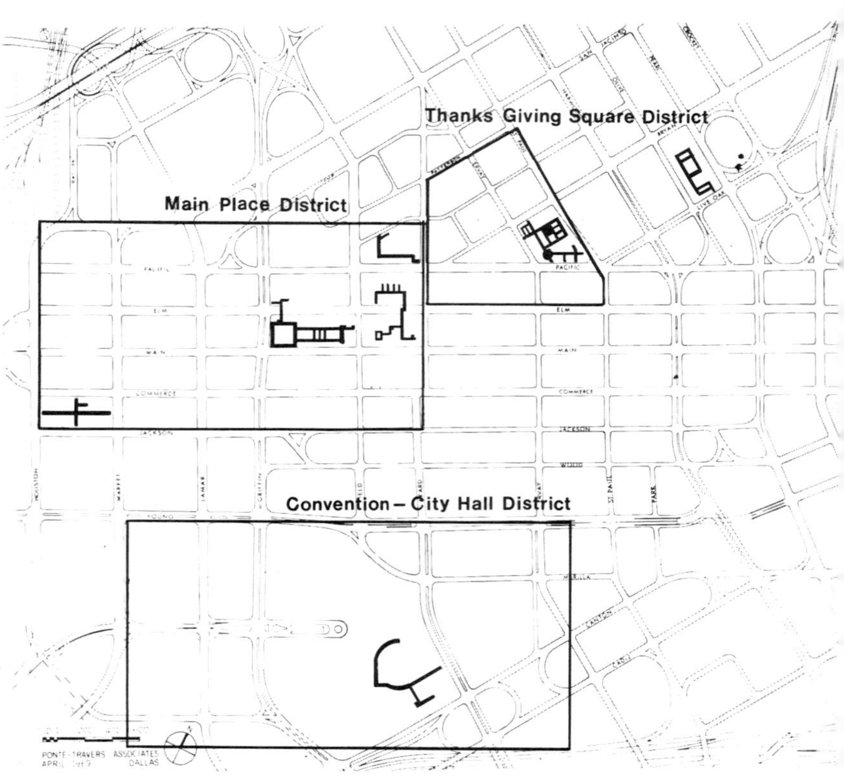

FIGURE 19   Fragments of Dallas pedestrian system, 1968.

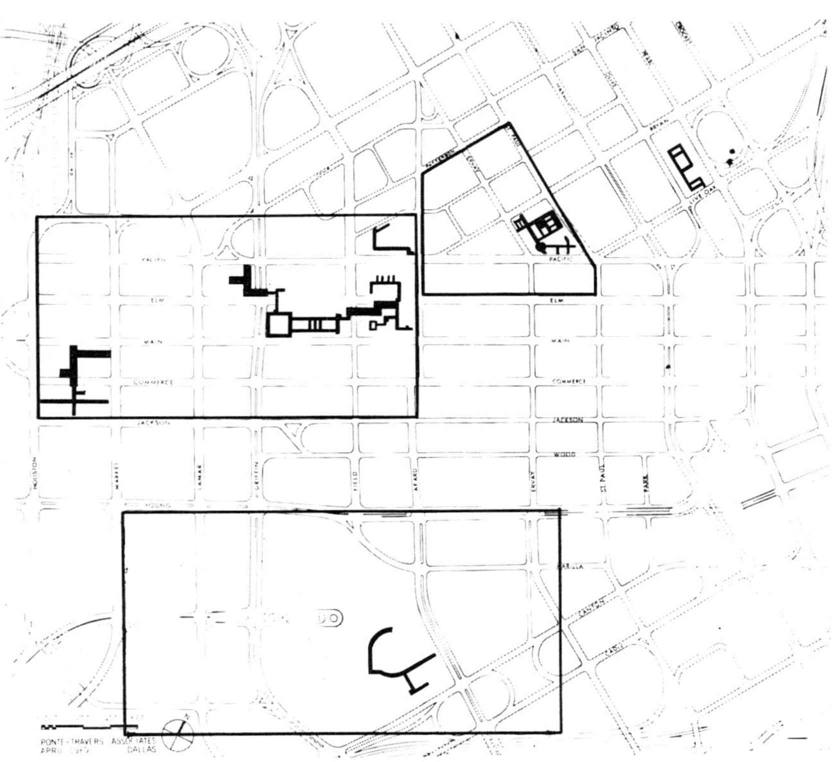

FIGURE 20   Fragments of Dallas pedestrian system, 1970.

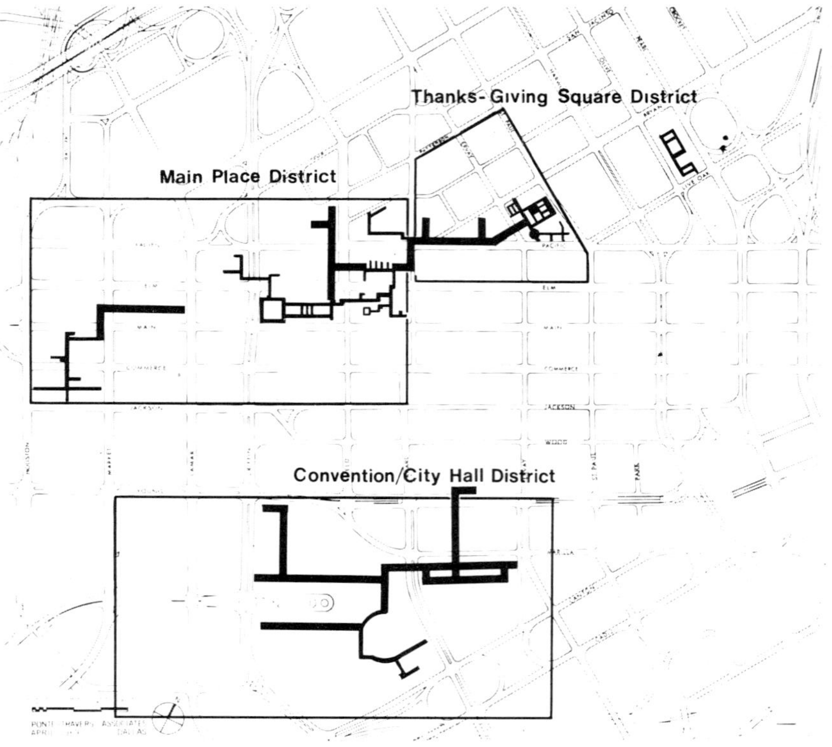

FIGURE 21   Fragments of Dallas pedestrian system, projected 1975.

library, the County Court House complex, and the downtown branch of the city's junior college.

If Dallas were to stop here with these three pedestrian units and not build one other walkway after 1975, it would be an impressive accomplishment in itself. But Dallas need not stop here. Within the Dallas Action Triangle, other big land developments have already been announced for 1975 to 1980. The first three pedestrian units just described will serve as points of departure—extending themselves across intervening blocks, as these in turn come into play in the accelerating process of urban growth. In time, with the sustained momentum of its growth, a single pedestrian network will weave throughout the downtown grid within the next 20 years (Figure 22).

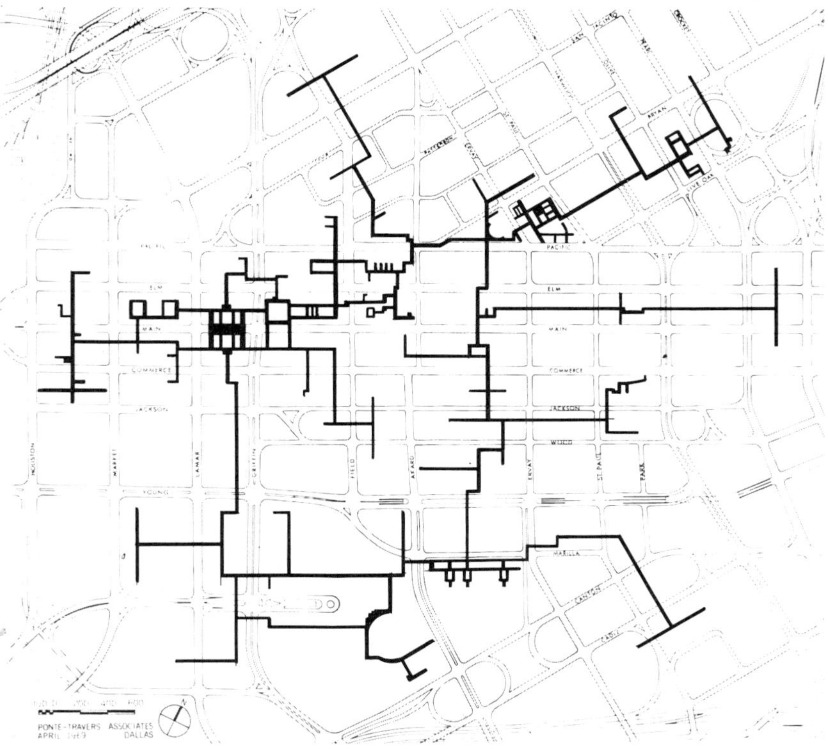

FIGURE 22   Downtown Dallas pedestrian system, projected 1975–1995.

Such an extensive plan for the whole 150-acre zone of the downtown looks ambitious when it is charted beyond the year 1980. But only its ultimate configuration is speculative. Its size and extent are well within practical feasibility. Likewise its cost. The central fact about such a network is that the vast portion—nine tenths of it, specifically—lies within private property and will be constructed by private enterprise as an integral part of future development. Of the 5 miles of the overall downtown network only 2,500 feet will actually become the city's responsibility to contract. This consists chiefly of street underpasses and overpasses that tie the various private units together from block to block block. Since the system will extend itself gradually, Dallas can, with an annual investment of $200,000, buy itself a pedestrian network that will

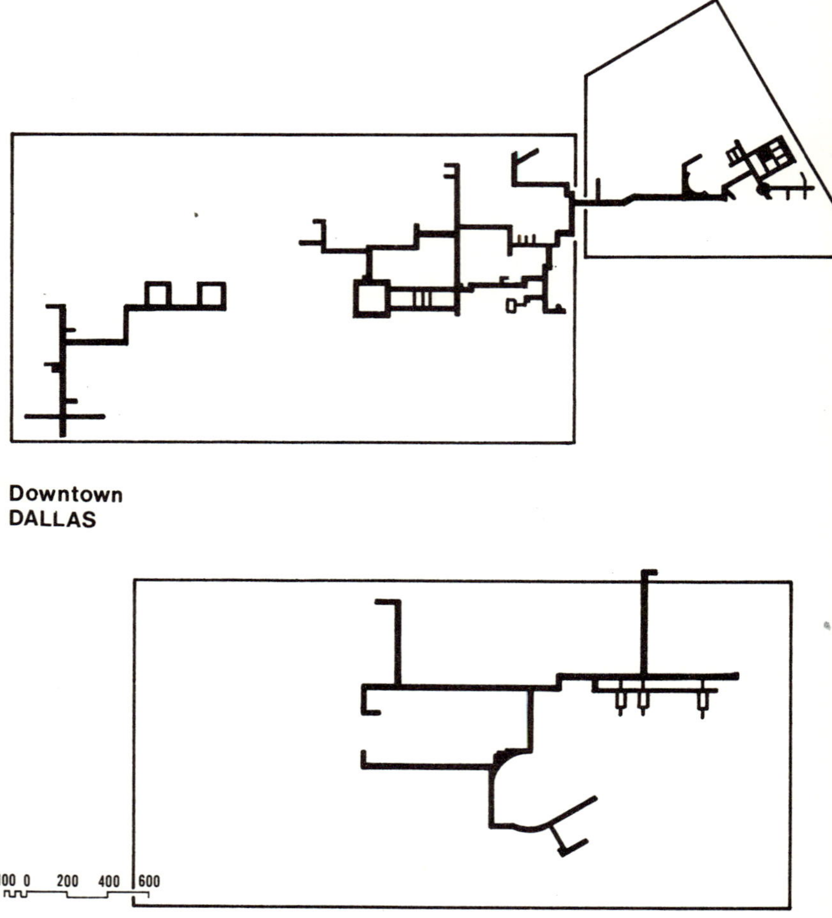

FIGURE 23   Scale of downtown Dallas pedestrian system, projected 1975.

will place it in the forefront of modern cities in the struggle for safety, efficiency, and convenience in its downtown center.

To appreciate more readily the potential scale of the Dallas pedestrian system (Figure 23) one may compare it with several well-known antecedants (Figure 24) that illustrate the different kinds of pedestrian elements that have been woven together into the fabric of the Dallas system.

The forerunner of the multilevel system in North America is Rocke-

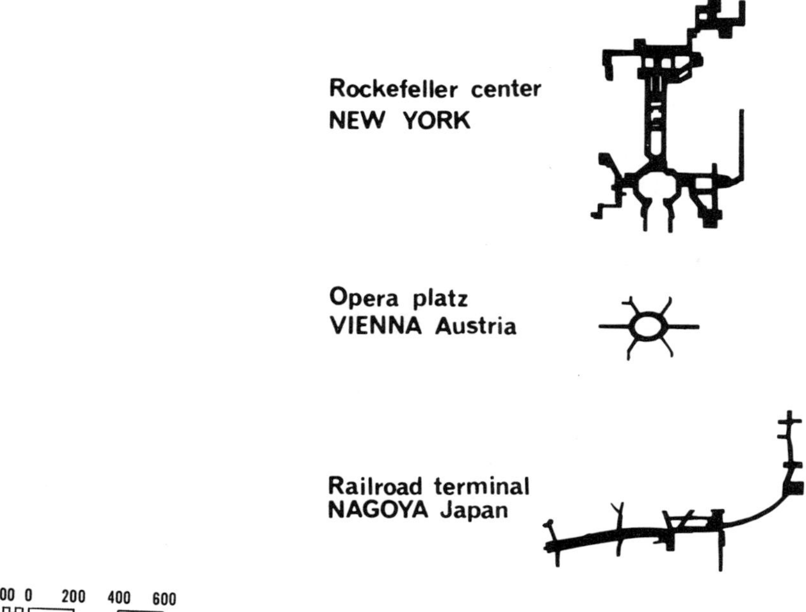

FIGURE 24   Scale of some international pedestrian systems.

feller Center. Other postwar examples of separating people from traffic at street level are the limited intersection solutions as in the Opera Platz in Vienna, or the Tritone in Rome, or the Magen David intersection in Tel Aviv. In Japan more extensive units are inserted into the city fabric by tunneling under streets for a considerable distance, lining the new walkways with shops, and tying into existing buildings on their flanks. Some 25 such "Chikagai" exist in Japan today. The Rockefeller Center system serves some 20 acres. When the northern unit of the Dallas system is completed in 1975, it alone will serve a built-up area twice as extensive as Rockefeller Center. In the southern sector of the core—the City Hall area—the system will serve another 49 acres of land and all the public buildings on it. While work proceeds on the pedestrian system, steps are also being taken to establish an underground trucking system to service the same area.

Trucks unloading and loading are a massive nuisance and another direct cause of congestion in downtown Dallas. The inconvenience

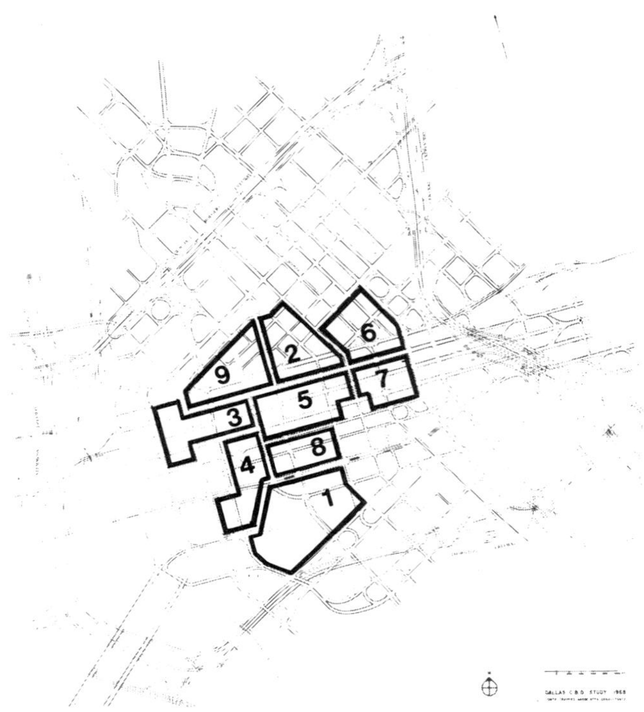

FIGURE 25   Nine underground trucking "compartments" planned for Dallas.

worsens each year as more office buildings are built in the core, doubling and tripling trucking movements on already overcrowded streets. Traffic studies show that by 1980 some 2,000 trucks daily will have to come into the busiest portion of the core.

Obviously, that many trucks cannot be allowed to unload at curbside as so many do today. This means that at least 180 additional off-street docking spaces will have to be made available in this one area alone, according to zoning requirements. But off-street loading docks only solve part of the problem. The 2,000 trucks will still have to use the busy streets—further slowing down traffic, even halting it, and interfering with pedestrians as well while they maneuver in and out of docking areas.

The underground trucking system planned for the core is designed to

FIGURE 26   Four trucking "compartments" ready for immediate development, to be completed in 1975.

solve all these difficulties. The approach—once again on a piecemeal basis, as with the pedestrian system—is to design separate trucking systems each serving a cluster of contiguous blocks comprising 10 or more acres. The core thus becomes divided up into nine trucking "compartments" (Figure 25). Four of these compartments (Figure 26) are ripe for immediate development and will be completed by 1975. The first underground trucking units (Figure 27) will serve all buildings on some 70 acres of densely built-up land and will require only five trucking portals, located on streets at the edge of the core. If the same 70 acres of land were allowed to develop in the customary fashion, i.e., each building supplying its own off-street truck dock, the city center would have to have an additional 80 separate off-street truck portals. The remaining five trucking compartments, when built, will be connected to-

FIGURE 27   The first trucking units planned for Dallas.

gether to create a unified underground system complementary to the unified pedestrian system above it (Figure 28).

By creating underground trucking compartments, Dallas can reasonably expect to have a complete and integrated trucking system for the entire core within two decades. The piecemeal approach ensures that funding will always be a manageable budgetary item, since the system will be financed over a period of years, compartment by compartment. The timetable, of course, will depend on the rate of overall development, because the trucking compartments will come into being as part of the normal growth process in the city center. This program will also ensure that its fulfillment will be functionally appropriate to each successive stage of the city's growth and also economically sound.

Over the next 10 or 20 years, as Dallas grows and suburbs multiply, some sort of commuter rail service will inevitably be needed. The first

FIGURE 28   Design for the Dallas underground trucking system.

regional transit link with downtown is likely to be a line from the airport. Coming in from the west, it would extend as a subway only
through city center in the bed of Elm Street (Figure 29)—the most
favorable corridor because it is almost free of underground utilities.
The system will be supplied on the outer limit of the CBD to two huge
garages.

The regional transit line would be supplemented within the CBD by
two shuttle lines (Figure 30) with a large garage at each end. The shuttle
lines can be fully automated. Small-scale, light-weight equipment will
permit a tight turning radius and a narrow right-of-way through built-up
sections of the downtown. The paths of the two shuttles will cross at
two points within the CBD.

Both elements of the mass rail transit—local shuttle and regional subway—will be closely tied to the downtown pedestrian system (Figure 31).

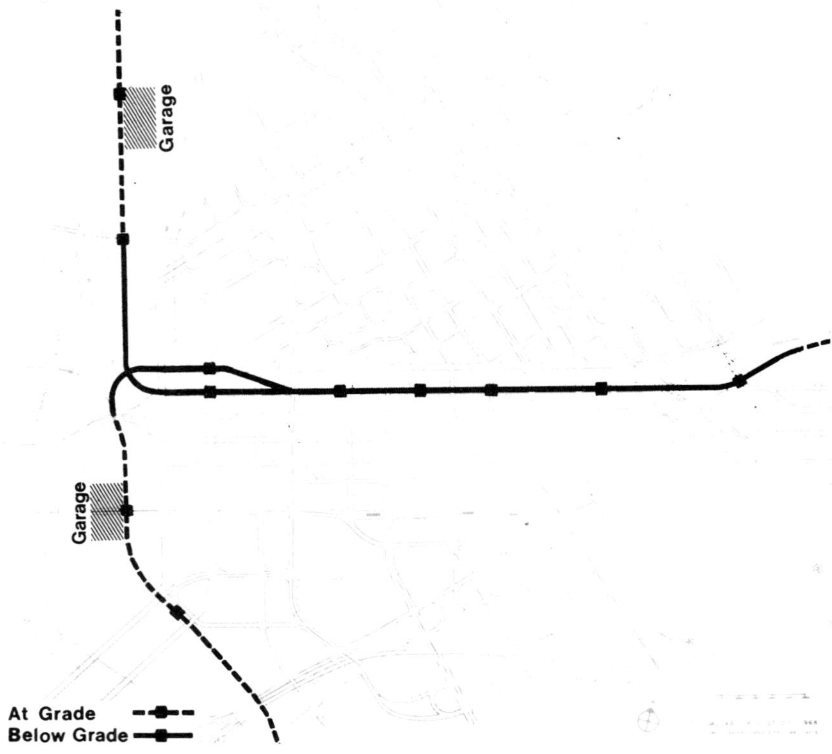

FIGURE 29   Proposed alignment of the downtown subway.

Every transit stop and station will be connected directly to one or another sheltered walkway, so that anyone may move from any point within the downtown area out to any of the parking garages on the inner or outer ring without once ever encountering street traffic or having to step outside of an exclusively pedestrian environment.

Turning finally to the question of vehicular access to the core, the internal distributor roads from the freeway loop will lead to peripheral portals of the underground trucking system, keeping to a minimum all truck circulations within the core itself. The same distributors lead to close-in garages (Figure 32) that ring the core in a fashion similar to the peripheral garages that ring the CBD. The core and CBD garages together will supply 44,000 stalls, all of them directly accessible to the core's pedestrian network.

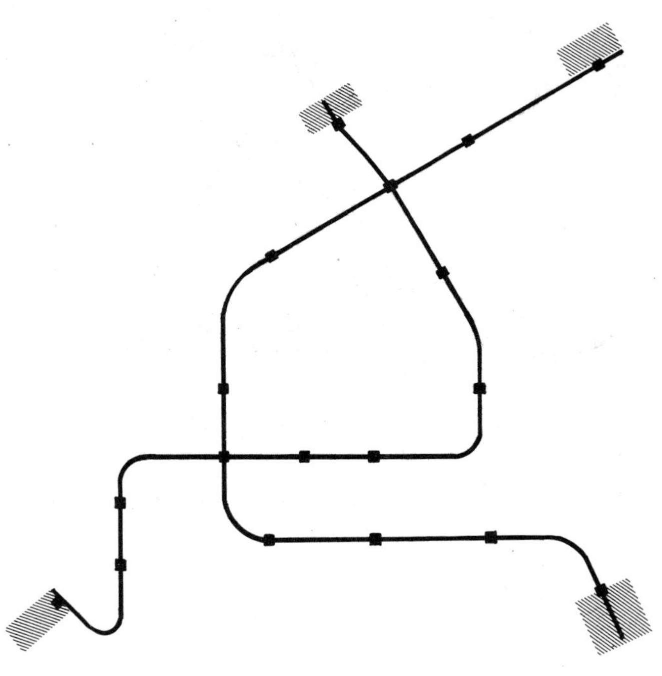

FIGURE 30   Proposed alignment of the downtown shuttles.

The freeway loop itself (Figure 33), started in 1950 and soon to be completed, has already alleviated downtown traffic problems by detouring 40 cars out of every hundred so that they need not fight their way through the local streets. The remaining 60 percent of the traffic—whose volume steadily increases—is still enough, however, to overburden the local street system within the CBD, which has seen only a scattering of street improvements since the grid was originally laid out 80 years ago. Any effective reorganization of the old street grid to absorb mounting traffic would obviously entail enormous public expense and a massive disruption to existing investments. The multilevel reorganization of downtown Dallas, therefore, presents the only reasonable solution to maintain free circulation within the core and the CBD.

The CBD's freeway loop is the hub of nine radial highways reaching

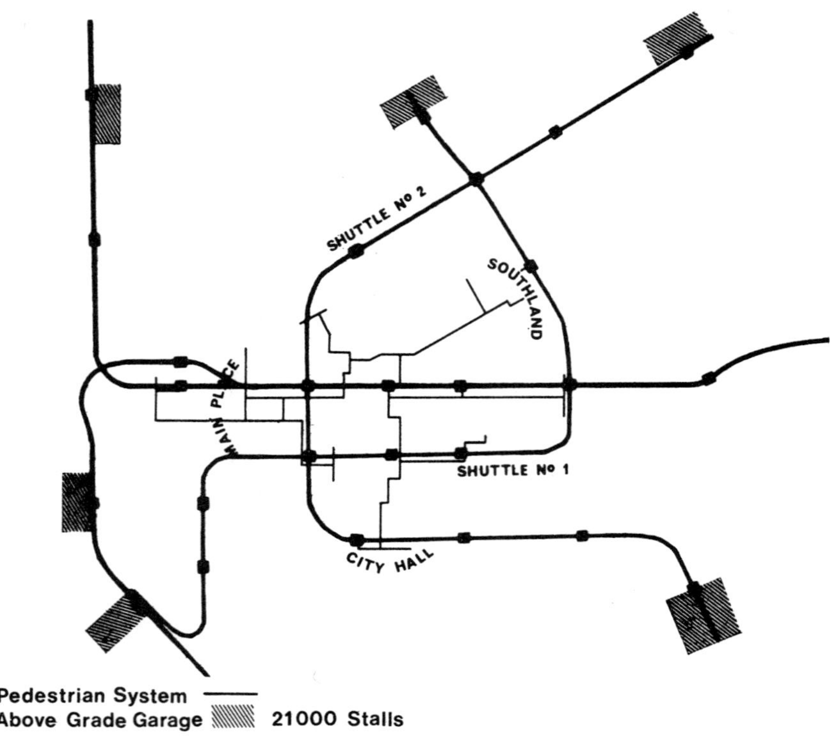

FIGURE 31   Connections between CBD peripheral garages, mass-transit stations, and the pedestrian system.

out into the region. That highway system effectively funnels traffic into the city center from the surrounding region.

Rivaling the regional highway system in completeness is a legacy of railroad rights-of-way also focusing in on the downtown (Figure 34). If present trends toward consolidation in the railroad industry continue, some of these tracks are likely to be abandoned through merger. These lines form the ready-made basis of a regional transit network. As already mentioned, the trackage of the Rock Island, connecting downtown Dallas with the regional airport and Fort Worth, is the most immediate and obvious target for conversion into a rail transit line. While only an estimated 15 percent of arriving air passengers will be heading downtown, even this number will become significant as passenger

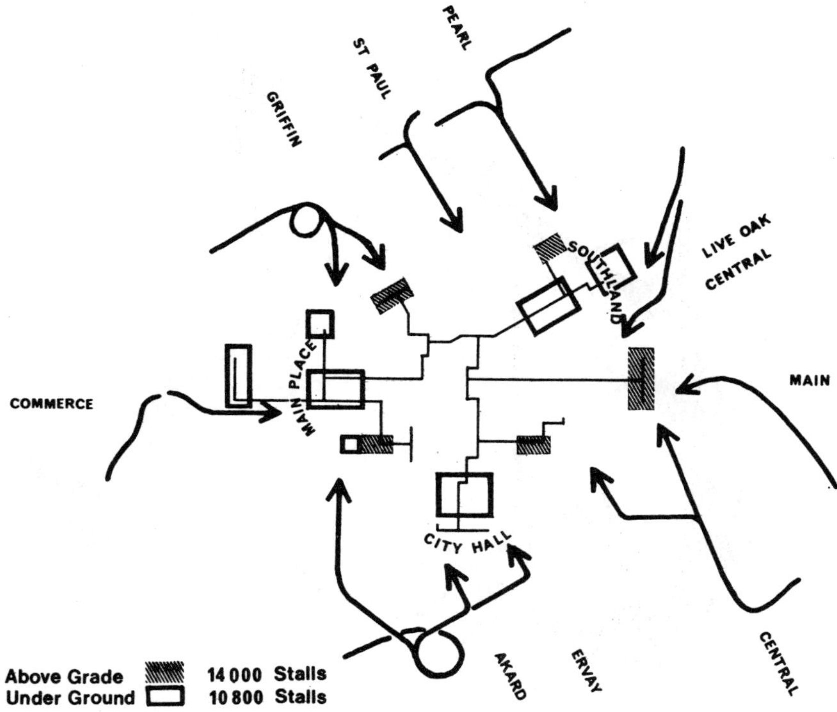

FIGURE 32   Core parking linked directly to the pedestrian network.

volume grows. Besides passengers, there are airline and airport employees and a massive payload of mail and air freight.

Thus, mass transit, underground trucking, reorganized parking, and
a pedestrian system separated from conventional street circulation—all
these are inseparable and indispensable elements in the multilevel city,
the only structure that will effectively prepare Dallas to meet the problems of downtown growth in the decades that lie ahead.

This whole ambitious program in Dallas got under way about 8 years
ago, when Mayor Eric Jonsson, concerned over the dangers of chaotic
growth, initiated a broad and searching study of the Dallas long-range
and short-range goals. In this, Mayor Jonsson was doing what countless
other city mayors have done, but he didn't stop here. Believing as he

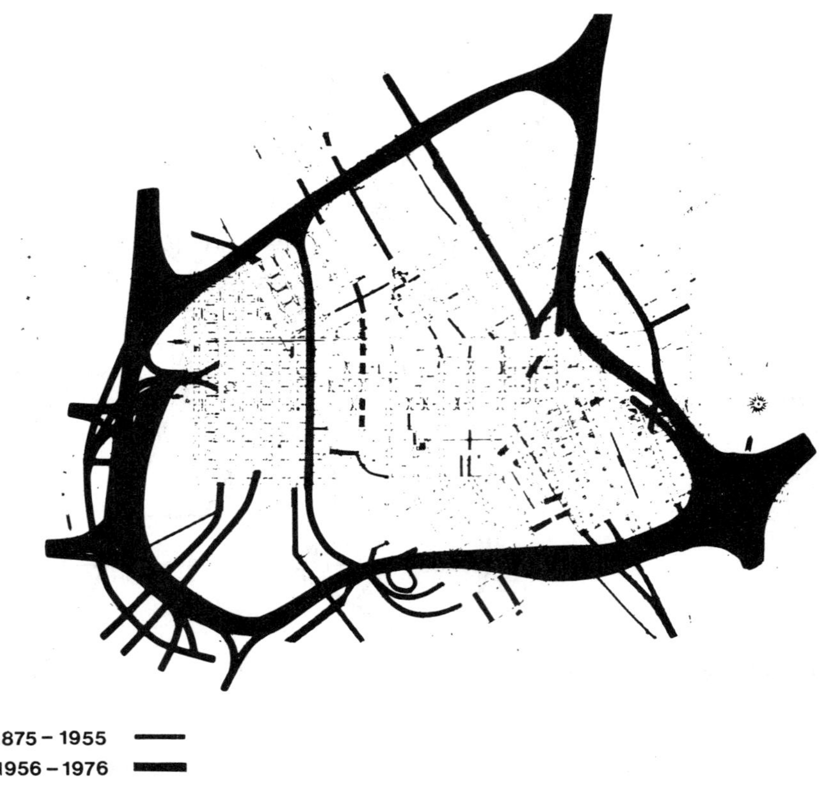

FIGURE 33   Street improvements.

did that planning cannot be left exclusively to specialists, Mayor Jonsson took the unprecedented step of inviting the entire citizenship of Dallas to examine an extensive program of public improvements, known as "Goals for Dallas," and to criticize 114 items covering the entire spectrum of civic concerns.

Over the last 5 years, the "Goals for Dallas" program was accordingly deliberated by every interested citizens' group. More than 100,000 people to date—professionals, businessmen, housewives, and young people—have become directly and personally involved in the important task of deciding on their collective destinies. The result was a broad consensus on what the city's goals should be and a massive rallying of public support, whose initial fruit was the triumphant passage in 1967 of a $175 million bond issue to launch the program. It was the largest civic bond

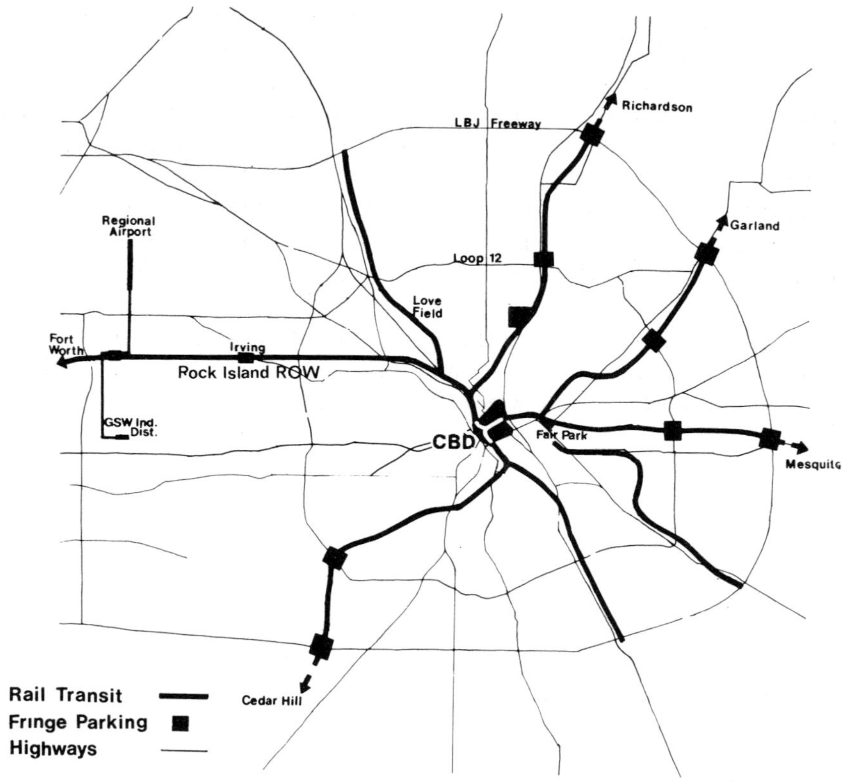

FIGURE 34　Proposed regional system (rail and road).

issue ever put before the voters in the Southwest. And the momentum did not stop there. Just this year another $170 million bond issue was approved by the voters.

Popular support and local financing would not be sufficient by themselves to realize a program as ambitious as the one in "Goals for Dallas." State and particularly federal aid and support are bound to play a major role. Indeed, federal funds have been forthcoming from different governmental agencies and departments for a variety of improvements under this program, particularly in the area of transportation. More will hopefully be available in the future.

The existence, however, of a comprehensive plan for the city's future, a plan that was worked out not merely by a handful of politicians and professionals, but by the masses of the citizenry, has played a major role. It has performed the indispensable task of focusing, harmonizing, and coordinating the separate financial contributions of independent government agencies to achieve a large common purpose. It is in the nature of our federal government, and individual governmental agencies, to provide aid strictly within the limits of their particular franchises without interference or trespass on those of the others. But at some level these separate items of aid have to be coordinated within the framework of an overall plan, and there is no better place to do this than at the local level, where the end results will rest and will have to be lived with.

Broad local involvement is the best and healthiest method of planning for the future of our cities, and the emerging experience in Dallas clearly shows a reasonable way to accomplish the task.

ROGERS: Vincent Ponte's description of the Cincinnati Walkway is quite right; it isn't used. I don't disagree with him at all, although I am the author of that plan. But what I found interesting was the reasons why it is not used. This again relates to an institutional barrier, in this case politics.

We were permitted to put the walkway in the system only if we put it on the alleyway system where it would not compete with the existing investment for retailing and other uses at the street level. The streets in Cincinnati are very, very narrow indeed; there was no way to create a pedestrian system at the grade level and separate it from the automobiles.

So we took a chance, with the blessing of the city that paid for this. We did put the system in, and, now, free enterprise being what it is, a lot of stores are beginning to tap into it. My prediction is that in 4 or 5 years this may be directly competitive with the present retailing and other activities at grade and at that time will become very highly used. However, the reason it was built and not used was directly due to a political constraint.

GORHAM: When I left the government in 1965, the then mayor of Dallas told me about the failure of an attempt to develop a joint airport between Dallas and Fort Worth. Mr. Jonsson some years later did bring together the two cities and ended that pressing problem in the airport field.

COMMENT: As one who attends meetings like this from time to time, I would just like to commend Mr. Ponte for what I think was a quite fantastic presentation. So many presentations are so poor it is very nice to get a really good one.

ROGERS: One general comment is that while a great deal of the earlier discussions related to planning in terms of future projections, without any real description of the implementation, both the Chicago presentation and the Dallas presentation are obviously real. I thought that was reassuring.

Two personal points: Mr. Pikarsky's very poignant description of the unacceptable risk of failure—we talked about this yesterday—the loss of the American tradition of trial and error, the fact that nobody, particularly the government, which has resources, is willing to deliberately pay for failure and learn thereby; and the overload of application forms that are really designed to make certain that failure is not even in the picture. I found that a very haunting account coming from somebody who has to live with these problems in his own city, and I certainly hope that at some point we will find institutions that are willing, if not to encourage failure, at least to accept it.

BERRY: I have a question for Mr. Pikarsky. He commented on the problem of the local–federal relationships, but "local," as I gathered it, dealt mainly with the city of Chicago, and I would like to know how the complexity increases as you also think in terms of metropolitan area agencies. How does the city of Chicago tie in with the metropolitan area agencies there in planning and transportation?

PIKARSKY: If I seemed to indicate that by "local" I meant Chicago, I did not convey the impression I wanted to. We do have a consortium of agencies that operate in the metropolitan area. What we are really saying about local–federal relationships, and this bears some note, is that there are individuals at different levels of government and from different areas who are trying to prescribe a single form, or general form, that can be universally applied. We are saying that the prescription should be the coordination of modes and of performance criteria at the federal level, which by its nature comes to the least common denominator of 50 states; the individual states then can prescribe more rigid or more desirable attributes of transportation planning in their areas.

However, to say that you must have a single form or one single regional planning and transportation agency is something that we disagree with very strongly. We don't have that, and we think that is one of the strengths of the Chicago area. I dare say that this issue, the resistance to formation of one single metropolitan agency, as urged by the Office of Management and Budget and by the highest levels of HUD, is one reason for the vitality of the Chicago region transportation planning, which I believe is second to none in this nation at the moment. Of course I would add that there are certainly others who would perhaps differ with that judgment. Although we have resisted establishment of one single agency, we have a regional planning agency in Illinois, and it has not been given, perhaps, all the authorities it needs, but the agency is there.

The organizations and representatives work as a consortium. The governors of Indiana and Illinois have representatives. We have the Chicago Area Transportation Study; we have a representative from the commuter railroad lines. What we have done is to provide a mechanism for interactions with the legislative or the political leaders, the ones who make the ultimate decisions. We first, in a technical assessment, throw out those solutions for our area that are professionally unacceptable, and we then list the alternatives that are professionally acceptable. The political leaders then make the decisions, and the technical agencies optimize that solution. We feel that in this way we have been able to implement and progress.

We don't believe that you need one single regional planning and transportation agency. You can do it with a consortium.

BAUER: My question is perhaps the same as Dr. Berry's. I think Mr. Pikarsky's paper may leave some people with the impression that the city of Chicago either has gone or should be allowed to go it alone in resolving transportation and related land-use problems in that very important area.

I know, and I think the answers here have indicated, that Mr. Pikarsky doesn't take that position or believe that, and I was going to ask him how he believes the necessary areawide transportation and land-use planning should be accomplished, and I think he has at least given some indication of that.

PIKARSKY: I might comment that there is no doubt that we agree that land-use planning and transportation planning must interface or intermesh, without any question. It is an error to think that one can perform without the other.

GORHAM: My question to Mr. Pikarsky is: Why did you decide it was better to bring a shuttle bus in to tie the airport in to the transit system rather than extending the transit system itself to O'Hare?

PIKARSKY: It was purely a matter of funds. We have initially, in the construction of the Kennedy Extension, provided the right-of-way all the way to the airport. In fact, that was done at city expense, without federal contributions of any kind.

We have a study, to be completed by the end of this month, on O'Hare Airport access to the downtown area. It will explore that type of extension as well as the commuter railroad lines that abut O'Hare Field. The decision was based purely on the lack of funding, however.

BERRY: I would like to make the general comment that I think the interplay of the architects and the engineers and the planners all working together, taking into account what the people say, is the right way to move ahead.

BAUER: I think the presentations of the papers were balanced, in that they provided usually two or sometimes three diverse viewpoints. This morning we heard different approaches to the institutional structure for planning and plan implementation; we heard papers that dealt with new technology and its concepts, and Mr. Browne told us that in his view there are going to be for some time to come, primarily two modes—the auto and air transportation.

I think on the whole, when the *Proceedings* are published, an interested reader will see a very balanced viewpoint from this symposium.

SUMMARIES

John A. Logan

SYMPOSIUM OBSERVATIONS

PURPOSES OF THE SYMPOSIUM

1. To advance the recognition and understanding of the impediments to urban transportation progress through a review of the efforts made in regions and cities where significant accomplishments have been made.

2. To propose, where appropriate, means of overcoming these impediments that relate to the interfaces of transportation modes with urban transportation systems.

3. To identify the key factors selected and used by private enterprise in helping to overcome institutional barriers to transportation progress.

4. To stimulate urban transportation innovations and foster improved urban growth patterns.

5. To identify information useful in the improvement of transportation decision making in the public and private sectors.

SUMMARY OBSERVATIONS

1. Transportation is not an end in itself, it is for people; and our ultimate objective is the improvement of the quality of life.

2. Transportation planning and urban planning must be on a regional or areawide, rather than local, basis and the two must not be separated.

3. Transportation planning is not an end in itself. There must be sufficient funds and appropriate organization to implement some of the concepts and some of the plans through coordinated action.

4. Transportation and urban planning must include the decision makers, that is, the political and business leaders and the citizens' groups, and it should be multidisciplinary.

5. Any plan that involves a transportation system must be concerned with competence or capabilities as well as efficiency of the proposed system, and the plan must be economically viable and must take adequate consideration of aesthetics. There must be equilibrium for the system within the environment, and, last, it must directly involve the people.

6. Based upon the above, there appeared to be general symposium agreement that institutional barriers have and will be overcome and that it can be done as was outlined by the speakers through a wide variety of institutional arrangements permitting effective planning and development.

Morton Hoppenfeld
Vincent Ponte
D. David Brandon
Walter A. Scheiber
Milton Pikarsky
Paul C. Watt
and
Archibald C. Rogers

URBAN TRANSPORTATION AND URBAN DEVELOPMENT APPROACHES

For the convenience of those particularly interested in the several different approaches to urban transportation and urban development used in various municipal areas, this brief summary of the speakers' views is included.

The process of planning and development followed by The Rouse Company was one primarily conceived, funded, and implemented through a private developer or developers.

In the Dallas case, metropolitan officials instituted the plan and guided development but enlisted the private urban planners and the developers in the process as required.

The New York Urban Development Corporation approach is an example of a corporation formed by the state government to provide the powers, a part of the capital, and the expertise for areas unable to initiate needed development without outside help.

For Washington, D.C., Chicago, and San Francisco, a municipal or regional agency or agencies created by the affected municipalities or regions guide planning and development. Varying degrees of responsibility and delegated authority are shown in these examples, with final implementation action in certain instances dependent on the success of coordination or a working coalition. Developers are then brought into the process in a variety of ways.

A list of observations and design criteria applicable in general to all of these processes, developed from experience around the world, is also included in the summary.

The approaches described are identified with the respective areas and authors, and a full discussion is included in the text of the address.

THE ROUSE COMPANY – MORTON HOPPENFELD

General Observations

1. A national goal should be to build better cities for people to live in. The Rouse Company calls it community development.

2. Community development must be an integrated process that includes planning, development, and then a repetition of these steps, or recycling. The process must provide for the introduction of the "new city in relation to old city" as cities grow and requires that the whole system must be considered.

3. The availability of long-term-risk capital, or "front end" money, is essential for the private developer.

Criteria

To create the kind of community development entities or corporations (public, quasi-public, or public–private combinations) that can succeed, the following conditions or criteria must be met:

1. All essential parties must be brought "to the table," that is, organized for action.

2. The planning must set forth a believable image for the region and provide a design that will work in service of its people.

3. Planning and a commitment for development must be united for successful implementation.

4. The overall process must include the recognition that social, economic, and physical planning and development are inseparable and must have social purpose, have a clear delineation of the economic implications, including an economic model, and must clearly identify the resources the people require to live a better life.

5. Physical development should be used as a force for positive social change through creation of opportunities.

6. The process must be undertaken on a large enough scale and not be fragmented. The objective should be to build whole communities on a scale consistent with desired goals.

7. Adequate initial and long-term funding is essential for the creation of values, land, aesthetics, etc. and their retention for the public good, rather than for gain of private developers.

8. A continuing process must be established.

DALLAS–VINCENT PONTE

General Observations

1. In any city, the "core" is the center of its energy and wealth. It embodies a city's spirit and reflects its pride.

2. The core is a compact unit, which seldom extends beyond 150 acres.

3. It has to function well, otherwise the whole city suffers. And what keeps it from working properly today and hampering its desire to grow is the familiar problem of congestion.

4. The multilevel city center, in which pedestrians, cars, transit, and trucks are separated into different levels is the only logical answer to control congestion and still keep a compact core.

5. Obviously, the existing core cannot be rebuilt in one swoop. The cost and disruption would be horrendous. It must be done piecemeal, as new development takes place.

6. Since redevelopment and self-renewal goes on continuously in any city center, bits and pieces of the future multilevel system can be inserted into the new fabric until the scattered levels multiply and finally connect together.

7. At the rate our cities renew themselves a corewide multilevel center, if initiated today, would be functioning long before the year 2000.

Criteria

1. A realistic plan that charts the location of the several levels of circulation within the core is needed.

2. Adherence to certain standards of function and quality, without which these systems may fail, is also a requisite.

a. To guarantee that people will willingly use a grade-separated pedestrian network, the walkways must have all the features that make the sidewalks interesting, such as shops, restaurants, and theatres.

b. Garages on the edge of the core, and mass-transit stops within the core, must all be linked into the pedestrian walkways connecting all major buildings in the business center.

c. As the core grows in density, complete intermodal linkups should be achieved to create a total terminal system.

d. The freight handling system may be built around an underground truck-circulation system incorporating well-lighted and ventilated areas to service as many as 6–12 blocks at a time, with access to underground truck-docking stations by means of two- to four-lane tunnel ramps separated on the surface from regular traffic.

3. To achieve a multilevel center the users must be completely united behind the plan. The entire citizenship must join in setting the goals and in approving the funding support plan. The public and private sectors must agree on the uses of the land to be developed in order to provide for improvement by connecting other portions of city into the multilevel system as part of a continuing process. Because of the nature of our federal government and individual government agencies—provision of aid strictly within the limits of their particular franchises without interference or trespass on those of others—coordination of this federal financial aid is required within the framework of the overall plan. This is best done at the local level.

NEW YORK STATE URBAN DEVELOPMENT CORPORATION — D. DAVID BRANDON

General Observations

1. Private enterprise is often unwilling to take long-term financial risk in the urban development area.

2. Government must take the risk, therefore, if progress is to be made.

3. UDC was created to work with private enterprise to facilitate their willingness to invest their funds in things that were considered to be in the greater public interest.

4. Ways must be found to provide low-income housing in a satisfactory way.

5. The problems of transportation, employment, and housing cannot be solved by dealing with the center cities alone. The problem must be treated by dealing with the whole urban complex, the whole metropolitan or regional area. There must be recognition of the need on occasion to create structures that can deal with specific major projects such as the Welfare Island Urban Development Corporation.

Criteria

To make such a development corporation possible, certain powers are needed that help overcome institutional barriers. UDC can: acquire land; condemn land; waive local codes and ordinances; override zoning; hire architects and engineers; choose builders and developers; utilize state, federal, and other assistance program funds; place mortgage loans; own and operate facilities.

METROPOLITAN WASHINGTON – WALTER A. SCHEIBER

General Observations

1. One of the greatest barriers to metropolitan progress is the diffusion of responsibilities at all levels of government, and clearly, improved coordination and simplification of federal requirements would help greatly to reduce the impediments to progress.

2. Consideration should be given to the reservation of transportation corridors and other landbanking plans.

Criteria

1. An association of local governments such as the Metropolitan Washington, D.C., COG, created for the purpose of alleviating the transportation and other urban problems that face various communities, in order to achieve effective action, must have provisions for:

   a. Coordinating a wide variety of interjurisdictional and areawide problems not only in transportation but community development, health, environmental protection, human resource problems, and public safety;

   b. Assuming the responsibility for comprehensive planning to include land use and transportation;

   c. Speaking for all the vested interest of local governments;

   d. Implementing the appropriate programs through combined action of the local elected officials and the respective governments;

   e. Identifying tradeoffs between center city and the suburbs that are compatible with the overall regional goals and objectives.

2. The COG must provide a mechanism for arranging joint funding by all interested agencies of appropriate programs to assure successful completion and necessary continuity of action.

CHICAGO – MILTON PIKARSKY

General Observations

1. Public transportation is an integral element of our societal system. Where we are talking about conserving the environment, protecting national resources, providing economic, social, or recreational stimulus,

or reducing hardship associated with injury and death on the highways, we are involved in some aspect of public transportation.

2. What is needed and what the public seems to want, but does not yet adequately support, is a balanced ground transportation system.

3. Public transportation is a public service. Consequently, public transit should be supported as a public service and not be expected to be self-supporting from the fare box. It is important to realize that transit riders are not the sole beneficiaries of public transportation; rather public transportation offers lasting benefits to both the cities and the nation.

4. Effective public transportation will not come about automatically. It will require an enormous effort in terms of legislation, financial stimulus, and engineering advancements. It is imperative that the engineering and scientific community enter into the dialogue on legislative and administrative matters to bring about this transformation.

Criteria

1. To achieve the goal of a balanced transportation system, it is essential that the nation's legislative policy be redirected toward an effective ground transportation system that includes both private and public transportation needs:

a. Financial assistance for both capital equipment and operating assistance is the most critical need that timely legislation can provide. It is imperative that there be a commitment to rebalance transportation modes giving increased emphasis to public transit and giving priority to fund public transit programs promptly. Such funding should be designed to permit local governments to use this support for whichever need is greatest—highway construction or public transportation.

b. Federal guidelines would be rewritten in those cases where the administration of the legislation hinders implementation of the legislative intent. Key among these is the example of the demonstration grants, which actually discourage transit operators from trying new services by the tacit insistance that the service be completely self-supporting from the fare box within a year time period.

c. Reductions must be made where possible in the bureaucratic processes to eliminate needless time delays, redundant review processes, and inconsistent grant criteria at various governmental levels.

2. To encourage use of public transportation, the following steps have proven to be effective:

a. Optimum utilization of existing facilities and equipment by systems analysis techniques for optimum routing, rehabilitation of abandoned lines where possible, and innovative scheduling and modal interfacing.

b. Development of new convenient and efficient intermodal facilities and transit facilities to coordinate with existing facilities.

c. Implementation of promising innovative concepts to increase convenience and dependability of public transit, such as preferential treatment for buses, as in exclusive bus lanes, and park-and-ride facilities.

SAN FRANCISCO–PAUL C. WATT

General Observations

The creation of regional governments offers the chance of bringing innovative institutional approaches to transportation problems into existence sooner within urban areas.

Criteria

A Metropolitan Transportation Commission that is essentially a planning and coordinating organization concerned with land-use–transportation relationships, regional versus local considerations, institutional and resource allocation matters, and the environment is another creative way that can be effective if there is provision for:

1. Creation of a master transportation plan, adopted by law, that carries a provision precluding future construction not included in the overall plan;

2. The combination of transportation planning and land-use consideration under the formulation of urban development–transportation objectives;

3. Creating a public transit fund through gasoline tax or other levies with allocation authority vested in the MTC.

DESIGN CRITERIA–ARCHIBALD C. ROGERS

General Observations

1. For effective action a united team is required, consisting of:

a. A multidisciplinary design team including both technical and social capabilities;

b. A decision-making team, including legislative and executive representation;

c. The community team, involving affected groups and the citizenry.

2. Accept the tradition of the trial and error experiment, i.e., permit experiments where final judgment of feasibility requires full-scale trial and assessment, in order to stimulate progress toward improved transportation and other urban systems.

3. Four basic concepts relate directly to transportation design:

a. The planning concept should incorporate the concept of the completed trip, including the transition from, or interrelation of, one mode to another.

b. The design concept should be multiuse and have the objective of minimizing the need for transportation. To approach this objective, for example, design high rises with offices, apartments, shopping, and schools or horizontally group in close proximity shopping, residential, recreational, and light industrial facilities.

c. Transportation must be a part of a total corridor system. The total corridor should be developed and put in place ahead of time.

d. The amenities should be considered and included.

Criteria

1. Designs must include the external capability to do the desired job as well as provide for internal efficiency.

2. Economic viability must be provided but on a broader matrix of costs and benefits. The consumer may have to pay for diminishing the ecological damage and for ameliorating social disruption.

3. Aesthetics must be considered.

4. The design must be in equilibrium with its natural setting. Everything should be designed to minimize consumption of natural resources and the damage to the environment.

5. Community development and community architecture must be in sympathy with those who use it in all elements.

PARTICIPANTS

KURT W. BAUER, Executive Director, Southeastern Wisconsin Regional Planning Commission, Waukesha, Wisconsin

JAMES M. BEGGS, Under Secretary of Transportation, U.S. Department of Transportation, Washington, D.C.

DONALD S. BERRY, Walter P. Murphy Professor of Civil Engineering, Northwestern University, Evanston, Illinois

FRANK S. BESSON, JR., Board of Directors, AMTRAK, Washington, D.C.

D. DAVID BRANDON, Director of Program Development, New York State Urban Development Corporation, New York, New York

HARRY C. BROCKEL, Center for Great Lakes Studies, University of Wisconsin, Milwaukee, Wisconsin

SECOR D. BROWNE, Chairman, Civil Aeronautics Board, Washington, D.C.

HARMER E. DAVIS, Director, Institute of Transportation and Traffic Engineering, University of California, Berkeley, California

WILLIAM L. EVERITT, Dean Emeritus, College of Engineering, University of Illinois, Urbana, Illinois

HAROLD B. FINGER, Assistant Secretary for Research and Technology, U.S. Department of Housing and Urban Development, Washington, D.C.

BERNARD GIFFORD, President, The New York City—RAND Institute, New York, New York

ROGER H. GILMAN, Director of Planning and Development, Port Authority of New York and New Jersey, New York, New York

ARTHUR GOLDSMITH, Chief, Technical Division, Office of Telecommunications, U.S. Department of Transportation, Washington, D.C.

SEYMOUR W. HERWALD, Vice President, Engineering and Development, Westinghouse Electric Corporation, Pittsburgh, Pennsylvania

MORTON HOPPENFELD, Vice President, The Rouse Company, Columbia, Maryland

J. ERIK JONSSON, Honorary Chairman, Board of Directors, Texas Instruments, Inc., Dallas, Texas

JOHN A. LOGAN, President, Rose-Hulman Institute of Technology, Terre Haute, Indiana

WILLIAM L. MERTZ, Director, Office of Highway Planning, Federal Highway Administration, U.S. Department of Transportation, Washington, D.C.

RENÉ H. MILLER, H. N. Slater Professor of Flight Transportation and Head, Department of Aeronautics and Astronautics, Massachusetts Institute of Technology, Cambridge, Massachusetts

MILTON PIKARSKY, Commissioner of Public Works, City of Chicago, Chicago, Illinois

VINCENT PONTE, City Planning Consultant, Montreal, Quebec, Canada

STANLEY P. E. PRICE, Director, Systems Analysis and Evaluation Division, Office of Research, Development, and Demonstration, Urban Mass Transportation Administration, U.S. Department of Transportation, Washington, D.C.

ARCHIBALD C. ROGERS, Chairman of the Board, RTKL, Inc., Baltimore, Maryland

WALTER A. SCHEIBER, Executive Director, The Metropolitan Washington Council of Governments, Washington, D.C.

PAUL C. WATT, Executive Director, Metropolitan Transportation Commission, Berkeley, California

ISBN 0-309-021